1986

Gregory Rochlin, M.D.

THE
MASCULINE DILEMMA

A Psychology of Masculinity

LITTLE, BROWN AND COMPANY   **BOSTON / TORONTO**

First Edition

The author is grateful to Sigmund Freud Copyrights Ltd.,
The Institute of Psycho-Analysis, The Hogarth Press Ltd.,
and Basic Books, Inc. for permission to quote from
"Analysis of a Phobia in a Five-year-old Boy" in Volume 10
of *The Standard Edition of the Complete Psychological
Works of Sigmund Freud* translated and edited by James
Strachey and to A.P. Watt Ltd. and Macmillan Publishing
Co., Inc. for permission to quote from "Crazy Jane Talks
with the Bishop" from *Collected Poems* by William Butler
Yeats, copyright 1933 by Macmillan Publishing Co., Inc.
renewed 1961 by Bertha Georgie Yeats.

Library of Congress Cataloging in Publication Data

Rochlin, Gregory.
  The masculine dilemma.

  Includes bibliographical references and index.
    1. Men—Psychology. 2. Masculinity (Psychology)
I. Title.
BF692.5.R62   155.3′32   80–16618
ISBN 0–316–75335–1

BC

Designed by Janis Capone

*Published simultaneously in Canada
by Little, Brown & Company (Canada) Limited*

Printed in the United States of America

To Helen, who accompanied me with love

ACKNOWLEDGMENTS

FOR HELP WITH THIS WORK, I am indebted to friends, colleagues, and students, whose contributions became incorporated into this book in indecipherable ways. What I owe each one cannot be calculated properly either by acknowledgment or gratitude because the bounds of their generosity were so fully exceeded. I am grateful and steeped, but blessed, in such poverty.

There are particular ones among my creditors. From the outset, as she had before, E. S. (Peggy) Yntema nurtured my efforts with affection, literally fed me suggestions, administered editorial criticism, and soothed me with enthusiasm, often while she was no less free-hearted with the products of her well-known culinary art. Early on, Robert Lee Wolff, Coolidge Professor of History, Harvard University, a friend who knew what I had begun to turn my hand to, gave me a fistful of his unpublished manuscript of some of his research in Victorian fiction. My friend and long, close associate, Dr. Herbert J. Goldings, generously furnished me with his penetrating clinical criticism, together with some of his clinical material to corroborate my own. Anne Bernays virtually took me by the hand and led me out of my thicket with almost a ream of manuscript pages to the publishers, Little, Brown and Company. There, Richard McDonough, editor, by tempered patience, coupled an ear for dissonance with an intuitive judgment, and carried me through enough drafts of the manuscript to get through their fat to the flesh. What remains of its obesity is my error, not his. Channa Eberhart had the especially difficult task of threading my way through the maze of material I gave her to prepare the manuscript, check its footnotes, and all of that test of skill with it that Ariadne would envy.

G.R.

INTRODUCTION

THAT WE ARE BORN either male or female is a simple biological fact. For all its unambiguity, our lot gives us too small comfort. Only in the human does gender become a matter of distress. No one escapes unaffected. Although it creates emotional problems that most of us manage to solve, none of them are either simple or fail to make their mark. Born biologically male or female, we must prove our birthright. This is particularly the case, as I will show, with the male as he tries to define and secure his masculinity.

While scientific scrutiny of human emotional experience has burgeoned in the last century since its systematic beginnings in Freud's work, there have been few explorations into the psychology of masculinity. The available literature is suggestive of the parts but not the whole that characterizes the masculine experience.

We have seen in recent time studies of human cycles without reference to gender. Certainly we are all interested in the human condition and already there are passions, concerns, and vicissitudes that are common to both men and women. But the vital fact remains that there are differences in biology and resultant experience from them. Hence, enormous leaps of supposition are needless to suggest that psychological processes and imperatives are often different between the sexes. Literary sources from early myth and the Bible through Lawrence, Joyce, Yeats, and Lessing among other modern writers have often been more incisive in their explorations of human emotional differences than have psychologists. Much of the contemporary work of those studying childhood, youth and maturity, while invaluable in exposing commonalities of experience, avoid the confrontation, often a political one, with the fact of gender difference begging psychological difference. Just as the literature of the Victorian period distorted the view of children by treating them as miniature adults rather than as evolving human beings, so too have those psychologists who study the human condition ignored sexual differences.

I intend to show that the notion of the resolution of some central early turmoils in later life is fallacious. Indeed the dilemmas that are endemic to the masculine experience are played out again and again; the purchase of masculinity is never fully secured.

To begin fully to grasp the nature of masculinity and a man's interaction with his society, we must scrutinize our vast legacy about it from pre-clinical time left us by the myths and legends replete with accounts of the importance to masculinity of prowess, mastery, and achievement. It also entails what only close consideration will yield as to what it means to be masculine and what it must be unconsciously; how it is to be tested, felt, and undergone. This furnishes unyielding evidence. Our understanding of it discloses masculinity to be an endless trial. It is a predicament without a lasting resolution. In many respects, it is like an ordeal of Sisyphus or an Augean task in the actual living through of events whether they are real or imagined. And the rub is that it is bound to affect the judgment and the feelings, even while some are utterly unconscious, but nonetheless dictated by an unrelenting, compelling self-assessment of masculinity.

The experience that precedes a man's maturity is a seamless, perceptibly woven web of performance, prowess, mastery, and achievement. They are the operative elements. What may be latent or potential ones give no comfort to his ego, which is actively bound to each. With the ripening into maturity, still another element critical to a man is the relationship of each of these components to work and women. The ever-present dread of limitations finds expression in both, which uniquely affect masculinity, as the fears of impotence. Whether in its development or in its maturity, masculine narcissism, as I shall show, is especially vulnerable. It is, for instance, Joseph Conrad more than psychoanalysts who commented that a man's self-esteem remains precarious and demands that he put out of sight all reminders of his folly, of weakness, of morality; they all make against efficiency — the memory of failures. I must add that in these characteristics the boy was never more father to the man.

Precariously footed self-esteem being the condition, masculinity is beseiged — prone to injury, sensitive to and fearful of limitations. Aggressiveness and at times a ready hostility, typical of ever-vigilant masculinity, issue easily to its defense. The unique vulnerability to failed expectations is the fatal flaw in the masculine ego. It grows up in the shadow of a socially promoted and compliantly willing self-fashioned Herculean ideal. The expectations make the ego thrive. But they also feed its worm. It makes a readiness to turn on oneself in despair with railing against circumstance or Fortune a denial of one's unbearable intolerance of limitations. It often furthers a firing incentive toward achievement to rescue a self that lacks lenience to ignominy. The result may be creative or destructive; at the extreme it carries the quickly germinating seeds of self-destruction. The testing of masculinity knows no bounds. Hence, the warrant to prove oneself remains a lifelong necessity. It is the case as much in manhood as it was in boyhood. It gives rise to many of man's anxieties and failures as well as to his often extraordinary achievements. We shall find this the timeless case in a boy's adventures as in a man's enterprises.

From its outset, the *masculine experience* is a challenge—
"there's vinegar and pepper in't." It may also turn sweet. It is
this mixture that makes it wanton.

G.R.

THE
MASCULINE DILEMMA

Chapter 1

THE PHALLIC SELF AND
GREAT EXPECTATIONS

THE SOUL, the ancients said, as the slave of the body, is subject to its temperaments and risks being driven to delirium and denied its judgment. We may say no less of masculinity, which is held in its own thralldom "bound fast in that seat of endless chance and change, the body."[1] However, unlike the locus of the soul that forever escaped all who sought it, what animal spirits embody masculinity, where its juices arise or effervesce, or by which of these influences it waxes or wanes, may prove to be not so elusive. Few have been drawn to its emotional wellspring, to plumb its depths or to scrutinize its qualities.

Although the extensive research in human genetic codes in recent years has succeeded in uncovering the formulae for maleness, the canons ruling masculinity have not been revealed by them. Studies of our blood circulating its burden of sex-linked hormones demonstrate that some of these hormones, which characteristically belong to women, are in men, and that others, characteristically male, are found in varying significant proportions in females. However, the combined determining influence of a genetic legacy, physiology, and

3

anatomical structure that makes for maleness does not produce masculinity.

Although the sources of masculinity remain obscure, its emergence does not. It is the human condition to evolve inner defenses against our private, often ill-defined, emotional conflicts, and men, even as boys, are prone to particular defenses in regard to their masculinity. The most persistent, disturbing, and anxiety-provoking are those associated with the never-ending need to prove one's masculinity in the face of doubts as to its degree. Thus, we find at all stages of manhood — young boys, whose defenses of masculinity are developing; youths, whose masculinity is being tested in reality; and men, whose masculinity needs a constant reaffirmation — alarming fears that return in varying forms as even more distressing wishes. Principal among these are the fears and wishes to be feminine or to engage in what once may have been associated with notions of femininity. Such reverses of the "normal" conscious imperative of masculine striving, set off by the eruption of unconsciously rooted desires, call out vigorous defenses: most commonly striving to be and to seem more "masculine." Each age, period, and culture has its criteria for how such defenses will be socially delivered. The expressions are revealing. Faergeman, among others, has found that:

A man expresses his desire for femininity in all ways at his disposal — in dreams, in behavior and movements, in the way he dresses, in slips of the tongue . . . character traits; he may even in conscious fantasies experience the "sweet masochistic thrill of being taken."[2]

Masculinity is not a stable condition. Again and again, as we shall find, masculinity in its various periods of development must be reasserted over myriad recurring doubts that just as regularly must be dispelled. In a boy's early emotional development, such conflicts ripen sufficiently so that his need to free himself from identification with a woman becomes compelling. In this context, we mean by "identification" a desire to be

4

like a woman. Most analysts assume that a man's abhorrence of his identification with a woman comes only from that earliest emotional tie with his mother. This original, natural association is further assumed to have a continuing powerful influence and to give masculinity its double-mindedness. However, this deterministic view neglects the fact that it is merely the original agent of a lifelong process. Moreover, that it *is* lifelong fails to be explained as simply recapitulating of the infantile model throughout one's existence.

Present studies describe the boy's naturally developing an identification with his mother, or, in some instances, with an older sister. And they support the findings of analysts' studies of adults that took place early in this century. This early work was particularly concerned with those conflicts that derive from boyhood during the ages of four to about six years, which period analysts have designated as the oedipal phase. We have far fewer direct studies of boys in the younger, or pre-oedipal, period, which begins somewhat before three years of age and goes to about five years. But they, too, show that at this age a clear identification with mothers has taken place. In these studies, the emphasis is put on the residues of attachment to the mother and on the child's struggles toward independence that is in conflict with the more infantile longings not to separate from her. Such studies, both popular and scientific, which focus on the mother and child in their mutual dependence, do not note whether the child's sex matters to either the mother or the child. It follows that no note is taken of the specific effects on masculinity brought about by the continuing identification with one's mother. Hence, these analysts conceive of the boy's later development, when he wants his father's love and wishes to take his mother's place with the father to gain it, as related to that previous time without consideration of the role of his continuing dependent attachment to her. The developmental dynamics of his earlier identification are given at best a secondary role. The supposition is that it is the original dependence or so-called attachment to the mother rather than identification with her that governs the nature of the boy's relationship with her.

The most definitive studies of homosexual men during the past quarter century tend to give prominence to these subjects' suffering some lack of proper "separation" from their mothers at an early age and failing to establish their "individuality." It is further supposed that, as a consequence, this undifferentiated or inseparable "attachment" with their mothers impedes the normal development of their masculinity. Thus, the recurring conflicts that a man experiences throughout his life because of the identification with his mother are inclined to be neglected.[3]

We regard emotional development much as we do human embryological development, where the distinction between male and female is subsumed to the development of the species. During the past half century, analysts, and particularly child analysts, have turned increasingly to search for the deeper roots of libidinal or instinctual development. The focus on the infant's libido has led to simplistic reductions in reasoning and theory. They range from the assumption that a mutual psychology existed in the relationship between mother and infant to the idea that "regressions" of adult narcissism reflect that state which prevailed during early childhood, which has somehow continued and become anachronistic in the later years.

Such views reflect ignorance of the early conflicts that demand to be met within the self. These conflicts are self-contained and are not simply the sum of infantile experiences to which a set of reactions are developed. From such equations, the notion is that a direct passage must exist from physiological need to psychological wish and even emotional need, and that we have only to find that path to complete our passage of human psychological development. In both cases, the formation of the self, independent of neither wish nor need but evolving from a child's solutions to his conflicts, escapes the field of study. Instead, the expectation is that our mere observations of the infant's condition must coincide with the infant's view of himself.[4] The emphasis, so heavily weighted on what is presumed of a child's so-called instinctual life rather than on the study of the development of the self and, in this case, on a masculine self, has sacrificed proper study of the early and important formation of a child's ego, its lasting conflicts, and its increasingly sophisticated defenses. The distinction of a boy's ego from a girl's is lost in the anonymity that is unwittingly created by the failure to distinguish the masculine from the feminine psychology.

With rare exceptions analysts have tended to put aside, if they do consider them, the narcissistic conflicts that normally occur in and have a large role for small boys and girls as young as two and three years of age. Such conflicts are expressions of the issues that the self associates with gender. For instance, it is difficult to exaggerate the enormous pride that a small boy takes in his becoming masculine, yet it is overlooked in scientific studies. This is especially the case when attention is paid to the broader but shallower considerations of a child's ego. As a consequence, the private, inner, unobserved emotional conflicts of the ego in very young children are largely disregarded. The emphasis instead is given to the relationship of the child to its mother, and we have clinically couched generalizations that sacrifice the child's individual psychology.

Such studies depend on observations of the mothers and infants rather than on psychoanalytic material. Nonetheless, it is stated that the mother's conflicts, which she somehow conveys to her child, may be accurately deduced from giving close attention to her behavior. From these studies, put forth chiefly by analysts and those who follow their work, the idea is formulated that the psychology of the young child mirrors its mother's. By noting the emotional experiences of the two of them, referred to sometimes as the "nursing couple," their mutual effects on one another may be discerned. However valid the claims of such investigations may be, their flaw becomes increasingly plain as we attempt to find the missing early, individual psychology of the young child. We have long

7

known that both the conscious and unconscious influence of the mother in relation to her child only to a degree can be revealed by the closest scrutiny. Brazelton's original studies notably bear this out.[5] Attempts to fashion her child's ego definition from her influence are not fruitful.

These works place importance on the fact that giving birth is emotionally more than interrupting a mother's connection with her newborn. We learn that the attachment, which is naturally exacerbated, profoundly affects the infant. Here is the earliest emotional tie with another, and it begins in the nursery. There a mother — the person critical to the well-being of the infant — becomes a part of the infant self. There is the beginning bond of identification. The emotional experience, it is theorized, becomes a deposit in the self or in the ego, to be revived from time to time. It is one associated emotionally and intimately with the delightful gratification of our earliest appetites. Given the conditions of certain burdens and strains, the ego, we are told, reverts for relief to these archaic pleasures. But what distinctions, if any, may be found between the masculine pleasures and the feminine escapes such hypotheses, which rest on the notion of an ill-defined childhood in which frustrations are relieved through merely turning back to the gratification of primitive desires.

Thus we find a bedrock of deterministic theories that have found favor for about a century, since our inner life began to come under scientific scrutiny. Some of the theories are founded on our biological structure, others add considerations of hormonal effects, and some allow for the unpredictable role of circumstance. Except for some of Freud's early biological theorizing, this is not far from his original discoveries of how much our sexuality was at the core of our existence. In this immense psychoanalytic literature, scientific as well as popular, a general assumption remains: some ill-defined, primordial state, instincts, or passions exist in us, and we are lured to them by nostalgia. How else are we to understand the universally observed reversion to infantile or childlike states?

In this welter of writing, the infant's emotional destiny is conceived to be expulsion from a uterine Eden. A child must live then in anguish, condemned on its own account, sweat its existence, and yearn for some once natural and perfect union.[6] As this Rousseauistic argument has hung less over philosophy, it has been draped more over psychology and even further over psychoanalysis to influence heavily the present generation of analysts, as it had the older ones who passed it on. Freud was not an exception. He was deeply concerned with these issues, not so much for their philosophical considerations, although he did not neglect those, but for their merit in his theory that civilization is an intolerable imposition on our nature. The self-curtailments and the emotional privations it exacts of us, he thought, formed an irreducible kernel of hostility that we harbor against it. As a result, civilization permanently arouses in us more, rather than less, aggression. The myth of the Fall, the humanist tradition, and the modern Freudian theory of our resistance to civilization have in common the idea that we are the victims of our own instrument. To live in civilization, the only condition in which we can exist, exacts the penalty of forgoing aggression. We seem not to want to pay it. We see ourselves as compulsively fleeing the threatening embrace of civilization by way of regression to the archaic state we were obliged to repress; while there we snatch what relish we may enjoy before the dictates of convention intervene, censure, and bring us to heel.

These dynamic concepts and theories come from a century's collection of clinical scientific data. The conclusions regarding character formation, however, have not escaped being sentimentally affected, influenced unwittingly by a legacy of eighteenth-century humanism. With respect to our early years our theories are still more mechanistic than they are dynamic. They fail to explain how two distinct psychologies develop from childhoods that are supposedly undifferentiated. With no more distinction given than the struggles of "babyhood" or the characteristics of early childhood discerned in the emotional nature, for example, of a very young boy three years of age, we find no clue to the dynamic development of masculinity. No definition, no psychology of boyhood emerges. Theories of masculinity remain arrested in debating its possible origins. We commence direct explorations of its development beginning in early boyhood. We make that effort here.

*   *   *

For a boy, the identification with his mother never altogether loses its significance in relation to his becoming masculine. It gives rise to conflicts, affects behavior, and brings on some transient as well as lasting complex reactions and defenses against them. This caught Freud's direct attention as early as 1896,[7] although it was not until a decade later that he was able fully to grasp what a problem it was for a boy who under certain conditions naturally wished to be feminine.[8] However, Freud's lack of clinical experience with young children led him to omit the fact that with a boy's emerging masculinity his inevitable identification with his mother has particularly lasting connotations that are repugnant to him. This is not to suggest that they are identical to the original implications for him, but, throughout his development, it is unlike what little girls experience.

It is the boy's and the man's need to reject the identification with his mother that cuts a different course in emotional development from that of girls and women. It starts shortly after he emerges from the nursery.

It has been supposed that in cultures where women are employed equally with men the boy's notion of his mother will be different. We need but be reminded that a boy's assessment of his mother is not dictated simply by the nature of her tasks. This is apparent in observing agricultural societies, and perhaps even more so in preagricultural ones, where women traditionally have been and are still actively engaged in the labor force. The boy's resistance to being identified with his mother goes far deeper psychologically than what her chores suggest to him. A boy is most profoundly affected by the nature of his mother's relations with a man.

In early boyhood a boy attempts to rid himself of his identification with his mother, albeit unconsciously. He variously experiences it as an abhorrence of the passivity in relation to a man with which he associates her. Paradoxically, his conflicts to win his father's favor culminate in wishes to be in his mother's place with his father. Such aims contradict and oppose his masculine imperative to free himself of his identification with her. Much of the next phase of boyhood has this as its task.

From studying boys as young as two and a half to three years, I find that their intense need to assert their masculinity is associated with their own, self-induced, threatening fantasies and notions, which result from what being a woman means to them. The reaction of emotional defenses that issue from such ideas and the identification with their mothers quite naturally produce many of their fears, prohibitions, phobias, and a driving incentive to prove themselves masculine.

A small boy has no conception of masculinity as a function. We learn from him, beginning when he is about two years old, that what he perceives about himself, among other experiences and to which he attaches considerable importance, is his male anatomy. Its significance for him lies at first in his inevitable perception how he differs from those who are otherwise endowed. He is no less attentive to those who are like him. While this is meaningful, it does not carry the same heavy impact on him that the difference suggests.

Regardless of what explanations are given to him to satisfy his curiosity about the genital differences he sooner or later observes, the explanations that he retains are his own and will be at odds with what he is taught. Like any child, he keeps two sets of mental ledgers: one contains his emotional calculations, the other his learned accounts. It is a popular assumption and, to some degree, is held as a scientific supposition that a child is openly receptive to such information. My experience, however, dictates that, although there is no doubt he is eager to learn, he also holds to his own conclusions. Their emotional importance

11

to him requires that he do this. He may appear to accept what he is told, but it does not dislodge what he *believes*. He illustrates what we have long known about young children: they are not given to relinquish readily their own beliefs in favor of "knowledge." This is especially the case when what a child may learn is disturbing, contradicting what he observes to the point of being alarming and incomprehensible. There is nothing in a small boy's experience that prepares him to find acceptable what cannot be explained to him. For instance, that the differences he observes between himself and women are merely the accidental conditions of life. Such ideas promote a threatening, dismaying, and early self-conscious feeling that significant differences exist. A young child's conceptions of causality stem more from his own powers of observation. He can make little active effort to be reflective about the world in which he exists until his natural egocentricity and self-absorption give way to further development.

To examine the enormous power of beliefs that rule over the dictates of reality is beyond the scope of this work. Nowhere in human experience is it more striking than in the power of a small boy's beliefs about women. A child is especially concerned with the integrity of his own body. From it, in early boyhood he derives the conviction that those who are unlike himself are inferior. The tendency to claim superiority over others, a bar to intimacy, stems from a variety of motives, all of them self-serving and at bottom narcissistic.

A small boy's view of his penis is of lasting and greatest importance to him. Its urinary operation is soon understood as a function, and its association with excremental acts gives the penis an added and conflict-ridden significance that I shall later illustrate. The natural identification a boy forms with his mother by the time he reaches the age of three years brings him into direct conflict with his own self-image. This is sharply brought to his notice by his penis.

The penis is a performing organ. While the social emphasis may be placed on the act of controlling urination, to the boy this is of secondary value to the control he learns to exercise over his penis. The further advance in phallic importance comes with its unique concentration of erectile tissue. The penis's characteristically sensitive reactions to touch, as a source of feeling, and its remarkable, if seemingly incomprehensible, independent behavior soon promote it as a focus of interest and mystery. Moreover, the penis behaves as if it has a life of its own, unconstrained and self-determined. As the boy's possession, it is prized. The fact that a part of himself is novel and prized carries, as I shall show, an abiding meaning that has a direct bearing on shaping and maintaining a lasting narcissistic image of himself. Should his thinking better of himself be given exaggerated support for the prize that is his, making it more explicit that others lack it, he is bound to further self-elevation. His private vanity thus reinforced, confirming that others share his notions of himself, he thinks less of those lacking his good fortune. His tolerance of girls or women is not promoted.

A young boy's observation that only his penis distinguishes him from others has a disquieting effect on him. Given the proper conditions in which he may spontaneously express his views on such matters, as during the course of his play, we learn that he believes that those who lack an organ like his somehow have been denied it, or, once having had it, are now deprived of what he considers essential. It must have been a severe and cruel experience, he believes, to have been the victim of such a disaster. In a manner limited only by his capacity for fantasy and daydream, he spins out explanations for this catastrophe. They will be dictated by his social and cultural level, the experiences he has had and those he witnessed or learned about with regard to losses, deprivation, and punishment. The main issue here for the boy is that he regards women as having been victimized. It would be no less true of himself had he such a misfortune as he thinks is theirs.[9]

As I shall point out later, small boys react strongly when they come into a playroom and notice that a bin of toys contains some that are broken. The toys need not be only dolls that have lost some part. The boy puts forward the same questions and even at times shows distress about inanimate objects, such as a motor car with a wheel or some other part missing.

In the course of everyday events, the questions a little boy puts to adults about his observations that concern him, especially about losses, oddities, or perceptions that may often reflect his own anxiety but are expressed casually only as curiosity, usually get a reply addressed, quite ordinarily, to the simple facts. While superficially the boy's curiosity may be satisfied, the deeper implications, of course, are not ordinarily considered. Even though a psychoanalytic understanding on the part of the adult might be available in a response, addressing the boy's reaction to what is actually a conflict rather than a mere question would evoke his resistance and more than likely turn off further inquiry from him. When a young boy asks questions about his observations, he is not necessarily soliciting information but rather is first giving voice to a puzzling dilemma that he is far from bringing to a solution. Thus we find operative, especially early in boys, the ability to refer to oneself an alarming physical condition as well as an equal and opposite one of denying such eventualities. At some later phases of emotional development, the same question, and usually still unspoken, continues to be revived. The little boy will provide himself with additional, but not substituted, reasons for the genital differences between himself and girls and women. It is not incidental that he has a time to go before he understands that girls have a genital; he believes they have nothing or a "hole." But a "hole" is no genital. Rather, it is some sort of aperture. It is alien. It is, therefore, troubling to a child's mind, which is naturally resistant to the unfamiliar and the conservative dread of the unconventional as defined by itself.

Reflecting these experiences to himself, a boy is alarmed by a woman's condition. He does not make himself an exception to what he observes in others; they are the exception. It follows that he will privately be concerned for himself. The escape from the fate of others, especially when they are different or alien-seeming, calls on one of the earliest human mental functions: the ability to deny our own perceptions, realities, or beliefs. How soon in our early years we acquire this function we have as yet no way of knowing. But when a child is thirty to thirty-six months of age, he has it as a well-developed, readily elicited, and easily demonstrated ability that requires little clinical skill to reveal.

The knowledge gained that the structural difference between the sexes is a natural phenomenon adds to a boy's understanding and, for a longer time than is supposed, to his bewilderment. The lasting conviction from his own familiar, private conclusions, not readily given up, also continues to be carried for a surprisingly long time. The issue here is not to detail some interesting notions that boys entertain. (I shall take them up later in this work.) What is important for our purpose is to realize that these long-standing beliefs are not *inert*, finally, with knowledge and maturity, to be dismissed and dispelled with other childish notions we once entertained. These enter into a boy's psychology and are conveyed into his understanding of masculinity.

Masculinity thus self-defined has elements of fear as part of its development. The boy's primitive logic of self-reference, which I have just described, leads him to an inescapable belief, albeit a self-deception, and by it into another source of dread. What he believes has happened to a girl, he is no less convinced could be his fate as well. These early anxieties of masculinity compel him to find a solution. It must be one that will be adequate to alleviate his hidden concern that his mother, the woman he so values, is also critically deficient. To temper his concern for her plight is not from compassion, rare in a young child. He has a self-directed reason. It is that through his identification with her, he, too, might suffer her deficiency.

This is central to his anxiety. It is a powerful, ordinarily intransigent incentive to dissociate himself from femininity as menacing.

Uninstructed in these fears or in the ramifications of being identified with a woman, the boy seeks his own answers. No one teaches him that a girl is misshapen because she lacks a feature he possesses, nor has it been suggested to him that she might purposely have hidden from sight that which is so manifestly unseen. As a small boy, he has not read, nor has he heard the timeless myths about women who have displaced this organ to some other feature of their bodies and are, therefore, possessed of influential menacing powers. Yet, from ancient legends these are seemingly universal beliefs, fears, and explanations that men hold about women. And young boys hold identical ones. They make their own myths. The monotonous yet marvelous similarity of the myths tells us one important route by which they endlessly travel. They are autobiographically developed. They are the expressions of the early masculine self. Such influential notions are commonly carried into adult life by some men consciously and many more unconsciously who perceive women as inexplicably alien-formed and inferior, or, in contradiction, as those who for reasons of their deficiency, employ mysteriously dangerous powers.

The similarity is astonishing between these early boyhood impressions, images, and conceptions of women, shown to be part of the everyday psychology of masculinity, and the countless myths whose durability is remarkable.

Women as a peril to masculinity, to flocks, and even to plants is a conception not expunged fully from our own culture. Our celibate priesthood does not find such notions altogether alien today. And in many parts of the world, rather than in merely its remote corners, during important religious ceremonies and rites, men are obliged to shun the company of women for fear of impairing their own prowess or success. What is noteworthy is the virtual absence of myths or legends in which a man magically or mythically jeopardizes women. He may threaten women with violence, rape, or destruction. But he holds no magic or mystery over her. It is as scarce in mythology as it is in the play of little girls; to them, too, women, not men, hold secrets and concealments.

A boy's identification with his mother, as for all children, is necessary at first for a binding sense of security. But by his second year his gender puts him in a quandary. He ordinarily and unconsciously begins to wish to repudiate what gave him the comfort he required. His fits of temper and beginning efforts to be independent of her are in the service of attempting to be free from the constraints and significance that are suggested by being like his mother. However, much as these protests are voiced or the relation to her disavowed, they do not expunge his identification with her. Rather, unconsciously he needs to respond to it, to be like her, closely tied to her, and yet to begin to repress it. The comfort he enjoys from his mother begins to grow an insidious worm.

In later phases of his emotional development, these anxieties will return as the conflicts are revived. In play, the boy will express fantasies of being like his mother and even being in her place. Then, once more, the compelling need to expunge such ideas occurs. To that end, his becoming unconscious of them follows. The more we become familiar with the psychology of small children, the more are we aware that neither parallel nor similar developments take place in the psychology of girls.

From what he knows and thus judges, a boy attributes to his mother qualities of being lesser, weaker, and even a victimized being. She is seemingly no equal partner. Regardless of what she in fact professes socially, acts out professionally, or proves in the labor force, she fails to alter her son's thinking her deficient by a criterion she does not effect. Those women who are active and aggressive and in the boy's mind are more like men because of their pursuits begin to take on the legendary character of combining both sexes in themselves. In the boy's fantasies, his mother is phallus-bearing. The effect on the boy is not reassuring, but alarming. He takes her androgyny as a sign she has overcome being merely a woman, and that she must, like himself, find that being a woman is odious.

Because of her deficiency, it matters not to a boy how successful she is in comparison to men; he wishes to be like her no longer. Instead, he goes to higher ground, so to speak, where he can identify himself with those who pose no threat of being themselves deficient. It is far more desirable, we learn from boys — and who would say otherwise? — to associate oneself and be identified with the haves rather than the have-nots. The defense of the sufferer, compassion for the prey, or the sacrifice of oneself for another are only human achievements. They are acquired ones. There are instances when a child is altruistic and even highly moral in late periods of emotional development. But the young boy lacking inspiration tires easily of these ideals.

We know from experience a boy's great incentive is soon to be identified with the aggressor. It is a far more persistent and frequent propensity in him than it is in a girl; the difference that accounts for it is to be found neither in their instincts nor in their biology. It is in their psychology. After about the second year of age, boys make it readily apparent in their spontaneous play, fantasy development, and self-defined aggressive roles. In the course of observing this activity, I have attempted to have boys abandon such roles. My efforts were resisted, and as a rule they failed. The quality of mercy develops late.

By contrast, on a number of occasions I have asked colleagues who like myself were studying the play of little girls between the ages of two and a half and four years to direct them toward the sort of spontaneous play that repeatedly and typically engaged boys of the same age. The central theme of the boys was playing some sort of aggressive, assertive character: a soldier against a delinquent enemy; a person in authority establishing and maintaining law and order; a person in an occupation calling for prowess and achievement; or a person directing others, whether in projects, employment, or domestic life. The variety and elaboration naturally depended upon the level of a boy's development and social experience, as it did the degree to which he was emotionally invested in such play. Whether the choice was literally the army, cowboys, a role in law enforcement as the police, or as head of a family seemed to matter less than the pleasure derived from such action-oriented, aggressive conduct that was invariably morally justified.

Two elements appeared to be essential in the aggressive expressions: the sadistic satisfaction that was fully justified and associated with narcissistic pleasure in its performance; and a high moral purpose. Thus no guilt was entailed or violation of conscience breached. Our efforts to suggest that the play was to gratify cruelty, aggression, or violence were invariably resisted by way of asserting that such acts were fully in accord with meting out justice and required the exercise of powers and performance.

We rarely succeeded in persuading a small girl to sustain such play. When she would engage in it, the encounter was brief even if a boy enthusiastically invited her. It evoked opposition, antipathy, and a conspicuous lack of pleasure. The high point of one such occasion was reported to me by a colleague. A little girl who seemed willing to enter into an "army game" bargained on the condition that she could "bake an army cake." None of us succeeded. The roles the little girls chose, even at times when they were very aggressive, did not carry with them the boy's dedication to being *identified* as an aggressor. This is to be distinguished from being aggressive. Little girls were periodically aggressive but this distinctly was not a part that invoked aggression so much as it was a narcissistic reaction that sought and found expression in aggressive conduct. A girl might take the part of a witch or drive a tractor but it was clearly more out of necessity than satisfaction, justified or dictated by circumstance. It might mean abandoning being a girl for a boy's role. However, once she engaged in such a part, she would play at it comfortably for periods of enjoyment and return with relish to resume the role.

There would, of course, be frequent references to the fact that she was only pretending not to be a girl, but playing the part of cowboys, Indians, male characters from science fiction, or girl companions to boys and in that way being indistinguishable from them all proved to be sources of pleasurable activity. This was especially true of being a girl in a boy's role. However, only exceptionally and not for long could a boy be persuaded to take a feminine part, and, unlike a girl, he never embraced it eagerly.

It is commonly and naively supposed that simply by changes in behavior, by the parents' sharing more equally the burdens of the nursery, a child's own deeper psychology would correspondingly be affected. The notion is that the child's emotional life is governed merely by what part the parents choose to play out before the child, as though he were a passive, uncritically receptive audience. The idea is altogether familiar from the eighteenth-century writing of Jean-Jacques Rousseau to the effect that there was no better way of guiding children than by emulation. Moreover, it promotes a presently popularly held belief that in the early years of a child's experience, parents, even if distinguished as mother and father, like their children, are not sexually identified and are virtually interchangeable in their roles. Further, it is believed that, as the parents' character parts are altered, the child's unconscious, if it is included in this reasoning, will somehow surely follow that course. The assumption is that the unconscious determinants of the child and the parents may be circumvented by a conscientious effort to redistribute deliberately the everyday functions ordinarily assigned by society and culture to a mother or a father so that neither parent would be defined sexually by chores performed. While this may easily succeed in making chores or duties free of being sex-linked, it can hardly be expected to affect the course of sexuality. The two are currently and broadly confused.

For a host of both social and emotional reasons, in some recent cultural shifts a man may be obliged, wish, or attempt to take a mother's part, and a woman, a father's role. Does he in his maternal stint abandon his masculinity, being a father, and in turn take on femininity? And is his attitude toward his son therefore that of a mother? Does a woman who comes home from a "man's" job act in a fatherly manner toward her son? And can she thus quit being his mother? The boy's need to emulate his father or a surrogate, the more to secure his masculinity, is, as we have found, bonded to what supports self-esteem. What if the surrogate is the mother? Does the boy merely adapt to these varying, and at times bewildering, conditions in which each parent offers him an imitation of the other? From psychoanalytic study, we have long and laborious-ly learned that the tenacity of our unconscious aims is not readily relinquished, nor is it modified significantly by mere willing or even wishful alterations of conduct. When what is offered socially is at odds with a boy's unconscious aspirations, his conflicts increase. His solutions, as a result, may be obstructed or all the more difficult to find.

As emotional development takes place, a small boy normally wants to win his father's favor. This is not merely for his affection but for the father's recognition of the boy's masculini-ty. In the absence of the father, the boy conceives of what behavior his father would approve in him and he wishes to produce it. But would he also want additionally to identify himself with his father in the relationship with his mother? And does a boy want sufficiently to have his father's affection so that he thinks of being in his mother's place with the father? From the psychoanalysis of men whose unconscious boyhood experiences have been recovered and from boys about the age of four and five years, all these wishes have been shown amply to be the case. Ordinarily, these desires are temporarily enter-tained. It is a period when the boy is so laden with anxiety about his sexual role that the impetus to be masculine is heightened. With it, the enjoyment of being aggressive grows to an intensity above what he has previously felt. Moreover, the incentive to prove himself is enhanced. It becomes an intense

21

matter of self-esteem. The wish to identify himself with his father is greatly amplified. The boy is thus drawn into the oedipal triangle to take his father's place with the mother. But this enterprise is doomed.

The little boy's unconscious fantasy that he would be a man like his father is an expression of his extravagant aims that gives a design to much of his play and games. The deep-seated and heavily invested wishes for an exclusive relationship with a parent, even though dimly perceived, wield enormous power and immense influence in a child's ego-centered existence. Hence, the boy's narcissism is deeply hurt from the failure to fulfill his intensely held aims to identify first with one parent and then the other. In the case of being in his mother's place, his masculinity is threatened. And to be like his father menaces the feminine identification that, on the one hand, he wants and, on the other, he would happily give up. It also evokes the strictest universal taboo: incest with one's mother! The fact that this rarely occurs, except under extraordinary psychotic conditions, proves the point, especially if we compare how commonly the taboo is broken between a father and daughter.

In this trying period of a young boy's aspirations, the conflicts that are developed evoke fears, apprehensions, and, in some instances, phobias and other childhood neurotic manifestations of varying duration. They are often not without rages, which parents tend to regard as expressions of frustration attributed to the role of circumstance rather than to a boy's own conflicts that he projects onto an uncompliant world. The boy arrives finally then at an emotional confrontation with his limitations. They are the basis of his fury more so by far than the trifles of everyday life that merely set it off. The whole experience of the oedipal years unconsciously comes to a welcome, if conflicted and despairing, end.

* * *

Intimately associated with the phenomenon of identification is the young boy's close attention to physical performance. He is no mere observer. In the early years, he is defined particularly in physical terms with respect to what he is and in relation to what he does in connection with what he is. His and others' expectations for him are also expressed in terms of physical performance and the meaning attached to it in achievement. We will recall how early in a boy's development performance is sexually identified as masculine. His penis is a performing organ. It marks a boy for masculinity and associates him with performance. For example, a small boy does not simply urinate. He does it with his penis: a real, palpable, remarkable organ that he associates with himself. How different from a child whose urine merely issues from a "hole."

It was such a phenomenon, although not this particular one, that led first Freud and then the analysts who followed him to support his observation that our ego is first a body ego.[10] It is the self *physically* defined that is the earliest sense of self. Its global aspects and importance also came to Piaget's attention a decade later. He referred to this time as when "the world is explained in terms of the self."[11] In the same context, he meant that the world is interpreted by "the very young child in terms of his own 'I.'"[12] Others' expectations for him become his own and heighten the physical ones. In addition to eager learning and the ready acquisition of knowledge that a girl would be as prepared to gain, the boy is concerned with the exercise of skill, cleverness, and mastery of performance. These are the immediate engines that nourish the young boy's ego. Others are lodged beyond a child's short horizons. A child learns for the present rather than for some remote future. As we would expect, we find a boy's relationship with the physical world is as direct and immediate as its mastery is gratifying. The widely acclaimed work of Piaget, which he began to publish in the early 1920s, fully demonstrates this. From his findings, Piaget fashioned an existentialist child psychology (although he would not call it that), which is flawed by his deliberate exclusion of the psychodynamics or the results of psychoanalytic studies of the child. Nevertheless, he makes the child's relation to the physical world plain; yet its deeper significance is neglected. This is all the more conspicuous as he allows no distinction in his findings among children between boys and girls.

All young children are in some respect exhorted to perform. But in the case of the boy, performance, as we earlier noted, acquires a unique, lasting importance. To this chain of experience, the link between the boy's little feats of development and the reward of pleasing his mother is quickly forged. With it goes his association of success to aggressiveness. He easily connects aggressiveness and succeeding or performing with giving his mother pleasure. His own satisfaction with himself and hers with him are quickly bonded. She enters into the new equation in which the emotional elements of performance and prowess associated with being a boy are prized. In the earlier nursery years, during the ages up to about three and a half to four years, there were precursors to the new premium placed on prowess and achievement. Before, intimacy was fostered with each parent, albeit not the same quality or nature for each one; now, a son's passivity, which might have satisfied some of his wishes, lacks reward. Or, at least if it earns reward, it is not the same. Inasmuch as his perception is emotional rather than intellectual, the boy sees accomplishment or achievement as performing a feat rather than acquiring mastery of a skill that might be developed and for which he might later be rewarded. In short, as he shows prowess, he wins the immediate approval he so eagerly desires. His self-esteem rapidly comes to depend upon and thus be emotionally tied even more than previously to being endorsed for performance. The continuity from the earlier experiences in the same vein, even if on a still infantile level, is further consolidated.

The supreme narcissism of all young children naturally hinges on a parent's approval. The exception, autism, that condition of extreme self-centeredness or pathological narcissism that excludes all others, pointedly proves the rule. As a small boy's activity is cultivated in him it unconsciously promotes a gain over his passivity. Thus prowess and self-esteem are soon permanently fused, giving a boy's activity an indelible meaning to him. It is not a matter of indifference whether the nod of approval comes from his father or his mother. For instance, when the mother is the principal one who exhorts her son, it is to satisfy her wishes that he performs, shows prowess and achievement. As one woman commenting on this aspect of her relation to her son said, "I secretly want him to be my ideal boy. Even to be my mother's ideal boy that I was not and couldn't be. I want him to be my golden son or self that I wasn't, golden-acting and golden-looking. I still want to be that boy. I named him Eric because I recall that as a little girl it was the name of a favorite uncle who especially liked me. It was a name I wished I had. And I could be perfect. So I named my son Eric. He knows how upset I get with him when he doesn't do well." She was hardly aware of the extent to which she unconsciously is reborn through her son, his name, his prowess, his performance and achievement. This time better than before. She is quickly and, she knows, unreasonably angry when he performs poorly or not up to her expectations. But for a father, a boy's prowess and achievement lead to identification with him. The boy is not thrown into the same conflict as when he feels his mother wants to be satisfied. When she exhorts him that he can do better, he fears she only reminds him his masculinity is wanting. Whereas his father's prodding promotes identification with him. This is not to suggest that it fails to bring about conflicts, but they are not the same as the ones that the mother's wishes evoke.

It is prowess, later translated further into performance, achievement, and self-esteem, that are the central, permanent ingredients of masculinity. What constitutes prowess and its subsequent efforts to become achievement associated with self-esteem in one period of life will serve the same ends later. It is the durability of the union between the importance of prowess, performance, achievement, and self-esteem, whether in sexuality or in his other pursuits, that remains throughout a man's existence to define and measure his masculinity for him.

Chapter 2

A MOTHER'S CAUSE
IS HER SON'S

THE NATURE OF a man's endowment of maleness begins to be evident and to be employed in his earliest years. However, long before an infant boy is aware of his maleness, his parents, and particularly his mother (inasmuch as his early care is hers), bestow on the nursling boy the earliest attributes of masculinity. It is she who must help a boy acquire, not maleness, but *masculinity*. In this effort, she unconsciously draws on and is influenced by her awareness of what masculinity is and by those conflicts she associates with masculinity.

The following comment of Freud's is generally accepted by analysts and idealizes the relationship of a mother to a son. It "provides the purest examples of an unchangeable affection, unimpaired by any egoistic considerations."[1] Nearly two decades later he reiterated that the relation of a mother to her son "is altogether the most perfect, the most free from ambivalence of all human relationships."[2] The further supposition that analysts hold is that what a mother suppresses in herself of her "masculinity complex" may be compensated in the satisfaction she derives from having a son. Thus, we see the supposition that the birth of a son represents an unmixed blessing, exempt from serious conflict. When Freud romanticized the relationship of a mother to a son, he was not holding up a mirror to nature.

Pregnancy calls forth in a woman the unconscious fantasies about herself that she has held since childhood. As a rule, these ideas do not enter consciousness directly, but may be revealed only in dreams. She may dream, for example, that some obscure changes are taking place in her genital, or that she is being observed from below, as though something unusual called attention to herself, by a very interested spectator. The pregnant woman may also have pleasurable dreams of handling unaccustomed objects competently. On awakening, the woman customarily will dismiss such dreams or simply relate them to the pregnancy. She naturally assumes that what is going on below is of interest, that changes are taking place, and that she is an object of attention. These assumptions are, in part, her narcissistic expressions of the attention she is giving to the inevitable body alterations associated with pregnancy.

Closer attention or scrutiny through analysis shows these are normal self-observations. Unconsciously, the woman is the spectator: she sees the transformations, and she also wants them to be seen, plainly visible and on display. These ideas are also associated with the unconscious phallic wish. Because, in fact, the wished-for bodily changes are not there. Through analysis, these dreams are found to express long-held wishes that some changes would occur. The dreams refer not so much to the pregnancy, which evokes them, nor to a period of a woman's early adolescence associated with fantasies of being a "tomboy." The ideas, commonly found in all women, date back to a forgotten and repressed time of early emotional confusion over anatomical differences between being a boy and being a girl. The little girl reacts to this confusion by a wish structurally to be a boy. This period is in contrast to adolescence, when the girl often succeeds in demonstrating, principally to herself, that the structural differences are not important. Of course, the

27

underlying motives for this behavior reveal that to the girl the differences are significant. The physical prowess she demonstrates as a "tomboy" is intended to disprove what she well knows. During pregnancy, however, these fantasies take on the added importance of being associated with the contents of the uterus, which may now hold the promise of their fulfillment. The existence of these fantasies during pregnancy also shows what we have noted earlier: the durability of old wishes from puberty and from early childhood.

Nor do a mother's wishes for a transformation in herself terminate with a birth. They may continue with even more intensity because of the reality of the child on whom she projects herself and into whom her wishes are now extended. Freud first noted that long-abandoned and unrequited childhood, self-centered wishes were to be found in the affection that parents held for their children. These wishes tend to be revived with the child's arrival.

> Thus they [the parents] are under the compulsion to ascribe every perfection to the child — which sober observation would find no occasion to do — and to conceal and forget all his shortcomings. ... The child shall fulfill those wishful dreams of the parents which they never carried out — the boy shall become a great man and a hero in his father's place, and the girl shall marry a prince as a tardy compensation for her mother. ... Parental love, which is so moving and at bottom so childish, is nothing but the parents' narcissism born again, which ... unmistakably reveals its former nature.[3]

We are not here concerned so much with the emotional experience a woman may undergo in becoming a mother, well described elsewhere, but rather what it means to her to have a male child, and what a profound effect it has on the boy's developing masculinity. Despite the immense literature, both scientific and popular, on the psychology of women, this question has received so little study that no authoritative work may be cited.

There has long been a tendency to regard a woman's relationship with a child by paying attention to them as a pair, or as a "couple." While this can be true, there is a tendency to neglect the psychology of each as an individual. In fact, the gender of the child invariably evokes certain unconscious, inescapable emotional attitudes, conflicts, propensities, and idiosyncrasies, all of which have great significance.[4] For most women, a child is emotionally perceived as an extension of herself. However, that this view of one's child should remain as the only awareness a mother has or holds, without regard for the sex of the child, would test credulity. The role of her child's sex in fulfilling herself as a woman, although well known in history and scarcely less familiar to us in literature, has nevertheless had scant scientific attention.

The work of Helene Deutsch on the psychology of women, which was published more than thirty years ago, remains an exception.[5] Deutsch shows that a child may indeed fulfill a woman's egoistic needs. She points to the fact that women commonly experience a feeling of inadequacy that they relate to being feminine, and they often seek compensation by means of a child. In some women such a need to be gratified becomes so pressing that it extends into a child's achievements. But even Deutsch does not carry her work to the point of fully making the distinction that a boy's accomplishments have a meaning for the mother that is different from what a mother aspires to through a daughter.

The urgent need of some women to realize their own aspirations through a son drives them to push them, from infancy, by promoting the barest signs of development, by adopting training methods, and, later, by taking educational measures to advance him along to accomplishment and prowess. Women naturally engage in solidifying their identification of their children with themselves, but in the pursuit of their egoistic aims, these mothers scrutinize their children, seeking qualities the mothers either have or wish they had.[6] The child is coaxed, supported, and made to feel duty-bound to perform and to win. The boundaries of identity between a mother and the extension of herself into her performing child become less and less distinct for each of them. Neither the mother nor the child soon knows where one begins and the other leaves off.

We may catch glimpses of some of these "ambitious" mothers who have not been able to deliver themselves from this "feminine predicament." Such women hover in their pursuits about the edges of the skating rinks, behind the lines of the tennis court, near the diving boards of the swimmers or the benches of the gymnasts. In short, wherever children are in individual physical competition, we are likely to find these women. (Fathers often also have this role but the psychology is different.)

The feats through which each is to be redeemed are not exclusively physical. In sports, the spectacle is additionally important and significant, because the need to be seen on stage, acclaimed and loved by the crowd, has added its special value. Intellectual exploits can be given similar significance. The pursuit of intellectual goals carries the same intensity and need for distinction even when there is no court to play on, no actual races to run. Above all, it is the merit of achievement that is extolled and not so much, if at all, its substance.

For those women who muse that they would have made a "good" man or who otherwise reflect on masculinity as preferable to femininity, they disinter fragments of their archaic overvaluation of masculinity, which circumstance has not modified. A son is likely to be overwhelmed and overvalued by such a woman, as he is overburdened with what is expected of him. He unknowingly becomes for his mother literally a narcissistic object or vehicle for her own self-esteem to be carried in. This mother unwittingly places her son in some emotional jeopardy. She hopes to bring about the long-held aspirations she had not herself brought to pass. Her husband may not have been any more successful than her father. Her relation to them is by way of identification, but her son is more than that: he is an extension of herself. Ostensibly, she may seem merely ambitious for her son, or zealous for his interests, as she may well have been for her husband and, before him, for herself. While this may seem to exaggerate these ordinary conflicts, we see brought to light in clinical cases the psychology of daily life, which might otherwise escape our attention.

Despite — and probably even because of — the active envy and jealousy that many women are aware they have of men, they nevertheless enjoy them. There are certain types of women, however, who cannot take pleasure in men. This feeling does, of course, find expression in the relationship of the women to their sons.

A young mother confessed with considerable embarrassment during a routine pediatric examination of her four-month-old son that she had difficulty in bathing him. She very reluctantly admitted that the "trouble" was the necessity to wash his genitals. Unaccountably, this created in her anxiety and inhibitions, despite the fact that she knew she should regard it as she does his other care. After much evasion and embarrassment, the mother finally revealed that her son's occasional erections alarmed her. She feared she somehow stimulated their appearance. She wanted no role in this. In this case, the mother could avoid her own fears, because her husband wished to help with their son's care, and she eagerly enlisted it. Her fears were, however, stirred up through the repugnant, stray thought that she wanted to fondle the boy. It mixed her pleasure at the idea with guilt and anxiety.

The woman confessed her incestuous fantasy by way of explaining her self-imposed prohibitions. The guilt at her wish to breach them was sufficiently pressing to bring out her anxiety, but, beyond this conflict, she had an abhorrence of touching a penis. She said that bathing her son and seeing his genitals, which she could not avoid doing, reminded her of the occasions when she averted her eyes from her husband's sexual organ. The penis, even her baby son's, frightened her. "After all," she said, "I know about being a girl. I know from myself how to handle that." But a boy was not the same

31

extension of herself. Her conflict was unusual only insofar as giving birth to a boy was not the fulfillment it normally is to most women.

This mother wants the fulfillment, but she resists the temptation. She admits that she wants the penis that frightens her for her own to fondle. Unknowingly, it rekindles some of her oldest wishes. She does not in fact dread the penis, but rather has unconscious wishes for it, which are known to her consciously only as prohibitions, fears, and anxieties. She tells us that a penis is more than an organ of pleasure for her. Possession of it represents a superior condition. And she admits it gives her satisfaction that she does not want to forgo. She does not want, however, to acknowledge herself to be an active partner with her husband or her son in sexuality. In relation to her husband, her role is ruled by inhibition. In the case of her son, it is ruled by prohibition. Rather than fully participating, she prefers the lesser anxiety of being submissive, hindered, and self-denying. Some men enjoy their masculinity as a narcissistic exercise of self-assertion. It would be utterly alien to this woman to enjoy her femininity that way.

Her marriage to a fastidious, understanding, patient, and seemingly untroubled man is a good one. She enjoys her sexual life. However, it is confined to the dark of night. She refers to that as a necessity, as though she were carrying on some illicit sexual relations. What anxieties she associates with male genitals are obscured in the dark, put aside in the bed, where she enjoys a measure of freedom. But she cannot elude them with her son. How her unconscious conflicts will be conveyed to her son to affect his view of himself, which is first his masculinity, we must leave to conjecture. Her immediate fears and anxiety about her effect on him responded to reassurance. The deeper conflicts were not reached sufficiently to be resolved.

Women who cannot take pleasure in men often find their relations with women to be unrewarding. Their own femininity is oppressive to them. For instance, in the condition that most clearly and uniquely defines a woman — pregnancy — these women refuse to accept femininity and are most aggressive. While they can take a fierce satisfaction in being pregnant, this satisfaction is coupled with a pride in not being in the least hampered by pregnancy. According to Helene Deutsch, such women regard their pregnancies as "brilliant." That is to say, their denial of femininity can be so effective that even the ordinary negative elements and physiological burdens are not perceived. In such cases, the woman emphasizes her continued efficiency and well-being so that none of her usual activities are disturbed or compromised. She also rejects any implication of dependence upon the father of the child. She thus "proves" herself superior; in her looking-glass, her wishes are reflected as reality. Deutsch additionally states, "From the analysis of such women we know that their longing for pregnancy is often an expression of their wish for a bodily possession, a wish that conceals the old penis envy."[7]

But there are other considerations in "old penis envy." There is a normal phase of a small girl's psychology in which she wants to be both what she is and masculine as well. Ordinarily, this is a transient, rapidly repressed period that does not come to clinical notice. The child has some recognition of her wish and soon enough consciously gives it up. In the case of the woman we are discussing, few or no clinical signs of this phase need appear until she bears a child. At that time, it is as though we are presented with an archaic specimen. By a study of it we may authenticate what was once a normal phenomenon in a little girl's psychology, which now, if not modified, is anachronistic and of clinical concern. In dispensing with a man as a partner, the needed self-assertion comes forward. Here is no desire for an independent family, no pleasure of a shared experience with a man. The woman who wants the child solely to herself is deeply, emotionally androgynous. She entertains the notion that she has the best of both spheres, and that she is spared the vicissitudes of either one. In effect, however, she functions by disclaimers. She is psychologically hermaphroditic, as incapable as a eunuch, functioning neither as masculine nor feminine. Her discontent grows out of a continued repudiation of herself that once began as a child's fantasy and that she is now attempting to live out in reality. As a woman, she hopes to gain finally what as a small girl she believed was denied her. She is no more prepared than she was as a child to share her baby with its father or a husband. An image of herself that would satisfy her narcissism tantalizes her to reach for what is beyond her grasp. If we are to believe that Aphrodite has among her powers as goddess of marriage, family life, kinship, knowing the kindling of love as well as how to keep it away, then such a woman is the object of Aphrodite's vengeance. Like Narcissus, she is cursed to be solely engaged with her own company. As we might suspect, she needs a son to complete herself. Should her child be a girl, we may be sure she will not be spared sharing her mother's curse.

*　　　*　　　*

A young mother brought her only child, a boy, for clinic help because he was too difficult to manage at nursery school. His teachers complained and would not take him back until he was less abusive and aggressive, not only to the other children, but to the teachers themselves. He was a very bright, well-developed, verbally precocious thirty-month-old boy.

In investigating this mother's history, I learned that she had become pregnant during the period when she was contemplating marriage. On learning her condition, she announced, to her family's dismay, that she had no intention of marrying the child's father. While pregnant, she continued an active occupation and lived out-of-wedlock with the man whom she had previously planned to marry. Although he wished to marry her, she now firmly refused him. The young man was not eager to press his unplanned paternity, and a few months before the boy's birth, the father disappeared, to the young woman's relief. He has since not been heard from. Of necessity, she gave the care of the baby over to her widowed mother while she returned to work part-time. The boy was given the full name of his mother's dead father.

We learned from the mother that she wanted her child only to be a boy. She was "certain of it" all during her pregnancy. In fact, she had known for a long time before she got pregnant that she wanted a boy. There was something, she admitted, about having a girl that she could express only by stating repeatedly that she "really wanted only a boy." She knew this was an unreasonable notion, but she "could not change it, not that she thought she would." She could not explain her "mind being made up just to have a boy." The thought of giving birth to a girl was so overshadowed by the strength of her wish that it relieved her of the anxiety.

The short time that the mother lived with the boy's father proved what she "always believed." Like other men, "he enjoyed himself at a woman's expense." Despite her feelings about him, she was hopeful that she would get pregnant. She felt that she had to submit to sexual relations she did not enjoy, and she felt helpless to resist the intercourse necessary to gain her reward. Her son's father, whom she had met shortly after completing high school, was the only man she had slept with. Although he wanted to get married and she agreed to it, she did not want it. On reflection, she confessed she had no real intention of marrying. Once the baby was on the way, she was "determined not to get married." She wanted neither to live with a man nor to have a husband. The young woman had her wish when the boy's father disappeared. She did not want to function either as a mother or as a woman. She unwittingly expressed this by her resistance to a man's appetites. To accede to them would force her to be feminine. Her long-held fantasy of giving birth to a boy was realized with her son's arrival. By way of her son she gained as well her unconscious wish to be masculine. We thus may judge what a powerful, rewarding determinant it was that made her willing to alter her way of life. With her son's birth, she was no longer a girl, or a mother.

She was launched in a struggle with the boy over masculinity. He was her unconscious masculine part or the masculine extension of herself that she produced as though by parthenogenesis. The man's role was disposed of.

The woman whose need for a masculine identification is not satisfied by a relationship with a man or with her son remains unconsciously feeling deprived. The deeper jealousy of men is repressed in favor of the socially rationalized attitude of deploring being, as Euripides wrote of Medea, "home-yoked." The young woman who is not content to be either wife or mother or woman would, with social sanction, be gaining her ends through a virtual emotional parthenogenesis. Then she feels she owes nothing to the man. The young woman in this instance showed us she had no intention of sharing with the father of her child her unconscious, narcissistic need to complete herself, i.e., by becoming masculine.

A mother who views dependence and passivity in her baby daughter as an undesirable trait is not, so to speak, looking at her child as she is, but is holding the baby up as a mirror to herself. Thus, she reveals her own unresolved underlying conflicts over her feminine relationship to men, in which dependence and passivity have remained issues of contention rather than sources of satisfaction. She unwittingly imposes her own fears on her child, and, in her daughter, she foresees an experience with men that she regards as being like her own. She conceives that the relationship to a man, especially its literal sexual aspects, requires her submission. In it, she is no equal partner. She feels that her anatomy dictates her destiny. Hence, she judges herself the inferior of the two. Whatever rationalizations a woman draws on from social and political institutions to support her reasoning, her earlier child's judgment had never been overturned.

When she regards her son as passive, her torment by it is associated with her own fears. However, it is in relation not to women but to men that it gives her the greatest cause for alarm. She sees herself in his place as giving in to be "used" by a man. She may, as many women do, find cause for a seemingly parallel concern when she thinks of her son as being dominated by a woman. That woman she views as the more masculine, like herself. She may deplore the balance, but she will not be fearful of it.

Women who complain about their sons' overactivity can be revealing their own conflicts about their sons' masculinity. When this is the case, the mother's report of her son's development in relation to activity shows subjective distortion in her recollections. As a rule, the boys did not commence their "restlessness" during the pregnancy or even at birth, when they are usually active, vigorous, and normal babies. However, by about two years of age, as they mastered walking, their activity began to create problems for their mothers, problems that derive from the meaning that some mothers attach to the ordinary aggressiveness and destructiveness of small children and particularly boys. These mothers are harassed at times by the fantasy that their sons may become delinquent and regard their little boys, even at so young an age, as already showing in their activity certain propensities for a threatening masculinity they fear. A mother might complain that she is the helpless object of the boy's attacks citing endless encounters with him to support her fantasies of masculine sadism. Her efforts to defend herself, she pleads, are remarkably ineffectual. She deplores her suffering, yet she seems unable to escape it.

A mother once described to me that her two-and-a-half-year-old son somehow had seized a large kitchen knife with which he pursued her. Only after she implored him did he drop his threats and stop brandishing the weapon. This was a huge woman, being menaced by a baby holding a knife, and only by pleading with him to abandon his intentions was she spared. The ludicrous incongruity of the scene entirely escaped her. This woman describes her relationship to the boy's father in much the same words. She fears her husband, not because he has given actual cause, but because she is afraid of what he might do. Hers is the conviction that men are self-serving and

37

that their activity, like her son's, is best understood simply as "masculine." Even while she was pregnant, she regarded her baby as a boy, not an infant; to her, being a boy is being violent. Her fantasy of him while he was in the womb was that his violence would only increase with his growth and strength.

Many women with this idea have the fantasy, usually unsupported by a search of the medical records, that the birth of their son was especially difficult and resulted in lacerations to their genital. These fantasies express what the women believe about men and often about the boys: that from birth the males want to inflict assaults on them. Rarely do these women complain that giving birth to their daughters was a tortured experience. These women feel themselves to be victims of men's sadism, to which they must surrender.

In this vein, one such woman related during analysis the following about her relationship with her husband: "It is my fault he treats me this way. If I was better in dealing with him, he wouldn't be like that. I know I am hard on myself. I expect a lot of myself. But, as I set out to do something that's important to me, I'm afraid I'll collapse. I haven't ever. I'm strong, actually, for a woman. But I fear I'm not. I put myself down at the tail of the line, or the back of things going on, or the fringe. If I protest, I know I believe a man will tell me to get farther back. And I'll go there. It's a feeling, to be honest, of not really deserving better. Any complaint I may make will be met with scorn and put down — more: somehow, I can't expect to be listened to. . . . This feeling about myself goes back as far as I can remember. It was always this way. Much as I suffer from it, I guess I know it can't be changed. And for me to ask, or to pray, as I used to do as a little girl, or want to be different is ridiculous. Some things can't be changed. Men would act better in dealing with me if I would not make them angry, and that comes from my being angry that it's not fair. I suppose I shouldn't complain when somehow I know it's my fault. I was always jealous of my brothers. It wasn't fair that they were boys and I was not. My mother was angry, too. But I blame her."

Even with the conviction that the wish to be changed from femininity may be in vain, these women nevertheless struggle against their fathers' and their husbands' and their sons' masculinity. They cannot allow themselves to enjoy complying to a man. They unconsciously compel men to force submission to them. Then only, over their own protests, can they ever be satisfied, free of guilty feelings of having been a willing participant in pleasure with a man. Theirs are left-handed marriages. These women feel that men are contemptuous of women because they are women — a projection of their own self-image and of course not unsupported by a residue of a man's archaic notion. Such a woman has a relationship with a man at the expense of her self-esteem. Her merit can only lie, she thinks, in her service. She serves her son no less than her husband. In her deep resentment of men and boys, whose lot she envies, she fears their contempt. She looks for and finds refuge among women. This is not a homosexual escape or attachment, as may superficially appear to be the case, although some unconscious element of homosexuality may exist. Rather, in relations with a woman a reprieve is provided from some painful, conflicted aspects of the nature of the relationship with men. Women correctly sense that men carry unconsciously, even in their honest aims for a woman's full partnership, a measure of contempt for them that is the unexpungeable, narcissistic pride of ownership, which is central to a man's sense of what he possesses. Such notions fit in with the common, universal view held by all children. Boys hold them with arrogance and anxiety of ownership. Girls, in viewing them with envy, create in themselves a sense of unfitness; and if they hold on to this belief later as women, it will be that they are lesser than men. The mere fact of being a woman, according to this ineradicable childhood conviction, is to take "the uneven allotment of nature that the male bird alone has the tuft."[8] It means that they themselves, too, scorn women.

Such ideas originate in the "boyhood" of girls; we find also that they persist. Behind the curtain of amnesia of women, under certain conditions and circumstances, these ideas reenter into normal neurotic conflicts that women may experience and that may develop into pathological proportions when self-esteem suffers. The disorders then tend to be those of depression, hypochondria, and severe anxiety attacks associated with expressions of aggression.

The kind of woman who fears the helplessness that she associates with being female dreads her femininity. She regards an infant's helplessness, need, and dependence just as she does such feelings in herself — as stigmata of femininity. Especially in her son, they call forth her disgust and resentment with him as with herself. She then makes no emotional distinction between herself and him. Her loathing of helplessness and dependence often leads her to rages and a bewildered hatred of babies and particularly boy babies. She has little patience with their growth and development; the child's babyhood is a period to be endured. Her fantasies about her baby boy run to him as grown, seeing him accomplished as a man and his achievements made. His competition won, she can now enjoy him.

On the one hand, to placate her little son will lead to the development of the excessive aggressive demands she fears in men; on the other hand, to indulge his wishes she justifies from her vexation at the passive role associated with being a girl. She is fated to discontent. By her well-meant intentions, she fails to lead her son to find his limitations and to gain the impetus to attempt to transcend them. The boy's surmounting discontent is not his own and is lost to him on account of his mother's intervention. What may lead to creativity, in which lies the expression of expectation realized, brings instead the enraging frustration that demands unopposed indulgence. This mother tolerates her own limitations with scarcely more patience than she does those of her son. She commonly erupts

40

into an unbridled anger over his infantile efforts that might prove resistant to her own wishes. As an extension of herself, idealized in him, she inadvertently cultivates in her son the attitude that there should be few, if any, limits. She fosters the idea that the adverse effect of conditions, circumstances beyond one's influence, misguided acts of another, and the no less likely movement of the stars, rather than oneself, hold one's fate. She and her son, in short, are hostages of the haphazard.

Chapter 3

OF WOMAN BORN

FROM THE RECESSES of a woman's psychology, a hidden variety of influences lie ready to be aroused. They tend to carry a powerful, lasting impetus. None seem to be more important or to affect a woman's psychology more profoundly than those exposed through her unique relationship to her son. It is through him that the resolution of some of her most repressed conflicts as a woman, at long last, may be realized. Her son thus holds hostage her fulfillment with respect to these conflicts. As the instrument that may give her femininity an added dimension, the son is an important investment for the mother, who, hence, affects his masculine development. A son cannot too soon begin to wear the mantle of masculinity his mother is eager to drape about him. Usually unconsciously, when she accepts the emotional reality of being pregnant, she commences to think of her child as masculine.

We have observed in boys that they take their mothers' ambition for their masculinity onto themselves. Analysts, hardly less than others, have conventionally put the importance of such aspirations as deriving from the identification with the father. Only a deeper probing of the boy's intentions, which for obvious reasons he is most reluctant to have uncovered, shows that he has earlier and tenaciously identified with his mother's wishes for his masculinity. The two identifications are not contradictory. The hazard for the boy lies in that he not only identifies with his mother's femininity, but he also retains it. Moreover, he perceives that he is the carrier of her masculine wishes that she would have fulfilled through him. Naturally, in a small boy such notions unwittingly fire expression in fantasies of being Triton among the minnows, the boy-wonder Hermes, or any conceivable variation of these ancient mythical marvels made socially contemporary. At no time of life is there more viability given them than during the early thralldom years of a little boy's intimacy with his mother. We may not expect a boy to find such elemental conflict through self-scrutiny. But for our search as to what is the matrix of masculinity, it is very important.

Concern may be felt that the examples cited here merely reflect the feeble comfort that life is unfair and that we are witness simply to suffering. Were this all, the condition of a woman as a single parent would indeed give us little more to be moved by or to understand than its limited and also probably often joyless existence. But a mother as a single parent of a son together make a couple with jointly engaged particular emotional conflicts. While on the one hand their mutual problems are commonplace, on the other, they also tend for each one to become invariably intensified. This is to say that what for the son is ordinarily a transient conflict with regard to his mother becomes prolonged. For instance, a boy's identification with his mother naturally is promoted, but under these circumstances an excess of resistance to it is evoked as a reaction. At the same time, the opposite occurs. A resolution may be deferred indefinitely. A boy's identification with aggressiveness in a man gains an inordinate importance. But it is by way of fantasy more than through the tempering real experience of a relationship with a man. The result is less moderate. A son's prowess and marks of his achievement are always critical to his developing masculine experience. But as they are drawn into the service of the intimacy of a mother's wishes, she becomes less inclined to distinguish them from her son's needs. The effect promotes a boy's dependence on his mother especially at a time when such elements of his development should be bringing the opposite effect. The bill of particulars is long and burdensome to both in this "couple."

To return to the case history begun in Chapter II, concerning the mother who had a son out-of-wedlock and had no interest in having a long-term relationship with a man, we concern ourselves here with the effect on the son of the mother's attitudes. When the boy, whom we shall call Marty, was a year old, the mother and her overindulged son moved to their own apartment, out of the grandmother's house. They were still, however, near the home of the grandmother, who continued some of the care of the child while the mother was employed. When the mother returned from work, she regularly found her son in a fury. Marty complained to her that when she was away she was engaged in activities that she placed ahead of him. His demands frightened her into impulsive indulgences, as well as arguments and punishments that were equally impulsive. Often, she admitted that she was no less angry than he, and she expressed it to him as readily as he did to her. The mother dreaded the boy's temper and at times placated him for fear that in his "fits of temper he'd fly at me." When he would flail at her with his little fists, she had vivid images that he would assault her seriously. By his second year, matters grew worse. Marty had begun to add his verbal facility to his cruelty. He was often very abusive and flung back at his mother her own occasional angry obscenities and some he had picked up at a nursery school he now attended. His demands increased and were "overbearing." Few men other than relatives visited them. Aside from occasional male attention, the child was his mother's sole companion. She treated him so. He demanded to be served first at mealtimes and became enraged if she asked him to wait so they could eat together. He went so far as to require her to give up the use of the toilet to him; at times, as he saw her intention to use it, he pushed himself ahead of her. On these and other occasions, she freely admitted, his behavior often led to absurd fights that were like brawls. She usually capitulated.

When Marty came to see me, he was dressed meticulously in clothes that seemed more appropriate for an older boy. He gave the appearance of a little man, when in fact he was hardly more than a baby. He organized his play with me with a precocious concentration from which he would only with great reluctance permit himself to be distracted. In this way, he not only controlled the time during his visits but also showed his determination. His chief interest in play was the various toy "toothy" creatures: he selected lions, tigers, and bears, and, with clay, he fashioned "snakes." He also chose small dolls and soldiers, which, individually or together, he engaged in very aggressive, destructive encounters. In the course of these skirmishes between the toys, he forcefully asserted his wishes. He could be dissuaded from such violent play only briefly and with great resistance. In fact and in fantasy his activity was confined to aggression. When he arranged the animals in a way that they attacked the dolls, or when the soldiers were shooting animals or each other, he issued the commands they were to carry out. Or, he would make animal noises as though he were the creature attacking a defenseless doll. When I pleaded for mercy, for compassion, or for some extenuating circumstances on behalf of the victims, I could not persuade him to relinquish his purpose. Marty allowed no quarter, no pity for tears or misery. Moreover, he enjoyed the role he gave himself and would not give it up for any other. There were few peaceful moments among his toys. He allowed me only to follow his wishes in play; I was not permitted to exercise mine. When I suggested that we pretend the animals were not wild but in a zoo, he soon had them out of their cages menacing each other or people who were present. A suggestion from me that the animals were perhaps content, or that people would like to play rather than just fight, would be accepted by him in a perfunctory fashion and then he would quickly set one against the other.

In these struggles, control, authority, and aggression were inseparable from his fantasied identity as a man. He emphasized that whatever character he portrayed, or whatever animal through which he expressed himself, was male. He firmly refused my proposal to assign some of the parts to women or to female animals. The women were set apart; like his mother and grandmother, they were victims of violence. He would not in his play defend a victim, even though it was not always a woman, girl, "girl" animal, or "mother" animal. Although his mother's struggles with him were indeed characteristic of aggression, only men were allowed to be aggressive in his play. I suggested that women were also aggressive — if not in his play, this was the case at home with his mother. He rejected the notion of a woman's being aggressive like a man and flatly denied the situation at home.

After many sessions, although Marty did not give up his identification with the aggressors as men, he admitted his fears of violence. In the course of this admission, he permitted himself for brief intervals to be the little boy he was. But still he needed to retain his fantasied excess of masculine powers. Although he was only three years old at this time, he was certain that as a little man he was in far less jeopardy than as a little boy. While his masculine powers were ill-defined in his mind, he illustrated all the extravagances of "Superman" qualities in their simplest form as expressive reactions of just the opposite condition. Later in this work we shall see the same conflicts and defenses somewhat more developed and sophisticated. But their elaboration will not obscure that what this small boy plainly shows is at the foundation of particular masculine conflicts: first, that violence or forms of aggression are early narcissistic reactions associated with threatened masculinity; and, second, that prowess and authority are denied to women. In Marty's anxiety over what is at stake — the withdrawal or loss of his mother's love — he is obliged to test and provoke her. While this is a concern of all children, this exceptional little boy illustrates the norm dramatically.

The mother of this boy is unaware that she cultivates in her son what she wanted to be free of in his father. She promotes in her son, paradoxically, the model of a man she resents. Independent of the boy's father by way of her son, the wry jest is that the boy is seriously threatened by her will and cannot share his masculinity with her. She does not enjoy his having it alone and he does not and cannot give her any of his satisfaction in it. By cultivating in her son her own wish to be masculine, she includes her own unconscious aversion to women and to femininity. Had Marty not had unmanageable rages at nursery school, which his teachers would not tolerate, his mother would most likely have found excuses for her son's temper tantrums, violence, and aggressiveness, and would not have brought him for treatment.

He demeans his mother and all women, whom he naturally would identify with her. He does not, however, fail to recognize that she is powerful and that he depends on her for his own security. His father's absence heightens the anxiety he shows. However evenly explained, the absence of a parent leaves a small child with the private conviction that the parent who remains or who is the survivor is the stronger. A young child also often has the notion that the absent parent was sent away or somehow was gotten rid of because of misdeeds, evil intentions, or whatever in a child's experience and imagination might bring about a loss of affection. Children are deeply troubled by such ideas. Thus, real events, which give such notions support, whether through the mother's fury, the boy's rages, or the father's disappearance, reinforce his normal fears of being abandoned.[1] In defense, the child identifies with the aggressor, claims extravagant powers, and overvalues himself. These reactions all develop in the service of quelling the dread of being abandoned, being helpless, and being too limited to relieve himself of the effect of such events. A child yields to fearing his fate by way of fantasy and play in which he

47

takes on the very qualities he lacks to make himself secure. By way of them, he disclaims his anxieties in declarations of being fearless and powerful. In this case, Marty asserts his willful, lilliputian authority over his mother, as he fancies himself a man.

It is generally true of all of us, but it is especially the case with children that they do not observe their own coming maturity. A child does not see himself changing in character or developing emotionally. Rather, he sees himself merely "growing up," by which he understands that his dimensions expand. Without further professional help, this small boy is likely to alter little emotionally. His masculinity is now a problem. In that respect, it is one of the conflicts associated with identification. Identified with his mother, toward whom he has an aversion as a woman, he also depends on her. As his mother, he is thus deeply attached to her, but as a woman he also fears her. On the other hand, he is identified with his absent father, a presumed victim and also an aggressor with whom he would associate in order to make himself more secure. Without being brought to a compatible resolution, the boy's masculine development, fraught with such continuing impediments, promises to remain neurotic. To add to the boy's conflicts, he is also unconsciously relieved to be rid of his father, who would interfere with his own wishes for intimacy with his mother. At the same time, he cannot escape the actuality that, like the mother, he was abandoned. It means to him that he, too, was rejected. This experience makes identification with her all the more alienating, and a natural intimacy, unconsciously dangerous. He fights off both.

One of the most familiar problems to analysts is that created by the early loss of a parent, whether by death, divorce, or separation, which results in the remaining parent's (more often the mother) absorbing the whole of the young child's love and, thus, promoting early, persistent sexual conflicts. In the case of boys whose fathers are absent, emotional disturbances appear and are usually of a particular aggressive nature. These problems soon become associated with their developing masculinity. Later, in many instances, during adolescence, homosexuality either becomes overt or strongly latent. This is to say it may be easily evoked or as readily bring forth a vigorous defense against its eruption. The presence of youthful homosexual conflicts has been significantly contributed to by those circumstances in which early maternal seductiveness played a role in the boy's relation to his mother. As a consequence of her unwitting seductive behavior, the boy responds to her conduct with more than the usual secret sexual fantasies. She is the unconscious central figure in them. They are unselfconsciously divulged and create premature excitement. Thus they are generated when the small boy is poorly defended against them. Such fantasy results in anxiety that furthers aggressive behavior. It also promotes his developing, unconsciously, as a defense, highly idealized images of a father who is extremely punitive, disapproving, and intolerant of the boy's masculinity. The rages at the mother are a reaction to her as an *agent provocateur* against whom the child must defend himself.

In our instance at hand, the mother is genuinely fond of Marty and is affectionate with him, in spite of their fighting with each other. While the boy's dependence on her does not diminish, she is nevertheless repudiated, as his play and behavior show. When a little boy, who necessarily depends on his mother for a sense of security, is obliged to scorn her, he tends to extend this scorn to all women. He will attribute to his mother that she hates men and that all women must be as she is. He thus is inclined to seek another object for his affection. His affections will carry with them the longed-for dependence out of which he did not develop. Paradoxically, the boy does not learn from his mother, who wants him for herself, to love women. Instead, he fears them, their possessiveness, their presumed hatred of men. A powerful incentive to turn to a man for affection, with whom a less hostile and conflicted relationship seems likely, is a commonly sought refuge, as development proceeds. The basis for a submissive relationship to a man is formed and will seem the more sexually attractive.

*   *   *

Although a mother may dread a man's aggression, she becomes anxiety-laden when she perceives in her small boy's behavior signs of passivity rather than aggressiveness. In her son's seeming passivity, she sees a dangerous quality: he is being feminine. She fears the boy is too identified with her.

Rarely is a son's passivity viewed as a natural outcome of the nursery experience. Often a father is enlisted to aid the mother's effort to lift the presumed ominous signs of passivity. Such parental aims are not lost on any child. A boy may readily adapt to them, but not without learning that passivity is a menacing condition. Adolescent boys commonly dread passivity. Late in youth and in young adulthood, this fear can create a serious condition of panic that borders on, and may in fact become, psychotic in its dimensions. These episodes tend to be brief. Their importance for our purposes is that the horror of passivity in a youth and a man holds its terror for him in that he experiences it as representing a homosexual conflict — the wish and the fear of sexually submitting, like a woman, to a man. These conditions are exceedingly uncommon in women and even more rare in girls. A homosexual panic in an adolescent girl does not hold the potential clinical malignancy for her that it usually does for a boy.

The son of a mother who regards his activity as having a fearful portent of masculinity seems manifestly from an early age to fulfill his mother's prophecy. She foresees in her son's daily behavior the growing masculinity she both envies and decries. This suggests, many analysts have supposed, that the boy somehow divines his mother's unconscious fears and is inexplicably under a compulsion to act them out and thus to confirm them. Presumably, it would lead a boy to fear his masculinity, as his mother does, and to reinforce through his fear his further identification with his mother. As I have shown, neither need be the case.

However, the boy responds to the fears a mother harbors by means of a remarkable and early reply: he becomes excessively aggressive. This aggressiveness is rarely seen in girls, for obvious reasons. All children develop the wish to be like their mother, but a boy also needs to repudiate such wishes because of what he comes to believe they represent. When a small girl needs to reject what her mother represents to her, the basis for it is not the same conflict that it is in a little boy. The effect of a boy's excessive concern with activity shows, on analysis, that much of his play depicts the rough, violent, and often destructive encounters that he believes occur between people. The boy plays them out with others and also with objects that symbolize them. As a consequence, when imaginative play is thus narrowed, the principal intercourse among people is seen by the boy to be strife. While the violence between relations is not comforting to him, he views kindly behavior as a sign of passivity. Although he may be receptive to it, he more naturally associates himself with the aggressors, inasmuch as passivity raises his anxiety.

From observations and analysis of play, we find that a small boy commonly regards individuals in relation to each other as aggressors to victims. This division begins to be expressed clearly toward the end of his second year. This is not to suggest that the distinction he makes is necessarily that men are aggressors and women are their victims. But, to a boy, masculinity is at a premium and seems to require aggression to assert it. When the separation between aggressor and victim develops in his mind, he reveals the normal exaggeration of everyday concerns. Whether he is concerned with authority and being subject to it, security and being dependent upon it, or his recognition of parental care that panders to his needs, the effect is to fail to distinguish one from the other. Although the division is made the rule, it is the balance of relationships between people, rather than their quality, that matters most to him. A boy quickly comes to associate self-esteem with being the aggressor or the authority with vested powers. The early recognition of the physical differences between himself and others continues its importance. A child's mentality resists yielding its perceptions to review and introspection. Moreover, the child has a stake in partiality. Carrying a penis, however estimable to a boy, is always a burden. Its association with the early self-ideal and self-esteem is set.

It has long been assumed that the identification with the aggressor is a simple psychological defense, typical of young children, as a natural defense against the fears of feeling helpless, dependent, and perhaps at times as a victim. All children experience these conflicts, which are founded on their growing awareness of their real condition as children. Girls, however, must be distinguished from boys, for they follow a different course in the way they unconsciously defend themselves against these fears. This problem of childhood does not bring them, as it does boys, to the issue of self-esteem. Girls' efforts are directed quickly to mastering their fears by means of achievement, more for its own sake than to prove femininity or to uphold preference. Their childish narcissism is satisfied in this fashion earlier and with less conflict than it is in boys. The widespread intellectual precocity of young girls naturally expresses their need for mastery.

The notion of himself as the victim is already a conflict to a boy by the time he is about two and a half years old. It is a part in which he tends to cast girls and women. Despite his eagerness to be identified with men and boys, he cannot expunge the early formed identification with women, and he remains haunted by it throughout his existence. It is this fear, an affront to masculine narcissism, which promotes his establishing himself in the role of the aggressor. A boy employs performance, achievement, and hostility toward this end. Most of his play toward the close of his second year and throughout his third year is in the service of the narcissism of masculinity. The aggressiveness that forms so large a part of his activity is aimed toward solving problems or conflicts. When the aggressiveness becomes an end in itself, the gratification of it is associated with a developing sadism.

A girl is no less observant by the age of three years, but her spontaneous play shows that she is not similarly affected. As a rule, she does not readily identify herself with the aggressor. Studied observation of the play of a girl the same age as a boy shows she uncommonly initiates taking the part of the aggressor with the intent of finding a victim. When she does, she tends to imitate boys. But the basis of her aims is not the boy's. His is to *secure* his claim. Hers is to *establish* one. In play the aggressive girl is engaged more in expressions of envy, greed, and discontent in a reach that exceeds her grasp. She hopes for magic powers to gain over a deprivation or loss. Her wishes are to be identified with boys and men; she is a victim in search of an aggressor with whom she would identify herself. The foundation of self-hate is buttressed. And it follows that the early identification with her mother is not an incentive, but, as we have observed in a small boy, it becomes a development to resist. A girl who needs to resist inordinately identifying herself with her mother and takes a narcissistic pride in how like her father she is unconsciously develops an impediment to her femininity. She may delight in showing skills that she perceives to be more masculine than feminine, take a narcissistic pride in being ignorant of so-called feminine domestic pursuits, and believe she has won her freedom from her small girl fantasy of femininity as an unfair condition. She is not liberated, however, from hating herself as a girl. She represses it. As she matures, her reaction may take the form of misogyny expressed as finding motherhood and a woman's conventional role repugnant or as ambivalence eloquently exaggerating both femininity and a *manqué* masculinity. In neither instance does she escape her childhood-repressed self-demeaned image of what it means to her to be a girl. It would be hard to imagine she would fail to pass her convictions to a child.

We are forced to the conclusion that the difference in gender profoundly affects the young ego, the effect of which is seen sooner than has been supposed. A course of conflict for a boy is set remarkably soon. His masculinity needs to be secured, asserted, and continually reaffirmed. A girl's femininity does not follow that route. In feminine psychology, as we have seen, a central conflict is in recovery from an early conceived narcissistic injury. By contrast, a boy's lies in the peril of one. Hence, taking the role of the aggressor, the side to which a boy is drawn, shows in his play that the natural process of identifying with one's mother is resisted artlessly as it is a source of conflict. Correspondingly, the little boy's eagerness to be like his father, whether in fact or in fantasy, whether the father is present or absent, is promoted. We shall see later on what develops when a boy unconsciously rejects being like his father and prefers instead to be identified with his mother.

There are varieties of aggression in little boys. When they are between the ages of two and five years, their "overactivity" is most commonly complained about. Characteristically, they appear to be driven. At times, they resemble some clinical conditions that are recognized as founded on certain uncommon brain disorders. Many physical studies have been carried out in these particular cases but they have revealed no organic or pathological findings. The women who complain bitterly of such activity often claim that their boys were overactive from birth; some are reported to have been so even before birth, while "in utero." For others, the activity was said to have begun as they started walking, at which time "they broke into a run," and, it seemed, they had been "running ever since."

There are boys whose aggression and identification with an "aggressor" in their early years is disrupted from the course their masculinity ordinarily is set on. Their deeper psychology is to be exceedingly demanding of indulgence. When these boys naturally behave aggressively, their mothers are motivated to abort the fury they fear will erupt. In their zeal, such mothers, unlike those we have previously cited who surrender to aggression, thwart their sons in it. Thus, they further impede or impair the boy's identification with the "aggressor" by placating and indulging his whims and wishes. They may wish to gratify their daughters no less, but a mother's attitude toward her son is different. When a mother indulges her daughter, she is often unconsciously motivated by a desire to compensate her for what she believes she lacks, rather than from a fear of what her demands evoke.

A little boy who is encouraged by ambitious parents freely to do as he wishes is soon persuaded that his childish accomplishments are certain indicators of his greatness. He experiences more conflict over his achievements than reassurance by them. His real limitations are pressing and contradict his immodest wishes. Risk and fear are combined with the excitement of demanding satisfaction from oneself, from something one may do, or from another person. A new, different, and untried venture naturally brings uncertainty and a confrontation with limits, hence, self-scorn. From such exaggerated expectations, which all young children begin to develop in their appetites, is added the fuel that demanding parents unwittingly supply, particularly to boys: that they can fulfill their wishes because they are so gifted or clever; it is as though there were no limitations. A zeal to achieve is thus promoted in the boy, but so also are conflicts over fulfillment from which inhibitions issue. What of the wish to violate a taboo? Unconscious parental expectations of a boy, especially the mother's, tend to be more immediate and less compromising than those of a girl, unless she is the "boy" of the family. A boy is encouraged to be more centered toward performance. And as the fear emerges that gratification may not be quickly forthcoming, a refusal to chance failure is common. The obverse may also occur. A small boy is often found to make prodigious efforts to overcome his fear of failing. He may continue in them, so that by the age of four and five years he cultivates secret fantasies that he is then reluctant to divulge of being a "superboy." As he becomes older, he is no less wedded to such aims. He cannot relinquish them without a risk of losing self-esteem with which such ambitions are very early fused.

The "superboy" identity of small boys, with its associated conflicts, is not necessarily abandoned with maturity. It often gets carried unconsciously into adult life. There it finds expression in compulsive work under the burden of satisfying the extravagant wishes of early boyhood. The hope to excel, the fantasy of being perfect, persists, associated with performing heroic deeds and thus winning the eternal love of an uncritical woman. Later, these aspirations may take the form of such conscious wishes as revolutionizing the world with marvels of one's discoveries, or being a Shakespeare, a Marx, an Einstein, or being famous as an athlete, a performer, or an astronaut (it used to be an Argonaut). With it all is the deep childhood apprehension, held in repression, of disappointing one's mother. The effect in boys and even later is a shirking and even a hatred of work. In it are the signs of an early tendency to despair that later often develops into periods of depression. It is the result of the impairment of self-esteem when one's efforts fall far short of achieving the childish ideal of grandeur that one formed long ago. However, from such anxieties we have also found great accomplishment may sometimes be wrested.[2]

If the father appears to have a small role in these early years, it is that in fact his is only adjunctive to the mother's. The father stands in her shadow as her surrogate. If he plays a larger part during such a time, the mother's limitations account for it according to the child's reckoning. It is the father's task, ordinarily unspoken, as the boy leaves the confines of the nursery, to rescue him from his mother's conflicts. It is a long, arduous course that continues to the boy's maturity. The father need not be a psychoanalyst to meet the challenge. Nor, if he were, is it any assurance he would be certain to succeed. To do so, he will have to draw from his own experience as a boy, from some awareness of his wife's needs in her zeal about her child, together with his own expectations as a father, different from a mother's, to ensure the success of his efforts. These efforts entail helping his son loosen his identification with his mother. It will be in order that the son may be less an extension of her. The alliance that the father needs to form with his son, on the one hand, will need to avoid being seductive and, on the other, to mitigate the boy's incestuous wishes. This irregular round of events will take the boy safely through the Scylla and Charybdis that threaten to catch him. True to the myth, no one escapes unscathed. We only hope that no arrest in development occurs in this odyssey, and that a fixation at some infantile level of masculinity will be avoided.

Chapter 4

MASCULINITY AND THE
WISH TO BE FEMININE

LITTLE BOYS HAVE deep fears. We know this from observing their play, no less than from ancient myths, legends, and rhymes. From prehistory to our own time, even the close confines of the nursery have not succeeded in excluding these fears, which have puzzled those who gave them thought. What in such early years grips a boy, for all his bravado, to make him timid and anxious and in dread while grasping for pipes and powers? Perhaps, like all children, he naturally entertains figments of what he risks to lose and somehow what would frighten: the world beyond his mother's skirts seems indeed menacing. Yet, this enigma was not truly penetrated until after the turn of our century.

One father's concern was aroused when his little son declared that he was afraid to leave the house for fear of being hurt. Urging him to do so produced an unyielding phobia against going out: the boy expected to be hurt on the streets so he shunned them. The father, a physician, was puzzled by these events and determined that it obviously was some sort of emotional problem, which he could not affect. He thus appealed for help from a new quarter, having no idea that he was setting into motion the opening of the untapped, uncharted lode of a child's mind. He wrote of the boy's condition to his friend Sigmund Freud sometime in 1906.

This inquiry presented an irresistible opportunity to Freud of observing firsthand what "we dig out so laboriously in adults from among their debris — especially as it is also our belief that they are the common property of all men, a part of the human constitution, and merely exaggerated or distorted in the case of neurotics."[1] This became the case of "Little Hans," "familiar to every student of psychoanalysis — which offered confirming and conclusive evidence of the startling discoveries about the unconscious role in [normal] psychic life of infantile sexuality."[2] In light of our subsequent experience in the analytic study of children, the case of Little Hans has an added significance that Freud could not have developed: the early relationship that a boy forms with his mother is a precursor of, and preparatory to, the later development of his relationship not only with his mother but with other women as well. Because of the particular nature of this relationship and its significance by way of identification with his mother as a woman, the little boy is pitched into one of the most serious conflicts that lie at the root of masculinity, and he begins a lifelong conflict that all men experience.

Freud was not unaware of the magnitude of this problem for Little Hans, even though the study of the boy was limited by what the father observed and wrote. Once familiar with the details of the case, Freud could say at the outset that when the boy was less than three years old, his typical concern was that he wanted an explanation for his mother's lack of a penis. It would be difficult to imagine the degree of consternation created by the publication of this remark.

The first reports of Hans date from a period when he was not quite three years old. At that time, by means of various remarks and questions, he was showing a quite peculiarly lively interest in that portion of his body which he used to describe as his "widdler." Thus he once asked his mother this question:

Hans: "Mummy, have you got a widdler, too?"

Mother: "Of course. Why?"

Hans: "I was only just thinking."

At the same age he went into a cow shed and saw a cow being milked. "Oh, look!" he said, "there's milk coming out of its widdler!"[3]

During the same period, "standing in front of the lion's cage at Schönbrunn Zoo, little Hans called out in a joyful and excited voice: 'I saw the lion's widdler.'"

Animals owe a good deal of their importance in myths and fairy tales to the openness with which they display their genitals and their sexual functions to the inquisitive child. There can be no doubt about Hans's sexual curiosity, but it also aroused the spirit of inquiry in him and enabled him to arrive at genuine abstract knowledge. When he was at the train station once (at three and three-quarters years of age), he saw some water being let out of an engine. "Oh, look," he said, "the engine's widdling. Where's it got its widdler?" After a while he added in reflective tones: "A dog and a horse have widdlers; a table and a chair haven't." He had thus got hold of an essential characteristic for differentiating between animals and inanimate objects.

Thirst for knowledge at this age seems to be inseparable from sexual curiosity. Hans's curiosity was particularly directed towards his parents.

Hans (aged three and three-quarters): "Daddy, have you got a widdler, too?"

Father: "Yes, of course."

Hans: "But I've never seen it when you were undressing."

Another time, he was looking on intently while his mother undressed before going to bed. "What are you staring like that for?" she asked.

Hans: "I was only looking to see if you'd got a widdler, too."

Mother: "Of course. Didn't you know that?"

Hans: "No, I thought you were so big you'd have a widdler like a horse."[4]

Hans's sister was born about this time, and his inquiries extended to her. Watching her being bathed, he noted she was lacking what he had, to which he attached such importance.[5] The unavoidable sight of his sister's nakedness brought Hans an added blow. It further compelled him to recognize that some people "lack" or are without a "widdler." Hans developed his famous "horse phobia" at the height of his sexual interest, curiosity, and excitement: here "we have the beginning of Hans's anxiety as well as of his phobia."[6] He became fearful of leaving the house and had to be coaxed. After he was calmed by his parents, he finally confessed that he feared a horse would bite him and even that it would come into his room. Freud wrote, "His affection for his mother must therefore have been enormously intensified. This was the fundamental phenomenon in his condition. In support of this, we may recall his two attempts at seducing his mother."[7] This is a reference to a scene in which Hans playfully was proposing to his mother that she take a special interest in his penis. And, on an earlier occasion, the father reported to Freud that Hans had amused his parents with expressing his wish to be in his father's place with his mother. He had displaced this desire to one of having an adolescent girl in bed with him, much as he witnessed his parents together in their bed.[8]

With these events in mind, the father had written:

Hans always comes into us in the early morning and my wife cannot resist taking him into bed with her for a few minutes. Thereupon I always begin to warn her not to take him into bed with her . . . and she answers now and then, rather irritated, no doubt, that it's all nonsense, that after all one minute is of no importance and so on.[9]

Freud commented that it was a triumph for the boy over his father's resistance when Hans says, "Call out as much as you like! But Mummy takes me into bed all the same, and Mummy belongs to me!"[10]

In the course of telling his parents how he believed birth took place, Hans stated he wanted to have a child himself, like his mother, who had shortly before given birth to his sister, Hanna. Is Hanna to the little boy the feminine version of Hans? Despite his father's repeated assertion that only women have children, Hans declared, "I'm going to have a little girl. . . . Yes, next year. I'm going to have one, and she'll be called Hanna, too." The father continued his reiteration that boys can't have babies. Hans, however, kept his up his insistence that he would have a child.[11] To the boy's expressly repeated wish for having a child, Freud added an important footnote:

> There is no necessity on this account to assume in Hans the presence of a feminine strain of desire for having children. It was with his mother that Hans had the most blissful experiences as a child, and he was now repeating them, and himself playing the active part, which was thus necessarily that of the mother.[12]

Throughout his work, Freud maintained that one's least conflicted early experience is that time of bliss as a son with one's mother. Nothing is gained through supposition as to what motives prompted him to hold this notion. From such remarks, however, he set into motion a romantic trend among some of his followers. It began to have its impact, as their numbers and influence grew, into developing a mother-child psychology as a paradisiacal condition ruptured by the intrusion of reality. As a result, the early and natural conflicts that arise between a mother and her child have tended to be neglected, as are the particular conflicts in the young child. The significance of Hans's playing the father was not in any way lessened by his wanting to be in his mother's place. We learn this from the neurotic difficulties that developed, such as his "horse phobia," which came with wanting his mother all to himself. "It was not until this happened that it became evident to what a pitch of intensity his love for his mother had developed and through what vicissitudes it had passed. The sexual aim which he pursued with his girl playmates, of sleeping with them, had originated in relation to his mother."[13] And was transferred to them, I may add, at the height of his oedipal conflicts.

Culminating this period of the oedipal attachment to his mother, Little Hans sought relief from the anxiety generated by his wishes to take his father's place and his belief that his father had no intention of relinquishing so desirable a relationship to him.

The bedroom scene, in which his mother is indulgent of Hans, the father is objecting, and Hans is defiant, bounds the triangle and sets the tone that follows. Hans appears to retreat. He seems to give up his demands and wants to be like his mother. If he were, he would thus win his father's affection rather than the hostility that would come with insisting on his intentions in the face of his father's resistance. This retreat or regression to an earlier phase of wanting to be like one's mother and make peace with one's father has been found to occur by most analysts since Freud. This is the passive feminine role in which masculinity seems sacrificed. What is overlooked is that all boys do not give up the identification with their mothers, but continue it. It is neither taken up again by regression, nor is it retreated to in the ordeals of the Oedipus complex. It is the heightening of the continuing identification with his mother that now threatens Hans through his wishes to be in her place; his masculinity is too menaced by that solution. Hans is on the horns of a dilemma. His great aspirations come to nothing. The severest blow is to his masculine self-esteem. The way out of both conflicts takes him into the next phase of his emotional development.

The original significance of the case of Little Hans, as the classic demonstration of a child's sexuality, has long since passed out of controversy into history. Little Hans is every boy. In view of what we have learned, the same case today shows more than the existence of early sexual conflicts; it also suggests how powerfully they affect the course of emotional development. Now we know that these conflicts have a profound bearing on the development of masculinity. Moreover, they arise out of ordinary family life. Freud said of Hans's father that he "united in a single person . . . both affectionate care and scientific interest."[14] He and his wife indulged their first child, and they had agreed to use no more coercion than was absolutely necessary for good behavior. Hans developed into a cheerful, good-natured, lively little boy. The parents' experiment of letting him grow up and express himself without being intimidated went on satisfactorily.[15]

The first reports about Hans date from the time when he was not quite three years old. His father then noted that from various questions and remarks Hans made he showed a lively interest in his penis. It was not, however, until a year or so later, and after his sister was born, that the father sadly wrote to Freud that Hans had developed a "nervous disorder." He was inclined to believe "the ground was prepared for it by sexual overexcitement" due to his mother's tenderness. Hans's father went on to describe that Hans

was afraid a horse will bite him in the street and this fear seems somehow to be connected with his having been frightened by a large penis. As you know from a former report, he had noticed at a very early age what large penises horses have. . . . I cannot see what to make of it. Has he seen an exhibitionist somewhere? Or is the whole thing simply connected with his mother? It is not very pleasant for us that he should begin setting us problems so early. Apart from his being afraid of going into the street and from his being in low spirits in the evening, he is in other respects the same Hans, as bright and cheerful as ever.[16]

From our present, broader perspective and deeper understanding resulting from more than half century of direct analytical study of children, the family scene that Hans's father describes is as natural as it is touching. Significantly, the boy's father, searching to explain the curious mystery of his little son's "nervous disorder," looks into his wife's role. He fails to conceive that the creature with the large penis who menaces Hans is actually not on the city streets. He lives in the house that Hans fears to leave. It is typical, when one is in such a fearful state, to displace the cause away from those closest to one that is more remote. Fortunately, by way of Hans's father, Freud helped the boy rid himself of his neurotic phobia. Through lengthy correspondence about Hans, Freud was able to guide the parents to resolve effectively the boy's difficulties. The change came about when Hans no longer felt himself to be the victim of aggression and confined to the house with his mother. He achieved a freedom that turned him away from his powerful obsession with his sexual wishes to giving them up as a lost cause. However, instead of identifying himself with his mother, as he had done before, he heightened his aggression, which he associated with his father, and thus unconsciously further identified himself with him. By way of this new identification, he advanced his masculine development.

There are few occasions in the psychological literature that embraces psychoanalytic work where a sharp line may be drawn between what is neurotic and what is normal, between what is strictly masculine and what is not — whether in children or in adults. Consequently, we find a large class of healthy men passing into neurotic states "while a far smaller number also make the journey in the opposite direction."[17] In the case of Little Hans, we have the best sort of example of the phenomenon: a healthy little son of loving, intelligent, and well-meaning parents. He enters unwittingly, naturally, and inevitably into, and passes through, a period of masculine development in the course of which he becomes for a time neurotic. With therapeutic help, he is then freed to embark on the next major phase of masculinity.

It may reasonably be asked what happens when the same events take place in which such help as Hans received is not available. Depending upon the role of circumstance and the quality of their family relationships, boys go through this phase with greater or lesser travail. Accordingly, they emerge with more or less of the residue of conflicts about their masculinity. As we observed in Hans, masculinity is defined by a boy as a competition he is intent on winning. However, it is a contest in which victory is associated with the most strongly tabooed injunctions, and it is against an adversary whom the boy fully expects has no lack of resolution to deny him what he wants. Giving up its aims therefore has its imperatives. Submitting to them, however, as we have noted, brings on wishes to take a feminine role, to identify with one's mother and unconsciously deliver oneself as a homosexual partner to the rival. Ordinarily, this is a brief episode associated with one's affections for a father. At the same time, it is a retreat from the grandiosely conceived world of manhood into a sense of failure, a loss of self-esteem, and gloom at one's limitations. All these elements taken together create a powerful impetus to quit this complex and get on to find relief. It comes in the next and new phase of boyhood.

Freud's presentation intended to show the vigor of a child's sexuality, which he indeed succeeded in doing, at a time when the sexual life of very young children was given the scantest attention. However, it was illuminating as well about masculine development. This case also dramatized the fact that the foundations of adult neurotic disorders were laid in childhood conflicts. Much as we have already gained from Little Hans, he demonstrates even more. He shows that in everyday family life a small boy's masculinity is at risk, and he reveals that a boy's dilemma in the Oedipus complex entails giving up a measure of his masculinity and thereby increasing his feminine identification. As we have seen, it is a heavy price for a boy to pay. He prizes nothing more highly than masculinity. The cost of sacrificing any of it is laden with anxiety, provokes various forms of symptoms such as phobias, fears, and nightmares (as I shall later show), and threatens to impair further masculine development. These vagaries allow no boy to escape unscathed. Not even Hans's exceptional opportunity permits him to come away from his experiences as though they had not occurred. From this period, without such help as Hans received, the journey made to the next phase of normal masculine development is necessarily more difficult. Augmented by a feminine identification, the fear of a compromised masculinity leaves its effect, and is present thereafter in all men. Masculinity may be considerably diminished by this fear which, characteristically, is unconsciously present in claims of accretions of masculinity. Thus, a boy's self-esteem is precariously poised and highly vulnerable. This is a condition he will carry a long time as anxiety in being associated with girls and women.

The masculine anxiety of being identified with femininity or a woman has a long history and a correspondingly voluminous literature in ancient myth and legends. For example, we find as common practice, in prehistoric, in ancient, and in many contemporary societies, a separation of men from women. Prohibitions are placed on men that suspend their ordinary tasks, impose abstinence from sexual relations — even isolation from women is required prior to special ordeals testing masculinity in certain initiation rites — often before contests and in anticipation of battle. This anxiety is expressed in religious beliefs and is carried out in rituals. Encountered commonly in the course of analysis of the anxieties of men, it is given considerable weight in contemporary psychological conceptions, not surprisingly psychoanalytic ones in particular. Experience shows that a man's dread of being feminine is so generally pervasive as to be a universal component of masculinity. Most analysts account for it as representing a return and with it a revival of our first identification with a woman brought about in the wake of the oedipal conflicts. Some hold, in addition, that the feminine identity harks back to the intimate days of the nursery. These assumptions do not explain why the seeming tranquillity of early infancy, with its assuring dependence and attachment, should, through suggestion in fantasy or with impulse and by unconscious desire, typically evoke anxiety states that are often intolerable.

As we well know, young children and, to a large measure, even adults are loath to give up their persistent infantile

67

wishes. Thus, infantile gratification and its associated identification with one's mother are especially tenaciously held. Yet, the feminine identification a man feels unmistakably expresses its deep, emotionally disturbing presence. With the exception of cases of homosexuality as a gratified perversion and thus lacking conflict, the experience of a feminine identity in some men may reach the severest clinical dimensions, even, at times, going on to murderous psychosis.

From the heightened phobic alarm in Little Hans we are led to conclude that, in turning from his extravagant wishes to take his father's place with his mother to be identified with her instead, his purpose was more than striking a sensible bargain to win his father's favor rather than his ire. He jeopardized his masculinity by taking this course. This is not regression, because there was no such previous condition. Earlier, masculinity as he recognized it was represented simply as the structural differences he observed between himself and others. His father's features of masculinity were to him immense, and his mother's or sister's were correspondingly absent. The little boy's confusion went along such lines. Little Hans, like the boys and men we have since studied, feared he could ill afford to yield any of his masculinity. Yet, a small boy's naturally exuberant masculine fantasies, firing his aspirations, invariably lead him to an impasse from which he is obliged to extricate himself. His strategy will be to retreat, and he will be relieved of the wish to triumph over the most formidable rival in his experience. It is the first major blow to masculine self-esteem. However, it spares a boy his further wishes to be seduced by his mother. Such incestuous intentions are fraught with inescapable hazards, not the least of which is to prove his masculinity by performance. Reality compels him to believe privately that such an incestuous role is beyond his powers. The mother who seductively encourages her son thus raises his anxieties, as we observed in the mother who kept little Marty to herself, and in the case of Hans, whose mother saw no harm in momentarily encouraging him to share her bed. In either case, the boy's masculine narcissism can enjoy only the illusion of being elevated. He is aware of the strictest of taboos that he may not violate, and he recognizes the fact that the task is beyond his reach.

A mother affects her young son's boyhood development when she seductively presses him toward ambitious achievement that unconsciously expresses her needs more than his. He believes her exhortations, and they become imperatives. He takes them to suggest that rivals may offer no match to his exertions or undertakings. He must defeat all to win the exclusive place for himself that he feels he was promised. Despite the assurances of his success, there are also wishes to fail and thus be relieved of the obligation to his mother. But such ambivalence holds the dread he may fail and himself be the victim. While he wishes his rivals to lose, he also fears that this loss could be his own fate. His efforts, not surprisingly, unconsciously take on an illicit aura in the collusion for success that he has entered into with his mother. Thus, he is not without the added anxiety that he has created desperate enemies, and that whatever he achieves under such auspices is of questionable legitimacy.

In effect, such a mother unwittingly makes a Faustian pact with her son. He naturally wants to grasp beyond his reach, and she further excites him to aspire to and beyond the summit of earthly ambition. The yearning for more than earthly satisfaction becomes irresistible. He has his own injunction to remain within the limits of mortals or ordinary men; egged on, however, he cannot resist his own desires. Too late, Faust revolted, but his fate was sealed. While a boy's destiny is not Faust's, the revolt of his masculinity may be affected hardly less fatefully by homosexuality.

The alternative, to accept the limitations of boyhood masculinity and not to succumb to its extravagant, narcissistic demands, compels the boy to find restitution while suffering the painful loss to self-esteem. This debacle is the most significant injury to self-esteem that a boy encounters. The

69

termination of the Oedipus complex dooms a boy's preposterously male chauvinistic wishes for himself, whether they are to exercise masculine powers with which he would magically rule events, or to enjoy limitless liberties with his mother's indulgence. His underlying fear is that he will be more identified with a woman than a superman. Under these common circumstances, a mother, in her zeal to gratify her own masculine aspirations through her son, pandering to his discontent, tends to be seductive. Rather than supporting his masculinity, she inadvertently succeeds in making him fear that identification with her will be the consequence of failing to be a superman. Thus, he would be in her place, which is to be androgynous. To the boy this means homosexual. Both its lure and its terror are installed, and neither is readily dislodged.

The commonest masculine reaction is to repudiate the entire experience. It appears in Nathan Field's *A Woman is a Weathercocke* (1612):

> I never dreamt of lying with my Mother
> Nor wisht my Fathers death, nor hated Brothers;
> Nor did betray Trust, nor lou'd money better
> Then an accepted friend; No such base thought,
> Nor act unnaturall, possess this breast:
> Why am I thus rewarded women, women?[18]

* * *

As we have observed, a boy's unique, deepening attachment to his mother is, by its very nature, bound to rupture. Before that, however, his final identification with her gives his masculine development its indelible stamp. In the case of Little Hans, his identification with his mother in its last aspects entices him to want to be a woman and even to be in her place. Rather than have a man's role, which he had wanted before but which casts him in a rivalry he is loath to be in, he is spared when he unconsciously fears what it would bring. Either the boy remains in an unconscious feminine pact with his father, or as in the case of Hans, he chooses neither to be identified as before with his mother nor to aspire to the extreme of his father's place. Given the favorable and usual conditions in which he is not induced too strongly either way, he will make a friendly alliance with his father and with relief will abandon the highly eroticized period that had brought such conflicts, anxiety, and phobias. Freud's clinical note, made years later after a brief encounter with Hans, who was no longer little, confirms that Hans, once again the cheerful, if chastened, little boy, went on into a further phase of masculine emotional growth.

At a much later time in a man's life, his identification with a woman and, with it, his powerful wish to be one may be revived, but not, however, without serious repercussions to his masculinity. But, as I have stated here previously, the wishes normally are repressed, to remain unconscious, at least to the degree that they do not impinge significantly on masculine functions in the course of everyday life. However, if conditions for the return to a feminine role become favorable, they may take on such vigor and distortion of conviction that they may reach psychotic proportions, which gives us some insight into their potential power. The vast literature in psychology and psychoanalysis has given us no clearer demonstration of this occurrence than the case of Judge Schreber.

A huge scientific outpouring resulted from Freud's "Schreber" case. What was powerfully illuminated by this work also cast deep shadows over masculinity. Using autobiographical material published by a man whom he had never met, Freud gave the first demonstration that psychoanalysis had versatility as both a research tool and method. Psychoanalysis thus applied could reveal the dynamic processes underlying deep-seated emotional experience. In this instance, it was Judge Schreber's description of mental illness, which, following his recovery, he published later as *Memoirs of My Nervous Illness*.[19] For Freud, the use of the judge's *Memoirs* represented a work that was a tour de force both as a test and proof of psychoanalysis as an applied instrument. With it, using only the autobiographical material, he was able to uncover the dynamic processes in Schreber's madness.

It was nearly a decade after Schreber, a presiding judge of the Appeals Court of Leipzig, had published his *Memoirs* that Freud began to attack the problem that was so candidly and uniquely revealing of Daniel Schreber's psychosis.[20] Fundamental to the case are two assumptions that Schreber made, and which were noted by the medical officer in charge of him. One of these was a view of himself as the Redeemer, which he shared with God, and the other was a view of his transformation into a woman. In his favored relation to God as God's wife, he made a union from which would issue a master race; and in his transformation into a woman, he felt that he would be no less a woman but would be exploited by men and thus degraded sexually.[21] The idea of being "transformed into a woman was the salient feature and the earliest germ of his delusional system."[22]

"I am able to evoke," Schreber wrote, "a sensation of voluptuousness such as women experience and especially if I think of something feminine at the same time." He then went on to develop the conviction that it was not he but God who was "demanding femaleness from him."[23] His fantasies or delusions of being a woman were consciously repudiated with indignant protests asserting his masculinity. At the same time, he expressed his fears of sexual abuse by a man. Schreber's known relationships with men were of particular importance to understanding his subsequent psychotic condition. He had been deeply attached to his cruel father, who died an untimely death, and he was no less close to an older, domineering brother. His dependent relationship with his doctor became associated with the quality of his relationship with both his father, who was also a doctor, and his brother. As he delusionally replaced these men by the superior figure of God, he conceived himself to be His wife. In these ideas his unconscious feminine relationship to men is revealed.

Schreber tells us that his self-concern became alarming, as his masculine idea of himself, threatened by his own passive acquiescence to men, became evident to him. He associated it with wishes to be feminine. With that, he began to regard men, the objects of his own sexual aims, as his enemies. To deny himself his passive feminine fantasies, he thought men were his enemies whose intentions were to use him sexually.

The judge revealed that his distinguished career seemed not to give him relief from his private burdens of self-reproach. Neither he nor Freud's study tells us what exactly brought on the serious disorder, which seemed to coincide with his being elevated to his high judicial post. We may reasonably suspect that when Schreber began to make reckless and inappropriately grandiose assertions, soon after he took his elevated post, they were preceded by the wishful feminine fantasy associated with his physician, the surrogate for his physician father and also very likely other men. Such notions need hardly all be conscious. But they evoke reactions to offset them; some may be extreme as Schreber showed.

It was at this point that the psychosis seemed to have been launched. The judge exalted the importance of his feminine, passive, dependent identification as a woman. No longer related submissively to mere mortals in his delusions, we learn that he did not quit the role of a woman who is servile to men. He overcame that humiliated state by regarding himself as a fit companion only to God. Rather than quitting the part of a woman, he retained it to adopt a megalomaniacal conception of himself. He, with God, through their union would bring forth a new super-race of beings.[24]

The crux of Freud's interpretations of Schreber's *Memoirs* is in his tracing the dynamic development of the judge's delusions to their origin in unconscious sexual wishes. Their particular nature in Schreber led him to his disastrous course. It was, in Freud's view, Schreber's wish to be feminine that was reinforced during the oedipal strivings that had taken place. We also saw them to be present in the case of Little Hans. In the boy's instance, this was a normal, temporary condition. And, no doubt, this was the case with Schreber. We are not told what kept these old wishes from remaining relegated to the dim past.

In showing the unconscious homosexual foundation in paranoid psychosis, Freud made a landmark discovery. His explanation of that disorder for the first time clarified its bizarre homosexual hostility and its derivative forms in aggressive delusions. Freud's conception, and that of analysts that followed him, that Judge Schreber's central conflict issues from the Oedipus complex in which he takes the woman's part of the triangle, while correct from the evidence, fails to go far enough. It does not take into account the powerful impetus drawn from a boy's earlier-developed, masculine identity, which takes being female as appalling. Thus, a regression to a longed-for relationship with a man, as in Schreber's case, turns invariably to identifying with a woman for a man's favor. But, such a compelling direction brings a contradiction with the earlier-developed importance of being masculine. When it succeeds over masculinity, without a loss of self-esteem, the homosexual solution is an important positive outcome. That is to say, a man who seems to be spared the necessity of yielding his masculinity altogether may enjoy his sexual relations with another man without being conflict-ridden by it. He becomes a "phallic" woman. We shall later see the further extremes to be the case in "Jan Morris" and the little boy who, like Morris, wanted no penis. Their identification with a woman for the sake of relations with a man went so far as to wish to remove the genitals. But for Schreber, however, it was the loss of self-esteem, which he associated with the need to be a woman, that became so menacing to him. It was to be at the cost of masculinity. In order to achieve his end and forgo the "degradation" of being a woman, he solved his dilemma by developing grandiose delusions of femininity that exalted him to the grace of a deity. Only then are his wishes to be a woman rewarding. The infantile aspects of the judge's character are further revealed in his unconscious view of the nature of relations between a man and a woman; the powerful man holds sway, is a brute who mates with an inferior creature, a woman. In his madness, we find this had remained Judge Schreber's model. It is one he formed long before he became psychotic. It belongs to early boyhood notions of masculinity.

We learn from this case and countless others since that the Oedipus complex evokes a phenomenon and a conflict developed much earlier in masculinity: a small boy's repugnance at being a woman. It brings him into conflict naturally with wanting to be like his mother. It will be expunged only consciously, while as a repressed wish it remains a viable hazard to masculine self-esteem. Repression of the wish to keep safe his masculinity is no choice, but an imperative. Hence, the identification with one's mother, evoked by the wishes of the Oedipus complex, is not new but is a revival or a renewal of old conflicts in which were wishes that call for repudiation.

Once again, the incentive is launched to denigrate women. It brings conflicts with a needed and loving relationship. The unconscious course is toward repression both of the hostility as a reaction and the love as a peril. Thus, central in the psychology of the boy is the identification with his mother. It also forms the basis of the earliest castration fears. Is to be like her to be without a penis? The emotional image of a woman as a disfigured man continues for a remarkably longer period of boyhood than would be surmised by most without direct experience in the study of boys.

Natural as it is to be agonized by differences among us, essential even to generate the process by which we gain our sense of ourselves, no distinction carries a heavier weight for a boy than the one he observes as setting him apart from women or girls. This threatens his self-image, which allows no alterations, abhors change, and tolerates no differences from his own body. We see this train of thinking in Little Hans, who inclines to take his mother's place and even, like her, to have babies. Hans would not, however, recognize that a wish to be his father's intimate sexual partner is a self-imposed denial of his own masculinity. In Schreber, we find this same phenomenon in its psychotic proportions. He clearly cannot tolerate the role that he longs for: to be more intimate with his father, his brother, and with the family physician. His purposes are gained, then, through reconstituting his self-esteem by way of delusions of grandeur and only thereafter embracing exalted femininity. Bonded with the wish to be a woman is the compelling need to elevate self-esteem, which is expressed unequivocally in Schreber's delusions. When he was to join with God to create a "super-race," Schreber arrived at the summit of his newly formed hierarchy. Freud's and others' interpretations, which ascribe this phenomenon simply to Schreber's unconscious homosexual wishes, are too narrow. Regardless of how bizarre, fantastic, or preposterously conceived were Schreber's delusions, analysts have failed to take into account that inherent in them was the driving necessity to inflate his self-esteem. The wish to be a woman demands an elevated narcissism. It is the *sine qua non* of homosexuality.

Another variation on the same theme is that a woman embodies a narcissistic defect that cannot be tolerated. If we may guess that, had Judge Schreber been able to reveal his further underlying conception of himself as a woman, he might have shown that he had in mind to be a "phallic" woman: a woman who lacks a manifest male genital, but who has one hidden. It is a notion that small boys as well as little girls commonly retain. Especially is this a boy's reaction to the intolerable notion that there are those who lack what he has come to prize so. He must believe, not from compassion but for his narcissistic comfort, that indeed a female phallus exists. The wish that no one should be without a penis carries a sufficiently powerful impetus that resists being given up. Although a confrontation with reality forces the conviction to be withdrawn, it is retained rather than abandoned in the dark closet of amnesia. It may reappear in dreams, fantasies, or delusions like the judge's or when a threat over the loss of masculinity occurs, such as that associated with circumstances of a man's anxious identification with a woman. For example, recent vasectomy procedures as a birth control method have met with what appears superficially to be unreasonable resistance in many men, and, as a result, this program for population control has had serious setbacks in many countries. While among the simplest of surgical procedures, vasectomies evoke fears that are not readily dispelled. Men fear their virility will be impaired; they feel that the termination of their production of sperm would diminish them as men. These are some of the voiced objections that hush the deeper disquiet — men's fear of a reduced masculinity. The tendency is to draw a fallacious parallel with sterility in women.

Little girls also harbor ideas that there is no real absence of a penis, but because their psychology with regard to masculinity differs from that of a boy, they ascribe a different significance to a "hidden" penis. Some little girls have explored themselves carefully in the expectation of discovering it; others have not dared the investigation for fear of not finding what they would hope to discover. While they suspected the truth, they hid behind an inhibition to search themselves.

*   *   *

A clinical case of Freud's that forms the cornerstone of the structure of infantile sexuality — "the most elaborate and no doubt the most important of all Freud's case histories"[25] — has gone unrecognized as contributing trenchantly to our understanding of the mental life of boys. It takes us to an earlier phase of masculine development than either Little Hans or the Schreber case illustrates. It deals with the outbreak of an infantile neurosis that Freud was able to show was the basis of a later disorder in adult life. As in the other instances of Freud's work cited here, he did not intend them to show aspects of masculine development. Freud's purpose was governed chiefly by the fact that psychoanalysis was still a fledgling science, and the unconscious was yet an unfamiliar entity in the psychology of everyday life. Further, he wanted us to understand that the resultant infantile sexual conflicts and neurosis formation were the basis of later disorders in adult existence. His success is now history. Perhaps it is all the more important to review for our purposes a case that has a prominent place in psychoanalysis and bears on our concern.

At the age of two and a half years, the "Wolf-Man," as he is familiarly known to students of psychoanalysis, was an easy, tractable, good-natured child. When his parents returned home to him after they had been away for the summer, they found that he had become "irritable, violent, took offense on every possible occasion and then flew into a rage and screamed like a savage."[26] They learned that during their absence he had suffered the torments of his sister. She had especially arranged things so that when he would see a picture of a wolf in a fairy tale that she teasingly called to his attention, he would be set off into screaming "like a lunatic that he was afraid of the wolf coming and eating him up." He also feared and loathed beetles and caterpillars, yet he used to torment them and cut up caterpillars. He enjoyed watching horses being beaten, although at times he was upset by such a scene. "On other occasions he himself enjoyed beating horses."[27] Freud could not say to what extent these contradictory attitudes persisted or one replaced the other. In the next few years, similar episodes of terror occurred. The little boy would follow such outbreaks by making the rounds of devoutly kissing holy pictures and then have blasphemous thoughts about the figures; "he used to carry out another peculiar ceremonial when he saw people he felt sorry for, such as beggars, cripples, or very old men. He had to breathe out noisily, so as not to become like them."[28]

The patient, who was recalling these events as an adult, reported to Freud that he suffered a repeated nightmare. He would awake in an attack of terror that he would be devoured by a wolf, as with the childhood fairy tale that his sister showed him to plague him. A long period of analysis showed that the fear of the wolf was the manifest dread of succumbing to the wolf's appetite, which was the creature's sexual desire. This turned out to be a fear of his father that had taken "the shape of a wolf phobia."[29] Throughout the period of analysis, the patient was either aggressive or felt himself to be the object of aggression; either he saw himself as a victim and identified with the wretched or he became aggressive and violent in defense of the very ones whom he feared he was like.

Freud's intent in publishing this case in 1918 was twofold. It provided conclusive evidence that infantile sexuality not only existed as he found it, but also that it was the root from which emotional disorders stemmed. No less important to Freud at that time was that he could level an irrefutable criticism at his most notable adversaries, Adler and Jung. As his editors wrote, "Perhaps the chief clinical finding was the evidence of the determining part played in the patient's neurosis by his *primary* feminine impulses."[30]

In light of what we now know, the "Wolf-Man" was not subject to some "primary feminine impulses." But we do gain some understanding of the conflicts in developing masculinity when identification with a woman is associated in a boy's mind not only with being victimized, but also with being deprived, mutilated, or crippled. Finally, the central theme of this case is the obsession with being attacked by a wolf, which through its appetite corresponds in the boy's mind to the fantasied ill treatment of a woman and specifically by his mother because of his notions of his father's appetites and of himself in his mother's place.[31]

Whatever other considerations may be ascribed to the patient's motives affecting his condition, his identification with his mother in a sexual scene that he often fantasied about remains central. Envying her intimate relationship with his father, he put himself in her place. But, as he regarded women only as suffering their sexual role, he was obliged to dread his own irresistible wishes. Thus, the conflict was joined. He regarded women as castrated and believed that "instead of a male organ they have a wound which serves for sexual intercourse, and that castration is the necessary condition of femininity."[32] The conflict between being masculine and giving it up for femininity remained with the "Wolf-Man" until his treatment by Freud resolved it.

These cases of Freud's, which have become classics in psychoanalysis, nevertheless leave obscure certain intimate aspects of the psychology of boyhood. However, we have learned from them that a boy's identification with his mother, when unconsciously held fast, profoundly limits his emotional masculine growth. These cases leave us largely to conjecture about the later development of masculinity. What throes of masculinity Little Hans suffered in boyhood, having wished himself in his mother's place, are not known to us. We don't know about the Wolf-Man's masculine experience beyond that identification with a woman was a menace to it. His recall of his boyhood was marked by a serious struggle between a devotion to pious rituals and the adoption of blasphemous ideas, which masked his dread of becoming passive and crippled, a state that he associated with the unconscious, persistent identification with his mother. Of Judge Schreber's boyhood we can suppose only that it contained an agony of being identified with a woman, which also must have been an ambivalent wish. We learned after the fact what led him to lengths of idealization of both a cruel father and an overbearing older brother, which he then transferred to his physician, all of which served to subvert his masculinity to a feminine, and thus demeaned, role. When these conflicts finally broke the bounds of repression into psychosis, he showed that he could tolerate the wish to be a woman only when he raised her, i.e., himself, to the level of a woman glorified.

All these cases convey the clear conclusion that a boy's natural identification with his mother, despite the intolerable anxiety it provokes at times by putting his masculinity in jeopardy, does not begin with the Oedipus complex, as has long been surmised by analysts. This identification does not altogether end with it either, nor do associated fears of being feminine, or what Freud called the feminine attachment to a man in a "homosexual enthusiasm,"[33] however brief a conscious episode, become expunged. Being thus left to supposition about masculinity in the boyhood years, before the oedipal period, and between it and adolescence or youth, analysts have not seemed to be encouraged to study it directly. I, therefore, can cite no authoritative work on these intervals of masculine development.

*　　*　　*

Boys masturbate during the oedipal period (4 or 5 to 7 or 8), but their fantasies associated with the activity are so self-censored that the remembered fragments of the daydreams are focused principally on the physical experience. The emotional content is elusive. We do learn from the daydreams that are associated with masturbation that the act is an assertion of prowess. However, especially during the immediate post-oedipal years, masturbatory activity alone, and with other boys, takes on more substantive importance. The boys begin to entertain fantasies of winning an older woman's favor. Conflicts arise between the wish to be immensely successful in seduction, which is narrowly conceived of as a physical triumph, and the dread of failure in so formidable an encounter. Moreover, with these conflicts, there is no escaping the strong taboo that strictly prohibits incestuous wishes and fantasies and condemns acts in which they are expressed. It is here that the basis of the guilt associated with masturbation is buried.

We are fully aware of the injunction that has existed at least since Genesis against yielding to the "evil desire." Nowhere does this injunction manifest itself more strictly than in regard to incest, the most "evil" of wishes. The taboo applies more to boys than it does to girls. Beyond the universal personal proscription, the prohibition against sexual wishes aimed at one's mother or a surrogate for her are at no time more severely self-imposed than in a boy of five or six years of age who is trying to free himself of his attachment to his mother and no longer be identified with her. This is a defensive reaction that reaches into aspects of a much earlier period when one's mother was likened to someone deprived, maimed, and viewed with disgust rather than with compassion. The early repugnance is added to that of incest. While the incidence of incest does not make it less of a taboo when it is violated between a father and daughter, it does not carry the same or a similar level of serious emotional disturbance found when it occurs between a mother and son. The father's incestuous conduct with his daughter has more of the character of sexual assault or rape. Usually, for him, it is more related to the fantasy of an exhibitionist who intends to astound the girl with his prowess, which is in question.

The early notions of a boy about a woman's "defect" are not as a rule well articulated during the second and third years, but are unconsciously present. When the oedipal period develops, the flawed feminine condition consciously is employed and brings it to term through once again demeaning women. Whatever took place with regard to conceiving women inferior to men before is now reinforced. During this phase, the fantasies are focused on the vagina rather than on the woman. This time marks the beginning of making coarse jokes and engaging in ribaldry in which the vagina is once again associated with anal or excremental functions and the organ as cloacal. One recalls a snippet from Yeats: "A woman can be proud and stiff / When on love intent; / But Love has pitched his mansion in / The place of excrement."[34] The vagina at this time is associated with sinister powers able to deprive the boy of what he prizes so highly. The further common reaction takes the form of designating the woman's genital as something devoid of significance, as a "cunt," "gash," and "snatch." Every language has similar expressions in which the "vagina is no meek asylum."[35] All efforts to be relieved of a relationship with a woman are associated with abjuring relations with girls or women for the presumed safer company of one's fellows. As we have seen in the case of the Wolf-Man, the triumph over femininity leads directly to conflicts in relationships with men, and unconscious homosexual fears are evoked by them.

* * *

During the first decade after analysis was launched, psychoanalysts began a continuing and searching interest in determining the unconscious basis for homosexuality. In laying the foundation for what would prove to be conclusive evidence of the role that infantile sexuality played in human emotional development and its disorders, Freud discovered in the same case material, although it was not central to his purpose, the unconscious genesis of homosexuality in men. The basis of this condition begins in the prolonged intense identification with one's mother, which, in a boy's later development, proves to be fundamental to male homosexuality.[36] It shows that a son's relationship with his mother is more than a tie of dependence, care, and affection, from which he struggles to be free. There is, as well, a powerful wish, even at times a need, to transform himself into her, to be like her, and, thereby, to attach himself to her the more completely and more securely. Thus, a boy's compelling development of his ego for an intimate relationship on which he most depends puts him into a vexing dilemma.

For the sake of his ego and his social development, the intimate tie and identification of a boy with his mother are critically important in contributing to the quality of his relationships in the future. At the same time, the boy's incentive to establish his masculinity is at odds with the compelling identification with his mother. The unconscious solution that a boy reaches is to retain his identification with his mother by repression and hold it in an emotional escrow. He then can pursue masculinity as his manifest choice. Here we have the key, given certain conditions, to the potentiality of the return of the repressed identification with a woman. As we have seen, a boy thus carries within himself a deep-seated ineradicable conflict, and the most serious menace to his masculinity is within him to hoist him by his own petard.

As we have noted, a mother who unconsciously promotes the earliest tie with her son extends rather than limits his fixation on her. In this case, the necessary modification of a son's identification with his mother, if she fails to cultivate or support its conversion, she unwittingly promotes his wishes to be like her. As his development proceeds, the feminine identification is reinforced. By remaining unaltered, its central importance both to the boy and to his mother gains. The boy's reaction to this condition will take the form of protesting strenuously his masculinity by increasing his overt social interest in boys, his father, and other men in whose company he is most comfortable. The homosexual gratification these relations afford him is meanwhile latent even to the point that he may be entirely unconscious of it. On the other hand, his being overly critical of girls and women with whom he enjoys sexually performing, because they lack the qualities he parades, plays the pander for his masculine ego. All this conduct functions to deny his underlying feminine identification. His masculine identity, thus flawed, is precariously susceptible to events that will breach his defenses.

Too often the clear distinction fails to be made between *being* masculine and *performing* as masculine. The emphasis on masculine performance gives scant evidence, often hardly even a clue, to the underlying motives it serves to repress. Thus masculine conduct may mask a powerfully based feminine identification in a boy and later in the man. The reverse is not the case. Boys who are more secure in their masculinity have little need or occasion to behave as though they were girls. However, the homosexual wish to relate to a man is where masculinity is being self-defined as competitive with men and wishing to give up the contest. As a youth said, "Being gay opts out as accepting failure. It's those men who have given up battle with men. They've submitted to men, retreated to the world of men who accept weakness, like in 'gays' who can't be self-dominating. Rather than take women, they take men on as homosexuals; 'gays' are victims of women on the one hand and of 'machos' on the other. They can't meet the standards of manhood. That takes incredibly high performance, competitiveness, winning all. Being 'gay' gets you out of the competition of manhood.''

A common explanation in a large literature about homosexuality that is more theoretical than real, developed during the past twenty years, argues that in the earliest nursery period some failure of emotional development must have occurred which arrested the child's evolving separation from the mother.[37] This explanation draws on the commonplace finding that adult homosexual men show an inordinate infantile attachment to their mothers.

The common report from homosexual men, in which they frequently complain, is of a long history of excessive intimacy with their mothers. This is not to suggest that such a relationship was necessarily expressed physically. Exhortations toward advancement and precocity of performance are the most ordinary forms of intimacy that a mother cultivates with her son. It has too often been assumed that such close guidance and care suggest warmth of affection and expression of tenderness. The contrary may be true and, to the boy, she may seem more like a coach, a tutor, and a guide who explicitly or by implication demands adherence to a program of self-improvement. Such a regimen develops intimacy bonded by performance. And a failure in performing threatens loss of intimacy, love, and thus self-esteem.

Whether homosexuality is manifest or latent, clinically significant as a perversion or compatible with a way of life that may or may not be socially questionable, there is generally agreement among all who have studied its unconscious structure, that this development in men lies in the persistence of the early-formed and unmodified identification with one's mother. It is assumed that the relationship that may have existed during the child's first year or year and a half somehow persists unaltered. The adult homosexual man, it is supposed, carries this arrested condition forward from his nursery.

The wide variety of inclusive studies of homosexuality show that explanations from actual, substantial clinical studies are lacking. Studies of latent homosexuality, in which there are few if any definitive clinical manifestations, are even more incomplete. The theories on homosexuality continue to out-run the data. For instance, in 1896, Krafft-Ebing supposed homosexuality to be caused by "inborn" characteristics of some excessive, as yet unidentified, substances that made up the hereditary composition of the brain.[38] Currently widely read are the ideas of Barry and Barry, who, nearly a century later, identify the cause of homosexuality as hormonal.[39] From this spectrum of supposition, we see that such popular and scientific theories that ignore the participation of the unconscious in the formation and the disorders of our character continue to hold a sort of unwarranted but stable currency.

While homosexuality has been shown in the past seventy-five years to have an unconscious element, scant scientific attention has been paid to its singular nature outside of psychoanalytic studies. It is no less remarkable that even with the penetrating psychoanalytic search of the unconscious begun with the turn of the century, there is a virtual silence on the development of homosexuality in women. The two most important works on the psychology of women to be published in recent years give it only perfunctory notice.[40]

The psychoanalytic studies of men have revealed that the nucleus of the wish to be desired by a man in the way one might be desired by him as a woman is normally repressed in the man's unconscious. Where a lasting, unmodified identification of a man with his mother is retained, associated with these dynamic elements, such a man is prone to be sexually attracted to another man who would wish to play a woman's role. In each one is a continuing, unconscious conflict of what a woman represents to a boy. Rather than explore these findings on homosexuality in men further, Freud commented that the temptation persists in "replacing what is left undone by speculation — the latter being put under the patronage of some school or other of philosophy."[41] Little scientific work seems to have been affected by his caveat of 1918. There is today elaborate speculation about biological bisexuality, which is reminiscent of the controversies of more than half a century ago when there was thought to be a psychological conflict in which masculine and feminine tendencies were opposed to each other. These new adherents explain, as did Alfred Adler in the 1920s, that homosexuality represents a struggle in man over which of his sexual tendencies will triumph, the masculine or the feminine. Suppositions in the decades since 1945 seem to have proceeded from the profound effect of traumatic separations in early childhood, about which we have learned directly, to philosophical, rather than palpable, constructions of what separation must have meant to young infants.[42]

Inasmuch as a prolonged attachment of a boy to his mother is associated with the development of homosexuality, the underlying assumptions are that conflicts over parental roles are discerned by the baby. Images that represent moral judgment of good and evil, it is also supposed, and reactions as well to frustrations are projected by the baby into aggressive and destructive fantasies expressed in anxiety, hate, and anger and are directed at the mother. Such ideas were elaborately developed by Melanie Klein, an early pupil of Freud's, in the 1920s.[43] Following considerable controversy with him and his adherents, she broke away to form her own school of thought. From studies of the play of older children, she reconstructed what she believed they conceived in early infancy to be the nature of relations between people, chiefly their parents. While the evidence for her notions has not been either advanced or developed by others, her theories have had a continued, unaccountable viability.

In recent years, especially since 1966, analysts, notably Stoller,[44] proposed that homosexuality was a problem of "gender identity." Stoller believed that this was due to a certain type of mother who was envious of men. Such a woman denied her son the intimacy a mother gives her child, especially in the first months of life. As a consequence, the infant boy somehow registers his mother's grief that she lacks the "maleness" that is his. It begins an estrangement from him that the baby experiences as a deprivation. Such an impoverishment, it is supposed, lays the foundation for a disorder in the boy baby's earliest identification. Hence, the problem of "gender identity." On the other hand, this mother does not help the child to "separate from her physically or to differentiate his own clear identity." This is thought to be due to her own feeling of "emptiness," i.e., grief over a supposed loss, that she received from her own mother and does not overcome. Further, she would have her son "cure" her of her penis envy from which she needs relief but fails to get it.[45]

Despite the large literature that offers many theories on the cause of homosexuality, those analysts who address themselves to the unconscious in no important respects disagree with Freud's original explanation of it: that the homosexual man remains unconsciously fixated on his mother, to a "mnemic image of her." He runs from other women who might cause him to be unfaithful to his mother. He pursues or prefers men, to whom he has therefore transferred interest from his mother. More explicitly, Freud wrote:

> In individual cases direct observation has also enabled us to show that the man who gives the appearance of being susceptible only to the charms of men is in fact attracted by women in the same way as a normal man; but on each occasion he hastens to transfer the excitation he has received from women on to a male object, and in this manner he repeats over and over again the mechanism by which he acquired his homosexuality.[46]

Freud was thus able to add that

> Psycho-analytic research has contributed two facts that are beyond question to the understanding of homosexuality, without at the same time supposing that it has exhausted the causes of this sexual aberration. The first is the fixation of the erotic needs on the

mother which has been mentioned above; the other is contained in the statement that everyone, even the most normal person is capable of making a homosexual object-choice, and has done so at some time in his life, and either still adheres to it in his unconscious or else protects himself against it by vigorous counterattitudes. These two discoveries put an end both to the claim of homosexuals to be regarded as a "third sex" and to what has been believed to be the important distinction between innate and acquired homosexuality. The presence of somatic characters of the other sex (the quota provided by physical hermaphroditism) is highly conducive to the homosexual object-choice becoming manifest; but it is not decisive. It must be stated with regret that those who speak for the homosexuals in the field of science have been incapable of learning anything from the established findings of psycho-analysis.[47]

The direct studies of young boys, during the past thirty years, have in no definitive way contradicted either Freud's work or that of others who have followed him in studies of the psychoanalysis of homosexuality in adult men. However, the great variety of homosexuals, the different conditions or circumstances of their development, and the diversity of their practices defy the simplistic generalizations most analysts hold. Moreover, homosexuals are not all clinically disturbed. I have earlier here called attention to mothers whose zeal for their sons' careers begins in the nursery. There are mothers cut from the same cloth as John Stuart Mills's father, but a mother in such a role affects her son's masculine development differently.

Most likely, through unwittingly reinforcing her own identification with her son, a mother, in an expression of her own needs, succeeds in making it reciprocal. That is to say, she identifies with his being a boy and he with her. What we know of the psychology of women supports that this naturally occurs, and that a mother usually is unaware that the need of her own fulfillment through a son has its lasting and pervading effect on his masculine development. The woman who finds this fulfillment in her relationship with her husband will look less for it from her son. It is through the clinical aspects of these common conflicts that we arrive at where the normal limits are exceeded. These mothers exhort their sons to perform as though they were their surrogates.

The son who has become closely identified with his mother begins to feel he is obliged to realize her needs through him. The boy, unconsciously, is in his mother's service. Under such auspices, the son's identification with his mother is not relinquished for one with a man. The later aspects of this in a relationship with a woman are reasonably predictable. The nature of his relationship with his mother tends to extend, with relatively little significant difference, to his close relations with other women. Whether homosexuality will remain latent, as is most often the case, or become manifest cannot be foreseen solely from a boy's attachment to his mother. But whatever circumstantial factors contribute to the development of homosexuality, none, it is generally agreed, has so great a bearing on it as the nature of this relationship.

Of significance is the inordinate difficulty that some mothers experience in encouraging their infant boys toward some independence, which to them is allowing a boy liberty at the expense of their own aspirations. They have little understanding of the nature of their difficulty, which is heavily masked by a deep devotion. They do not realize that it is their own narcissistic childhood sense of deprivation they would rectify through their sons.

Many analysts lean most heavily on the explanation that such a mother simply does not give up her original mother-child relationship, and that when a mother cannot help a child develop independence it is that which remains unmodified. The emphasis is laid on the question of separation of herself from the child. This theory, currently popular, extends to understanding homosexuality as produced by a mother who is "a chronically depressed bisexual woman who considers herself without value [and who] marries a distant, passive man." The husband is no model of masculinity and the mother "holds her perfect child in an endless embrace," and, as a consequence, "the child does not adequately learn where his own body ends and hers begins, at least in regards to a sense of maleness and femaleness."[48] This theory, only slightly modified by other analysts, holds to a global view of simplistic determinism that attempts to explain homosexuality in men as a condition rather than as a form of their development that may become pathological. There are parallel theories offered by scientists engaged in psychohormonal research. They attribute homosexuality to a biological aberration of some given hereditary endowment of masculinity and femininity from which homosexuality somehow issues.[49]

*   *   *

Masculinity begins as a precariously held, endlessly tested, unstable condition, uniquely invested with a mother's self-esteem and a father's narcissism. Each parent unwittingly thus assigns a burden of masculinity to a little boy. His responsibility quickly develops. The boy must prove the value conferred on his sex. There are not only special difficulties in becoming masculine but also in maintaining it throughout life.

Chapter 5

COOP'D FOR DEFENSE

THE QUALITY OF boyhood assuredly remains obscure and ill-defined so long as our accustomed concern with the early years of emotional life is fixed on the tenor of childhood and the sensibilities of children in general. This broad, shallow focus on childhood ignores the stage on which a boy plays out his masculinity — its emotional experiences, vicissitudes, and conflicts which give him his uniqueness. Scant attention is turned to the early cross purposes, breaches, and enmities, as well as the desires, loves, and appetites that are stored in the boy's unconscious. His is not an attic filled with experiences rendered inert by repression. It is a repository for a dynamic store against a time to come. Its contents carry on a continuing, even if unheralded, existence and influence on masculinity. And, finally, masculine narcissism, as vulnerable and commanding as it is an imperative, makes aggression into its most versatile tool.

The extensive literature on childhood fails to reveal what the "milk-tooth" phase harbors of the masculinity a boy has acquired, which he brings to the period of his life beginning about five or six years of age and lasting until puberty. What has he naturally repressed? What are his conflicts? What of his inner life is exposed in his behavior?

It is clear in watching a little boy's spontaneous play that, toward the end of his second year and more plainly in the next few years, his most commonly held and persistent concern is the fear of losing what he values. Associated emotionally with this concern, we know, is an earlier, dogged anxiety: the child's dread of being deprived and, even worse perhaps, abandoned.[1] The fears of being separated from those who have become familiar, intimate, and loved are present in all children.

In his second year, a boy is noticeably more affected by his fears than is a girl by hers. Although he is not specifically conscious of his anxiety at a loss, he is quick to express his concern about it. In its most manifest form, a little boy may inquire, in what appears the most perfunctory fashion, about why a toy was broken; moreover, he appears to have an disinclination for and usually refuses to play with articles or toys that are damaged or broken. In this same vein is the case of the Wolf-Man who was so frightened when a boy by the teasing of his older sister that he feared he would be mutilated and strenuously avoided the streets where he would be likely to see deformed or maimed men; often they were beggars. We are also reminded of Little Hans, who perceived no "widdler" on his mother or sister — although he did see them on horses and zoo animals — and who was frightened by the implications of such a loss.

These fears do not arise out of compassion for others. Rather, it is from his natural tendency to self-reference, i.e., to see himself in the same way that he sees those who lack what he possesses. To be without an organ, which is to say his sort of organ, is to suffer a monstrous loss. His subsequent understanding of nature's distribution of what he possesses fails to dislodge his fears. Egocentric demands, moreover, naturally arise in force as a reaction. In boys especially fears of loss or being deprived carry uniquely deep emotional meaning. They are associated externally with the imposition of limitations. They bind together into an emotional amalgam, so that, whether it be loss, deprivation, or limitation, each or all come to be given the same or similar meaning. As we are all little egoists, we are in hot pursuit of satisfying our wishes. At their curtailment, frustration at the feared lack of fulfillment thus falls on fertile ground. The manner not only of protest but, more important, the means by which we expect to restore ourselves and to make restitution to our egos, i.e., what we lose, or fear we may lose, especially as boys, evokes aggression.

The little boy's burgeoning aggression intrudes on his need for intimacy. It extends to those emotionally nearest him who necessarily place demands on him. His unconscious reaction to his own hostility evokes wishes for affirmations of lasting love and no less his own repeated immediate declarations of reassuring affection. He solicits affection from a rival sibling, from one or both of his parents, or even from the family dog he often tortures, all in the compelling need to elicit their affection and thus his worth. By this means he would mitigate his conscience-bound aggression. However, his egoistic aims are not compromised.

Little boys are supreme narcissists, as compared to little girls at the same age. While the early aggressiveness in boys defends their highly vulnerable narcissism, paradoxically it makes them susceptible to fresh fears. The ready satisfaction they associate with aggression and their quick identification with that quality in others, particularly in men, or the pleasure in prowess they so eagerly pursue, leave in their wake a rich variety of tormenting conflicts. All are associated with aggression. The anxiety that derives from the boy's needed defensive aggression brings an added unheralded development. As noted before, similar anxieties arise in girls, but, because a girl's narcissism follows another course, her development is different. His early problems with prowess and achievement call on the need to be aggressive or assertive. The distinction is not evident to him, the two are, for him, synonymous. He as readily assigns aggression to others while at the same time taking on himself that desired quality. This is to say, he very early projects onto others in thought and hence in play the quality of his own aggression, real or desired. He is truly caught in his own web.

Thus dissociating himself to a degree from his own aggressiveness by means of attributing it to others, he gets only some respite from the conflicts that issue as a result of it. However, because this leads directly to the expectation of being menaced by others, the cost of this unconscious effort is exacted in fears of aggression from others. In this way, the natural fears of an uncertain environment have added to them the conviction of the hostility of others, of becoming an object of their malice, and of feeling more acutely than before his own inferiority. He is compelled to seek relief. The result intensifies the need to defend himself.

There is no clearer statement of a child's self-defense than in Anna Freud's development of her father's original work. It is expressed in the use of the mechanism of projection, which

is quite natural to the ego of little children throughout the earliest period of infancy. They employ it as a means of repudiating their own activities and wishes when these become dangerous and of laying the responsibility for them at the door of some external agent. A "strange child," an animal, even inanimate objects are all equally useful to the infantile ego for the purpose of disposing of its own faults. It is normal for it constantly to get rid of prohibited impulses and wishes in this way, handing them over in full measure to other people. If these wishes entail punishment by authorities, the ego puts forward as whipping boys the persons upon whom it has projected them; if on the other hand, this projection was prompted by a sense of guilt, instead of criticizing itself it accuses others. In either case it dissociates itself from its proxies and is excessively intolerant of its judgment of them.[2]

Two unconscious courses open to a boy; he takes both from time to time. By one course he develops a dependent relationship that mitigates the fears brought on by being aggressive.

The other course causes him to cultivate a fearful relationship with those he identifies with aggression and, by way of identifying himself with them, becoming himself more aggressive. Much as passivity and dependence are self-fostered, so also are aggression and prowess additionally called upon.

The whole process of ambivalence over one's aggression is set into motion. It is not confined to early boyhood, but is one that begins with early masculine development. At no time is it entirely relinquished. The process that begins in girls is neither identical nor parallel. A girl's narcissism is not so focused. Her burden is not in having a genital, but in "lacking" one.

In our century, the discovery that enabled us to reach into and examine the profound influence that our unconscious, infantile-rooted conflicts continue to bear on the character of our adult life has led logically to the direct study of very young children for the deeper influences on their emotional development. Inexplicably, aggression has not been singled out as one of them. And it follows that a boy's psychology, in which aggression plays so critical a part, has remained as descriptive but unexplored behavior. For instance, despite the recognized importance of the study of dreams in illuminating the early and deep unconscious conflicts they contain, relatively little research has focused on children's dreams, especially their normal nightmares, which demonstrably begin to occur between two and three years of age. These aggressive encounters are typically dismissed even by the cognoscenti simply as a child's fright in sleep. That nightmares are among our purest examples of aggression, and the dreamer, in this case the young child, is its victim, has had little notice. Well known, but significantly neglected, is the fact that in boys nightmares occur far more often, are of greater intensity, and last over a longer period of childhood than they do in girls. A girl whose nightmares persist tends to be exceptionally aggressive not only during her sleep. It is carried over from her waking hours.

Early analysts' inexperience led them to think that a young child's dreams were straightforward expressions of social experiences and were not subject to the distortion found in adults.[3] Children's dreams, it seemed, needed a mere inquiry into their experiences of the previous day to learn their hidden wishes. Dreams, it was supposed, were "short, clear, coherent, easy to understand, and unambiguous."[4] No consideration has been given to which experiences or dreams would reveal the course of conflicts and which especially affect masculine development.

The dreams of young boys show they are prone in them to be aggressive and also show the disorders associated with aggression. Moreover, the anxiety associated with aggression in boys is not mild, nor is the aggression a simple expression of a child's so-called impulses escaping control. Aggression creates conflicts in us all, and we are obliged to resolve them. I have written elsewhere how nightmares give us a window into a child's aggression and that the veritable "zoo" of creatures under the bed in the dark corners of the night are expressions of it.[5] The commonplace appearance of the nightmare in the very young child marks the beginning of an important, lifelong process. It is in our nightmares that we first turn our aggression on ourselves. We do this to deflect to ourselves the injury first intended for others. The aim is unconsciously at self-injury; carried to an alarming intensity, this desire may culminate in self-destruction. The nightmare is a suicidal act: aggression turned on the self.

The authoritative study of nightmares by John Mack brings to us a research into some deep anxieties that young children experience.[6] A child's first nightmares, which are both common and normal, however disturbing to the child, "occur in relation to the child's earliest struggles with aggression as it arises within himself or is perceived as emanating from angry persons in the outside world or from more impersonal destructive forces."[7] Nightmares are well known to begin to develop during the second year.

Mack cites his earliest example of nightmares in a twenty-six-month-old boy, Sam, who, in the following eight months, had recurring episodes of nightmares. Mack explains the appearance of these nightmares as the child's means of resisting the social limits that, of necessity, were being imposed on him.

Struggles began between Sam and his mother over his resistance to her attempts to toilet-train him. "Also, for several days before the dream he had been particularly destructive, especially on the day before the nightmare, knocking over lamps and wantonly tearing up plants. His mother reached the end of her patience and had punished him, angrily closing him in his room on two occasions."[8] From his sleep that same night, he cried out in fear, and awoke trembling and crying for his mother that a "thing" frightened him. On another occasion soon after, and on a day following violent struggles with his older brothers, which provoked his father to angry words, the little boy again awoke from a frightening dream in which he feared and complained of being hurt. His play with a toy family of dolls showed that he was concerned with their being hurt, and he kissed them repeatedly. In the same vein of play, he pointed to a window, fearing the appearance of an animal intending to kill him. He also struck himself in the face.[9] There were more similar episodes in the weeks that followed, during which time the toilet-training continued to be a struggle. The child was still under the influence of nightmares and begged to be taken into his parents' bed, where his fears were relieved.

As the months wore on, the Sam's play reflected his persisting resistance by assigning to a puppet uncompromisingly aggressive and destructive roles. He also drew attention to insects that he pretended he saw and attacked and destroyed. His puppet was threatened and unmercifully punished with beatings and threats of being mutilated by "cuts." "Nightmares in small children such as Sam," writes Mack, "are sensitive indicators of their internal struggles and reflect in particular their desperate conflict over aggressions and hatred, perceived in the dreams in life-and-death terms."[10]

Observers of infants and young children since at least the

time of St. Augustine have called attention to the "willfullness of infants."[11] Rousseau, no less in agreement, regarded the child as egocentric in the extreme.[12] Mack and other analysts, by way of discerning the child's unconscious, call attention to aggression as a major problem in a child's life, especially in relation to those with whom he is intimate. Our most contemporary scientific opinion shows that this conclusion is as remarkably close to our oldest moral precepts as it is to continuing Darwinism. It argues that human aggression is part of the legacy of our "descent."

As we cannot support our existence alone in our early years, our "child-self" emerges during the time we are under administered gratification. The intensely egocentric nature of our "child-self," unknowing of given limits, is utterly dependent upon those who secure its existence. Conflicts necessarily arise. The curbs imposed on a young child are to it never entirely welcome. While they give a sense of security through placing bounds to doing what one pleases, nonetheless the wish to break them is not abandoned. Compelling parental authority extends to restrain rage, and more quickly than is recognized the child comes to fear its own fury at the imposed restrictions. These restrictions evoke aggression directed at those who impose their will. The issue is thus joined.

As Mack's example by chance shows, typically a child's gesture of an acquired self-restraint has been formed before he is three years old. This gesture takes the sophisticated form, at so young an age, of self-administered blows.

Like most, but not all, creatures, we may be provoked and made aggressive by restraints and coercion. We resist limits. We do not simply chafe at the shackles of our discipline. When we are very young, our resemblance to all creatures ends when, despite our loathing of limits, we begin to curb ourselves. We cannot claim this to be serving any instinctual function. But it does effectively prevent us from attacking those on whom we are so dependent. Nor are we lenient toward ourselves. The opposite takes place. Sam's violent, destructive, and anger-provoking conduct toward all with whom he was most intimate was founded on more than mere infantile resistance to his mother's wish that he deposit his stools in a receptacle of her choosing. Nor is it indicative simply of a phase in which a child cannot yet control his aggression. Some analysts fail to recognize that the turn against the self in the little boy has, even at his young age, sufficiently developed so that he directs at himself his aggression meant for his mother. Such acts, so admiringly approved, have been naively regarded as simply imitative of parental punishment. Instead, they should be credited to the momentous early beginnings of turning hostility onto oneself. We find that even so young a child leans heavily on finding scapegoats on whom to project his fury. Thus, it is not he, but the monsters, the creatures, and the things that go "bump" in the night who deserve his abuse.

Sam's mother infringed on his need for anal gratification, which, we have discovered, occurs in an early phase of our emotional development. We never altogether give it up. This anal gratification is associated with certain character traits and the discovery of their early unconscious origins which residually persist profoundly changed our views of obstinacy, parsimony, and their intimate emotional connection with aggression.[13] Analysts uncovered these qualities as closely related psychologically, when the direct study of children began to mature about fifty years ago. This led them to suppose that the often formidable resistance that children put up to social demands of toilet-training, expressed as requiring cleanliness and orderliness, was illustrative of the human unwillingness to curb a source of pleasure, in this case one of our earliest and our most primitive: the anal one.

Rages were commonly observed as indicative of the child's tenacity to anal gratification. This was convincing that what was at stake was the importance to the child of pleasurable anal experience rather than a limitation on a function early associated with gratification. It is well known that the problems with toilet-training and nightmares, which often go together, are far more common in boys than girls. However, we have only inconclusive explanations for what accounts for the connection between nightmares and toilet-training, what accounts for the difference in this experience between boys and girls, and what accounts for the aggression associated with anal functions when there is no demand for curtailment of pleasure. In brief, one naturally resists social demands that invariably fetter gratification, particularly of infantile needs. These demands are regarded as an invasion of the narcissistic self. Aggression toward whoever imposes restrictions or limitations on this self is the reaction evoked in defense. A boy's narcissism, uniquely vulnerable, readily mobilizes aggression to defend it. This is what a boy does about his aggression.

Early in masculine development, aggression is employed in the service of narcissism. In the same vein, it is the arm to prompt prowess, to help achieve mastery, and to make masculinity secure. As a rule, the more vulnerable masculine narcissism seems, the more readily is aggression mobilized in its defense. Whether the aggressive defenses are expressed as impotent rages or become highly sophisticated intellectual pursuits naturally depends on circumstance, the level of developed maturity possible, and the degree to which self-curbs or aggression turned on oneself develops.

Psychologists commonly feel that the hostility toward those on whom we depend, with whom we are intimate, and who impose their demands on us requires some form of disavowal of the anger, hate, and rage evoked. The mode of repudiating the hostility appears to depend on the level of psychological maturity that has been achieved. They place emphasis on aggression, its vicissitudes, and defenses of the self that will be employed.

However, the modes of expression of our aggression, once we are developed beyond the rages of early infancy, beginning in about our second year when aggression that is no mere discharge of rage becomes demonstrably present, remain basically the same. There are two principal ways in which we are unconsciously affected by our aggression. One is what we found in Mack's example: little Sam has nightmares, which show that as the dreamer he disowns his destructive wishes or acts and attributes them to those who he claims would attack him. His awareness extends only to the fears of the monsters and creatures who would destroy him. He awakens in terror as the victim.[14] During his waking hours, little Sam may have the same ideas, objectionable to himself, and project them to others, his "proxies." The second way in which we are affected by our aggression is unconsciously to relegate our intentions to amnesia or repression. And, of course, if our defenses such as they are cannot contain narcissistic aims and their aggressive implementation, as we observed in Little Hans and Marty, fears and phobias or other similar signs of conflicts appear during the day, much as the nightmares make themselves manifest during the night.

Conventional as well as psychoanalytic wisdom holds that a primordial struggle remains within us between the strength of our appetites and the force of social claims opposing them, as though the demands of civilization make us more violent than peaceful. In Mack's instance, we find this is also his reasoning. What escapes recognition is that the running away from carrying violence toward others with whom we are close, or committing monstrous acts against them, are not mere matters of conscience. In little Sam's case, his emotional development has not reached a level for conscience to be a ruling factor, yet he cannot tolerate his own destructive intentions. They are a menace to the "self." For his own sake, he dares not to menace others, but he cannot stand to turn on himself either.

There is another course to take that is the opposite of the disavowal. It is the early and familiar practice of carrying out one's aggression by identifying oneself with that quality in another. It gives legitimacy to aggression, and, with that, the matter of conscience, which only in its rudimentary form in the little boy is not called upon. Furthermore, to identify oneself with the aggressor reduces the anxiety over one's own hostile intentions and justifies victimizing others. Small boys can hardly ever be shaken from justifying their aggressive acts that they enjoy during violent play. Closer scrutiny into what in an older boy would be an act of conscience reveals that the younger one is not concerned with the moral issue. Instead, the little boy's concern is with meting out justice. But its scales he manipulates to suit himself. He discards such considerations as kinship, friendship, mercy, and engages blindly in retributive justice, poetic justice with partiality only toward himself. The wide spectrum of a boy's aggression demonstrates its importance as a defense of a vulnerable vanity.

The maturity of emotional development may not improve on these unconsciously formed modes of behavior, but does modify and alter them by the self-serving nature of our relationships. It has long been assumed that these emotional reactions, having their origins in childhood, give way with maturation. On the contrary, repugnant as they are to our growing conscience, they are by it more effectively repressed. When circumstances lift the repressive needs, they may readily reappear at any time of life.

The sense of "self" remains manifest in egocentricity; its needs resist tempting or restraint. "Only the coercive necessity of a relationship profoundly affects the 'self.' The foundation of our emotional regulatory devices is a social one and not biological. No creature model for such development descends to man. . . . Man's unique psychological nature is his narcissism."[15]

It seems to test credulity that we can find evidence for suicidal wishes occurring in a little boy. The need to disassociate oneself from hostility toward those on whom we depend and love is as durable as aggression itself. But the consequence — to take oneself instead as the object of fury, hate, and destructiveness — seems also inescapable. There is little in the scientific literature to suggest that in very young children, especially boys, self-destructiveness is related inseparably to our narcissism. And moreover, that it is an early and lasting part of the psychology of everyday life. Instead, it is assumed to be confined to its extremes and exceptions in suicidal acts. As a result, the unnoticed minor episodes of self-attacks, in an infinite variety of ways, which go on in our everyday existence, receive negligible attention. The ordinary injuries that occur are so readily attributed to accident, circumstance, and events, which exonerate motive. No aggression surpasses the fierceness of taking oneself as the ultimate victim. Nor is there either reason or evidence for not taking into account that young children as well as adults are prone to the same intent. This becomes clear when we carefully cull the fears, phobias, terrors, and nightmares of early boyhood.[16]

Psychoanalysts have known since the early decades of this century that those who were exceedingly narcissistic were especially vulnerable to losing self-esteem and were thus susceptible to self-destructiveness — not, however, before reproaches against someone loved had been turned away to oneself. "The riddle of the tendency to suicide . . . makes melancholia so interesting — and so dangerous. . . . We have long known, it is true, that no neurotic harbours thoughts of suicide which he has not turned back from murderous impulses against others."[17] To exempt another from the certain belief in the effect of one's destructive, intensely hateful wishes toward them leads to taking oneself as the victim of one's own hostile aims. By setting a value on another above oneself, one may turn to self-denigration and self-reproaches. They lead oneself to the expectation of punishment and torment as the object of disdain. We have the image here that the martyr holds of himself. This course of emotional events holds the key to the puzzling yet commonest disorder of adult life: depression, or melancholia. It was mistakenly believed that this condition was limited to the severe emotional disorders. To this day it is not recognized as a part of the psychology of everyday life, nor a part of childhood. Despite the highly egocentric character of young children and especially the vulnerability of a boy's narcissism, aggression as a defense of it is not adequately appreciated.

There is a tendency to regard depression chiefly in its most neurotic and psychotic proportions. This has led to neglecting transient episodes of depression that occur in daily life in connection with feeling slighted, neglected, disappointed, and even perhaps abused. All arouse feelings opposed to love or affection; anger, hostility, and wishes that correspond to them come into awareness. These experiences in relation to one with whom intimacy exists and dependency and love have been established bring on inescapable, hostile self-judgments that are not readily reversed. Reproaching oneself is unavoidable. The entire process is not confined to adult life or its disorders. It is present normally in a very little boy whose nightmares showed that the identical emotional events had begun to operate when limitations were imposed on him, as when an adult's hostility is excited toward someone intimate. Turning some measure of hostility meant for another to oneself seems inescapable.

Taking oneself as the object of our "slings and arrows" is a momentous step in our emotional development. Insofar as it means that a needed and valued relationship is ensured by sparing it hurt, it is in a clear sense "nobler in the mind." The fact that this may at times be a serious, self-destructive process does not therefore make it in certain respects any less a moral one. The cost for our social gain comes in making ourselves unconsciously vulnerable to our own attack. To meet a social need, we must become less egocentric, less narcissistic.

It would seem that every boy is psychologically unwittingly an Achilles who, except for his heel of narcissism that he must defend, is invulnerable. In legend we are told that Achilles was deliberately placed to grow up among girls, in response to a prophecy that his prowess, if early displayed and celebrated, would lead to his fall. Seemingly protected in the company of the daughters of King Lycomedes, the young hero is safe until he is betrayed and unmasked through his own irresistible eagerness to battle to prove himself. Was he not given the choice of a short but glorious life or a long and sure one in obscurity? Boys forever are inclined to make the Achillean choice and hope to escape its fate.

A boy is directed in somewhat the same way as a girl. He soon discovers, however, that he must alter his tendency to wish to be like his mother. At the same time, a mother's aspirations for her young daughter are very different from those she has for her son. The disappointment a mother may feel that her daughter is not a boy often leads her naively to encourage the little girl to think that her distinction from boys is arbitrary, negligible, and even deniable. This may be a set of ideas that a little girl, to a degree, has formed herself and holds long after she has discovered her allotment is not identical with that given to others. It would be extraordinary but illustrative, however, for a mother to have an inclination to persuade her small son that his distinction from a little girl is to be disregarded.

The Farbs, as I shall call them, were parents of a small boy, younger by eighteen months than his sister, and wished to treat their two children evenhandedly. They wanted not simply to apportion what could be divided, but in every other respect they conscientiously wanted to be "fair." It seemed to them that they had succeeded. When the boy was nearly three years old, he began to inquire about the anatomical difference between himself and his sister with whom he was often bathed. The parents held to their resolution: the boy was regularly told, in answer to his repeated and insistent question, that the difference he saw was not important, and that his sister, like all girls, had a "hole." To him, this was a predicament as he raised more questions than his parents answered; because a "hole" means no genital and calls on a host of disquieting judgments that we learned previously here are associated with being deprived and "robbed."

Bolstered by a currently popular trend that would make little of the sexual distinction between children, the Farbs, and particularly the mother, hoped to prevent "undue arrogance" on the part of the boy by paying equal attention to the children's needs. The mother was furthered in her resolve because the brother had begun to tease his sister during his second year with what he had and she lacked. The mother, steadfast in her aims, insisted that all the toys were to be shared as equally as possible. Because the children were so close in age and in size, she dressed them in similar clothing. To her pleasure, occasionally they were taken for twins.

During his third year, the boy began to want to wear ribbons and feminine articles of his sister's, such as the separate top she sometimes wore with her beach bathing trunks. At first, the parents regarded their son's wishes as mere play in sharing clothing the children had been brought up to exchange. Their closer and critical scrutiny was drawn by the boy's insistence on extending his interest into wanting to wear articles of his mother's clothing. They discovered him trying to wear her underclothes. When he refused at times to stand to urinate, the parents became concerned that their small son appeared to them to want to act as if he were a girl. His wishes were beyond their reach or understanding. The father especially became irate and demanded that his son not behave as though he were a girl. He was more troubled than the mother, who was privately amused by her son's "play-acting," as she referred to his conduct. When the boy was nearly five years old, his interest in feminine clothes had continued, although not so obviously as at first, because of his father's criticism and his mother's scolding. By this time, the parents no longer delayed recognizing that their son's behavior was a continuing source of difficulty for them. They determined that he should be treated by a psychiatrist.

The boy, David, was an attractive, well-formed, tall child, active, obviously intelligent, and curious. Within a few visits, his play began to focus first on objects he noticed were broken. He would fish them out from a bin of toys (the broken ones were not deliberately placed there, but they had not been removed either). He would pick up these broken toys and remark that the object was broken or damaged, but he firmly avoided any other comment. After a few more visits, David took more notice of the broken toys, going beyond his usual comments that this or that piece had been broken. Up to this point, he had seemed merely to be making an inventory of the damaged objects. He began to be persistent in asking exactly how the damage occurred. He wanted the details of the actual event. As the explanation was that such accidents occur in the ordinary course of playing with toys, that they can be repaired, and that missing parts happen to toys rather than to people, he seemed to lose interest and appeared indifferent, turning away to other objects even before the finish of a brief reply to his questions.

After a further series of visits, when he had gone beyond familiarizing himself with the various objects and had become comfortable, his play began to take a form that continued from one visit to the next. He joined groups of jungle animals, lions, elephants, giraffes, tigers, and a family of small, rubber dolls into confrontations with each other in play that became increasingly aggressive. The various animals attacked each other, or the family, in what appeared a rather indiscriminate fashion. Soon, it became evident that the attacks were at the instigation of one, whom the others followed. It turned out that the one who marshaled the attacks was the mother; whether she was human or animal seemed not to matter — she ruled. In this boy's family, although both parents were shy persons and his mother gave the impression of being timid and self-effacing, she was also the more determined in her views than her husband.

In the boy's play, the men or boys were ruled by women; females ruled male animals, mothers or girls governed the family. The men were also aggressive; in this regard there was no evident distinction. But violence, which was increasingly the conduct of the one who ruled others, was confined to women. He identified them as the "bosses," and himself as liking to be "boss." Over and over, he played that men were being "bossed," and when they were hurt, which also often occurred, they were the victims of women. He put himself in the role of such women. He resisted giving the role of "boss" to the men. The women would not allow that change to take place. When it was suggested that he was not a girl and that as he played it was safer to be one so as not to get hurt, he spontaneously declared that women had penises. When he was reminded that he knew they did not, he angrily insisted that they did. After a few such sessions, he admitted that he did not know where the female penis was. But he was sure they had it.

David was identifying himself with the "boss," that is, with the one who is aggressive. His insistence illustrates what psychoanalysts since Freud found in children to be the problem of the "widdler." The boy's doggedness that the penis exists where he failed to see it is indicative of the conflict illustrated here. The boy is identified with his mother, she being the aggressive "boss." However, to be like her is to be lacking, as women are, and is to the boy intolerable. His insistence, therefore, that there exists a phallus, even though it is not in evidence, shows the deep imperative the boy is under. He does not accept what he knows to be true and what he believes to be the only difference between boys and girls, men and women, males and females. To reiterate for him what he emotionally rejects only additionally reinforces the strength of what he must believe. In conforming to his parents' wishes, with no less or perhaps even more conviction than theirs, his stubborn claim that there is no difference between the sexes does not bring him to the conclusion that all are female or women or girls. Rather, he insists, as do all boys for whom identification with their mothers is a source of anxiety, that all are male, that is, phallic-bearing.

Although the wish to be like mother, the "boss," seemed safer, the need to have his father's interest brought out his competing for it with his sister and mother. It came out in anecdotes of jealousy of his sister, whom he felt his father favored and of whom the father was not so critical. Was it not better to be a girl: his sister was rewarded for *it*, and he was criticized for *it*? With these issues plainly expressed, he stopped wearing any of either his mother's or his sister's things to avoid exposing his wish. But he did carry about in his pocket some article, which was often but a pin or an ornament, of theirs. He also began to make inquiries about when his father was a boy, and he asked about what activities his father had enjoyed. He became more interested than before in play with the other boys at school. He had previously kept away from them in his shyness and reluctance to engage in their boisterous behavior. Now he joined them with a burst of activity and interest in their games, from which he had been aloof or at most an observer rather than a participant.

His readiness to form new relationships with boys took him outside the family, as did his visits to the office. They had become easily comfortable in the continuity from one session to the next. There were fewer indications of anxiety, rarely playing "boss," when earlier this form of play had been virtually a sole preoccupation. With this, the emphasis in play shifted toward activity rather than aggression.[18] As often happens when a child being treated improves dramatically as his underlying intentions are illuminated for him, the immediate symptoms, especially those disturbing to the family, often subside. The parents are so relieved that they terminate treatment. It ended here in this case.

A colleague, knowing of my current study, generously offered me the following clinical report. It has similarities to the one just described above. A six-year-old, bright, and capable little boy, with evident great difficulty and reluctance, informed his parents, to their deep dismay, that "he did not want his penis." During the previous year, the boy had made remarks that his parents reported were "obviously very difficult for him to say to us." They always considered him to be a very sensitive boy; his feelings were easily hurt. They said that once he began with his admission, he often spoke of not wanting his penis together with not wanting to grow up. This was spoken of particularly when he was angry. "He would point to his penis and say, 'I don't want it.'"

The mother spoke of herself as "too shy and too accommodating." She saw these qualities developing in her son. "I am too anxious, too," she said. "He makes me so mad at him when I see he is like me. With my burdens. I'm so insecure. And *like* me. I don't like myself. It gets me so mad! To hear him say he doesn't like himself and that kids don't like him. I see myself reenacted in him. All my life I battled it. If only he were more secure, he'd be fine. . . . He says such outrageous things. It's in connection with his genitals. He speaks of it like excrement. He's very critical, that is, self-critical. And he is too tied to me. I was so involved with him before. His closeness was with me. Now he wants a lot of attention from his father. He likes to talk feminine to us. I can get very upset when I hear it. He likes to dress up in my clothes. It get me when he wants to be so pleasing to his father. I get all nervous when he wants to wear my clothes, my hats, my capes. Sometimes it varies, and he changes to 'superman.'"

The father independently confirmed the mother's impressions of their son. He, too, expressed his concern that the boy made the alarming announcement repeatedly to both of them that he did not want his penis. The father's explanation of his son's wish was that it came from his having been absent from home for long periods on account of his work. He feared that he "had not been around enough to be a proper model" for his son's masculinity. Now, however, he was home regularly, and he noticed with pleasure how eager his son was to please him. He hoped this might prove to be an incentive for the boy to be more like his father.

An extensive study of the little boy's play showed a ready choice or preference to play with a variety of toys that represented people. He would show no more than a perfunctory interest in mechanical toys or mechanisms that usually fascinate boys his age. However, he was an imaginative, intelligent child. He tended toward being immature in his play; themes were simple, inhibited, and at first confined merely to depicting events that centered chiefly on domestic scenes of household chores. His characters expressed little thought about their experiences. Thus, at the beginning, he engaged in neither an elaboration nor a diversity of his ideas. He was not able to let an idea lead to an elaboration of another. Moreover, he resisted suggestions that would take him to develop his play beyond the limits he himself set.

As the treatment proceeded and the boy's inhibitions in his play diminished, he became less restricted to playing out mere events that befell people. His play spontaneously shifted to focus on characterizing the relations between them. He showed people to be hostile, aggressive, and destructive to one another. Once on this theme, it was evident that to him this was the only way people were associated with each other. He would not allow efforts to introduce a measure of tolerance, forbearance, or compassion, even to avoid such painful encounters or conflicts. He thus revealed his view of the implacable nature of people.

The boy also developed another element in his characters. Those whom he represented as suffering hostility or aggression as victims also had a moral failing and were additionally victimized by deprivation. An inquiry into their plight turned out to show that theirs was a self-imposed condition that they had somehow chosen. Moreover, they were to blame for having something prized denied them, or they searched and could not find it; it was probably lost and beyond being retrieved. These guarded ideas were gradually disclosed and thereafter repeatedly played out. The relations between people were principally hostile. This applied no less to women than men. However, women became the chief victims. The play took on a frank, sadistic excitement that the boy was reluctant to modify in much the same way that his characters were remorseless. He relished playing the aggressive character. He did so with exaggerated fury in his scenarios that never failed to end in tragedy. Even as he depicted himself in this way, he showed that his own violence was a reaction to his conviction that he was weak, even helpless, and wanted to be dependent on someone with force. The violence and fury were only masks behind which to conceal the desirable, but also dangerous, wishes to continue his identification with his mother.

When their son pointed to his penis and frightened his doting parents with his reticent declaration that he wished to be without it, he was simply stating in the most ingenuous fashion that he wanted to be a woman. Neither they nor he could have supposed that such an untoward, expressed wish would bring him to reveal a serious, unconscious conflict of his own making, and that its implications would have far-reaching, even if different, psychological effects on each of his parents.

It has been well known since some of the earliest psychoanalytic reports that boys about the age of this one normally go through a brief period of unconsciously wanting to be a woman.[19] But this period also revives the earlier identification with one's mother that the later interest of pursuing masculinity had caused to be abandoned. He must quit these feelings when his masculine aspirations are at their apogee and when their expression is directed at his mother. He is obliged to give up the deep-seated and heavily invested wishes for an exclusive relationship with his mother. Even though they may be only dimly perceived consciously, and their expression limited to earning her admiration by means of some achievement, or the promise of one, or her preference for him by his mere existence, all are doomed to failure. The effect falls heavily on self-esteem.

Narcissism, assiduously nurtured as masculinity and presented through aggression in pride, performance, and prowess, is in jeopardy. The extravagant wishes for himself to exercise powers, magically rule events, or to find no limits to his achievements and pleasures are brought down to scale. A boy's fate is to be struck by the strongest taboo men experience: incest.

113

Some recovery of self-esteem comes with the unconscious passive wish to take his mother's place in his father's affections. Normally, these are transient states, anxiety-laden, and withdrawn from awareness by repression into amnesia. However, in the boy that I have just described, we find that certain normal conflicts have been prolonged. Moreover, they are not repressed. His wishes to be a woman are sufficiently demanding to intrude into awareness and find expression. Their significance is plain. The imperative from them is to give up masculinity that calls for prowess, performance, sexual aggression for a compelling, passive, feminine role. It represents a solution to persistent unconscious incestuous wishes that resist being abandoned.

The mother's self-recriminations are revealing when she tells how much of her discredited feminine self she now observes in her son. We cannot here know how the identification of the son followed his mother's wishes. But we do know that the intensity of his reaction to taking his absent father's place as the man in his mother's life required strict repudiation. In short, the unconscious, incestuous wishes the boy entertains are not tolerable. A reversal unconsciously takes place. He disclaims masculine aims and supports his denial of them by recanting. He declares he wants no penis. He wants to be a woman. Moreover, he wants to be his father's woman!

Understandably naive, the father blames himself and supposes that by his absence he failed to provide his son with a proper model of masculinity. We cannot expect the father to realize that vacating his place at home promoted his son's masculine aspirations and intensified the boy's incestuous desires, which we may safely believe must have been furthered, in her husband's absence, by the mother's unconsciously being seductive with her son.

At the close of World War II, there were many similar situations, though they were often less dramatically plain, when a small boy, to his alarm, grief, and unconscious mixed pleasure, was told by his mother that as his father was off to

114

war, he was now the "man." The conflicts that were thus ushered in can be anticipated. With demobilization, the father's return was a mixed unconscious blessing for his son.

We have observed before that masculinity is an acquired state. Its particular conflicts arise in the earliest years of boyhood. During the course of masculine emotional development, they are largely brought, for each phase, to resolution. However, one disturbing element remains a continuing source of conflict, despite its being relegated to repression early. It does not remain there inert. Retrieved from amnesia in dreams, fantasies, or evoked by some circumstances, it returns to awareness to become again a vivid experience. This is the identification with a woman, the wish to *be* a woman. We have earlier here noted this phenomenon in small boys. In recent years, reports of the wish to give up masculinity, to be female, have been dramatically and authentically demonstrated.

An autobiography recently published tells of a man who did not want his penis.[20] The book is about how he got rid of it.

> By favor of hormone treatment and surgery (writes Rebecca West, reviewing the book), Mr. James Morris, a well-known journalist, and perhaps the finest descriptive writer in our time, of the watercolor kind, has become Miss Jan Morris. . . . Surely this is rather a record of a strange self-treatment for a neurotic condition.[21]

To a psychoanalyst, that a man wishes to be a woman is neither a mystery nor an uncommonly expressed unconscious desire. As we have seen here earlier, such notions are normally transient. But it is how Morris chooses to solve this riddle that is illuminating. In his writing the account of the painful vicissitudes he subjected himself to in being sexually mutilated, we must conclude that one important object was to be exhibitionistic. He wanted no privacy. But for this we would probably be deprived of a remarkably articulate account, first hand, of the persistent strength of the psychological motive in a man to rid himself of his penis.

115

More eloquent of course than what we have heard from little boys less directly, Morris writes:

> I was three or perhaps four years old when I realized that I had been born into the wrong body and should really be a girl. I remember the moment well, it is the earliest memory of my life. I was sitting beneath my mother's piano, and her music was falling around me like cataracts. . . . What triggered so bizarre a thought I have long forgotten, but the conviction was unfaltering from the start.[22]

More than the fact of his recollection is the important significance to him that the event holds. It is his small boy's desire to be like his mother. And we well know that this is a wish that all little boys, at one time, entertain. Morris says, "It is true that my mother wished me to be a daughter." He denies, however, that he was ever treated like one. But he gives us a fleeting glimpse that his mother's friends playfully wrapped him in "their furs and lavender sachets to murmur that with curly hair like mine, I should have been born a girl."[23] These experiences and similar ones are recalled to support that his early wish to be a girl should leave the reader in little doubt. Moreover, he wants us to understand that a correspondence existed between his own wishes and his mother's. It remained his purpose to keep this correspondence.

We know that in the early development of small children, whether they are boys or girls, they at first naturally find their definition through the wish to be like their mothers. This is not ordinarily a prolonged intention. The boy soon begins tc wish to abandon such aims to pursue what he sees as a less alarming and more gratifying course for himself toward masculinity. Boys who persist in going on being like their mothers, as did Morris, are not doing it out of a wish simply for conformity with their mothers but rather out of some satisfying and compelling necessity. To take on being feminine is usually a boy's reaction to masculinity that unconsciously has become prohibited, based on an earlier-seated identification with one's mother that

116

has been prolonged. In either case, the conscious aim of requiring femininity, when masculinity is too anxiety-provoking, is to take or carry on the safer, feminine role. This is not to suggest that the boy's incestuous wishes are altogether abandoned. They are not. The role of being more one's mother's little boy and to continue the close identification with her intensifies the unconscious, incestuous desires to make them the more intolerable. As we have seen, the little boy treated by my colleague unconsciously chose a feminine identification as the more satisfying and more secure solution to his tangle at the expense of his masculinity, which we saw he depicted as implacably dangerous to others and to himself. Morris appears to have forgotten that he, too, as a little boy, seems to have made a similar choice. We may suppose that in his case he was heavily influenced by the prolonged identification with his mother. His early boyhood history is too scantily given to permit us to reconstruct satisfactorily what contributed further in that period to his wish to quit masculinity for being a woman.

Morris tried to analyze his own childhood emotions, he writes, in order to discover what they meant when "I declared myself to be a girl in a boy's body. . . . I see it still a mystery." He adds that no one really knows why some children, despite all the physical evidence, carry the "inexpungeable belief," as he does himself, that they are really of the opposite sex. He finds no theory acceptable. It may be, he guesses, that the child's conviction of his sex is due to some constitutional or genetic factor, as some scientists claim, or perhaps a too-close identification with a parent, which many psychoanalysts think is the case, or perhaps it is an environmental element. As Morris believes that no one is born entirely male or female, he suggests that some children may be susceptible to the "imprint" of circumstance. It is, to him, a riddle. He takes his own case: he has had a "passionate lifelong ineradicable conviction" that he was a girl and that he must physically conform to the certainty of his choice.[24]

117

For many years, Morris remained physically a man. Yet, throughout these years he retained his boyhood wish to be a woman. He intended to characterize men when he writes about them, but he only succeeded in caricaturing them. He limits us to his Victorian schoolboy impressions of a masculine ideal. They seem more appropriate to his mother's generation than to his own. Although he was in this thirties, he could still write:

> Man was for hard things, making money, fighting wars, keeping stiff upper lips, beating errant schoolboys, wearing boots and helmets, drinking beer; woman was for gentler, softer purposes, healing, soothing, . . . wearing silks . . . and accepting admiration.[25]

In all these ruminations, he secretly enjoyed, as though he were a girl, the attentions he recalls that other boys paid him. He began on the strength of that to pray "throughout my boyhood . . . an appeal: 'And please, God, let me be a girl. Amen.' "[26]

The actual gratification of his wish began to be realized with the fuller knowledge that he was attractive to certain men.

> It was fun to be pursued, gratifying to be admired. . . . I enjoyed being kissed on the back stairs, and was distinctly flattered when the best-looking senior boy in the house made elaborate arrangements to meet me in the holidays.[27]

We may fully appreciate Morris's frustration in feeling himself "to be wrongly equipped."[28] He keeps repeating his lament that he was the "wrong body, being feminine by gender." He goes on to a further development of the fantasy that he is in fact a woman masquerading as a young man, "pining for a man's love." It seems no accident that his going into army service was for him an excursion into male society. He asks his woman readers to titillate themselves with the notion of being "successfully disguised as a young man . . . admitted to this closed and idiosyncratic male society."[29]

118

Nevertheless, he married, fathered three children, became a well-known writer, climbed Mt. Everest with the British expedition as a journalist, and, as he says, covered rebellions, famines, and earthquakes. He was all these years actively in male company. There he enjoyed being paid the frequent compliment by his fellow officers, expressed in various ways, that they wished he were a woman. He claims no actual homosexual encounters. He continued to suffer, however, since he felt imprisoned. A girl in a man's body. His obsession with being a woman became a compelling conviction that he must fit or alter his body to match his self-persuasion.[30] With that, he began his odyssey to find a surgeon who would modify him physically sufficiently to conform with his continuing boyhood wish to be a woman.

Morris fails to appreciate fully the power of his identification with women. In his eagerness to have his obsession realized, he became further enthralled to such an intensity that "I set my face against manhood." He withdrew from public life and went about "cultivating impotence."[31] His purpose brought him finally to Casablanca. There two weeks in a clinic after surgery, bandages, tubes and with supplementary hormones,[32] his boyhood fantasy seemed materially realized. He had become *like* a woman. What Morris seems not to understand is that what he really wanted was to fulfill his boyhood notion of what a woman was like. Thus, we find his fantasies are limited and directed to the physical aspects of a woman. We find nothing of a woman's character or a woman's psychology entering into his reveries. Such musings, focused on the woman's physical characteristics, are common to boys during their early pubescent years.

Morris leaves us ignorant as to what possessed him, after so long, to terminate his evident heterosexual life. Nor does he tell us he ever enjoyed it; was his wife the more masculine of the two? He makes it plain, however, that he did not, nor could he allow himself to, enjoy being a man. It was the reverse. His pleasure was the company of men. His satisfaction was

119

gleaned from their admiration, their approval, and their finding him erotically winning or appealing. He had enjoyed that role as a schoolboy just as he did in his adult career. As he says, he turned his face against manhood to look for impotence! When he found it, by the grace of surgery, his own childhood prayers were answered; not, however, by God's intervention, but by the impetus to put an end to being a sexual man. The extreme end, to make this point, brings Morris not merely to forgo his sexual conduct as a man but to abandon masculinity through the most childlike and primitive conception of it — by having the "offending member" removed. Morris does not become a woman as he would have us suppose. He becomes a woman *manqué*.

A boy's erotic bond to his mother and her concern with her son evoke in each of them powerful libidinal wishes, if we are to judge by the strength of the defenses that form unconsciously against acting directly on these wishes. In the case of the little boy who did not want his penis and showed early and rudimentary forms of being a transvestite, he illustrated at the age of five years what Morris shows us may appear thirty or forty years later. We may suppose that as his wife came into her full, mature, maternal years, Morris's unconscious conflicts became more pressing. He brought them to a resolution in such a fashion that confirms their boyhood character: the conception that masculinity resides in the phallus and being a woman is to be without a phallus. Like the little boy cited here, Morris wants to be seduced by men, much as the little boy wanted to be in his mother's place and win his father's favor.

Psychoanalytic writing on the subject of incest has been evenhanded in treating the incest taboo as a strict prohibition to which mankind submits.[33] The distinction that exists between incest as a boy sees it and a girl's conflicts about it has not been studied carefully. This may be due to the continuing failure to develop the distinction between masculine and feminine psychological development and as a consequence to remain with the psychology of the human condition. The examples show a small boy's need to have a share in a father's pride, prowess, and those qualities the boy attributes to him that represent what he wants for himself. For obvious reasons, the boy is never equal to the task he sets for himself. This is nowhere more evident to him than in the Oedipus complex. He puts so much emotional masculine capital into it, yet it has to be abandoned. He is confronted with a profitless venture in the pursuit of his wishes for the kind of exclusive relationship with his mother that he envies. It is also a humbling experience. Not only has his libidinal undertaking been dashed, but he extends this sense of futility to intellectual curiosity.

As a consequence of high expectations that are bound to come to nothing at this time and the resultant sense of loss, Freud wrote that he found lasting and even "crippling" effects that extended into adult life.[34] Whether "crippling" is wholly accurate is not so important as the fact that this effect is profound. Before a boy recovers from this period of his development, unaccountable fears enter his awareness; he expects attacks from others and as often complains that he is a victim. He is unconscious of knowing that the source of what menaces him is within him; he is indeed a victim. But he is unaware that the monsters he dreads are of his own making. As I have shown, he would in self-defense even sometimes abandon his masculinity.

The taproots of failure lie in narcissism. Those of recovery from the helplessness, the sense of limitation, and the oppressiveness of unfulfilled wishes are not less embedded there. The boy is not alone in this. His parents' unconscious narcissism and their conscious aspirations for him drive their son to recover his pride through performance, prowess, and achievement. The thrust of aggression, which normally arises to restore one's narcissism, is nowhere plainer than in this period of a boy's development. He is conveyed by it into the next phase. Usually, it appears at first merely as an unaccountable burst of activity. As little else is manifest, it is ascribed vaguely as a developmental change due to some set of circumstances.

However, it is the sense of limitation and a corresponding narcissistic injury that are generating efforts at recovery. The need is great. The boy seems propelled by his changing physical development, and, although this may be the case in part, the activity shows a powerful "responsive" effort. It is to restore self-esteem; the recovery from the "crippling" is at stake. It is at this time that the "little boys" and the "Morrises" may begin another course, as their masculinity fails to recover normally. The specter of feminine identification remains with them as desirable, rather than the opposite.

The daydreams, fantasies, and activities a boy begins are often all that he socially and culturally may have available to him, when he is not engaged with excesses of aggression, to lay the basis for constructive relationships outside his immediate family. There he may deploy his ambition and aggression in more realistic rivalries and competitions. By means of them he acquires a mastery and skill to become a part of a group in which his own egocentric needs are compelled to modify for the sake of the group. The libidinal intimacy with his peers is less intense than in the family and, where sexuality, at least in its more manifest forms, is diffused, less selective, or exclusive. It has led analysts to designate this time of development as a period of so-called latency, giving it the meaning of sexuality's being held somewhat in abeyance for the onset of puberty. We shall find instead it is a unique period of masculine narcissism, of sexuality that is repressed, concealed, and disguised, and yet coupled with pride, prowess, performance, and achievement. The boy begins, at least in fantasy, a new life of adventures, somewhat independent of his immediate family, with a band of fellows to take their earlier experience from their families and, as an unconscious template, be guided by it in their outside encounters.

Chapter 6

BOYHOOD IN RETROSPECT

DESPITE ITS EXTRAORDINARY growth in nearly a century of existence, scientific psychology has had relatively little to contribute to our understanding of boyhood. Our knowledge of the psychology of boys has its roots principally in literature rather than in clinical sources. It is in literature that we begin to see plainly how important a period boyhood is thought to be in the development of the man's psychology. While literary sources provide the most valuable perceptions we have as to the nature of boyhood, it is interesting to note that the characteristics of boyhood are illustrated by men who are ostensibly far beyond the development. Because boyhood is a time of vaulting imagination and a need to transcend limits, this is what we ascribe to our heroes. While the remnants of boyhood cause older boys and men to resist the knowledge of limits, they can no longer allow their imaginations to soar to such an extent. Thus, because science has failed to provide the knowledge of the true character of boyhood, we must look to our heroic tradition and literature for this understanding.

The ancient legends of Gilgamesh, for example, tell of the qualities that boys revere and eagerly exhibit. The Babylonian hero, Gilgamesh, shares his passion for adventure with a comrade, Enkidu. But for negligible differences, they are alike: chivalrous, strong, loving of adventure, and embracing hazards over which they test their mettle and prove their valor. We quickly recognize that theirs is a boy's tale of camaraderie, joint struggles, and shared triumphs.[1] Gilgamesh loses none of his authenticity for us even though he and Enkidu come out of the shadows of prehistoric time. They come out of "once upon a time"; they intend to do as they wish; they resist convention; as an act of daring, they violate what is sacred. As two stalwarts, they are impetuous for adventure, to defy a monster and ask themselves in the course of privation and tests of endurance:

> "Are we such puny weaklings as to be put out by the first mishap? We have traveled a long way. Shall we now turn back defeated? For shame! . . . Wounds will soon be healed: and if we cannot engage the monster in his house, let us wait for him in the thicket!"[2]

These are Gilgamesh's words to his companion. Each exhorts the other. Little distinguishes their remarks, their prowess, or their achievements from those of numberless boys' tales. The entire legend is a larger-than-life sketch of boyhood prowess, proving oneself in adversity, and gaining from it an assurance of manhood to follow.

Among the even earlier myths is "Hermes's Nature and Deeds." Hermes grew with astonishing quickness. As soon as his mother, Maia, turned her back once, even while he was an infant, he was off looking for adventure. All too soon he was full of pranks. He succeeded even in deceiving Apollo by "rustling" one of his flocks. A vigorous search for the culprit did not succeed. Hermes's prowess soon was broadcast. His inventions drew envy, and even Zeus noted his achievements. This brought from Zeus a fatherly admonition to the boy that he "must respect the rights of property and refrain from telling downright lies; but he could not help being amused. 'You seem to be a very ingenious, eloquent, and persuasive godling,' he said."[3]

Literature emerges from legend and myth with the Homeric epics, the *Iliad* and the *Odyssey*, poems of a mythical time of the sort that boys dream. These heroes have no boundaries to observe, and they rule over what they choose. They are regal but have no emotional ties of kinship. They depend on companions who, like themselves, are largely adventurers. Their faithfulness to each other depends on personal qualities that each aspires to in himself and admires in others as a reflection of his own ideals, qualities of strength, courage, and mastery. According to this view, the *Iliad* turns on a contest in which a king takes unfair advantage of one of his greatest warriors, Achilles. Enraged with humiliation, Achilles throws down his weapons, quits his allegiance, and goes into the most notable sulk in literature. Meanwhile, his dearest friend, not having Achilles at his side, is killed by Hector. Achilles is convinced that, but for his rage and self-concern, his companion's death would have been avoided. Guilt-ridden and in despair, Achilles cries out that he deserves only to die. Finally, he can but make some restitution in swearing revenge against Hector. Now he feels that honor by vengeance must undo the wrong, even though he knows that he risks his life. Achilles can barely contain his eagerness to redeem himself. This darling of the gods chooses the short but glorious life rather than the offer of a long one in obscurity.

With Odysseus we may hardly imagine a mythical character given over more to resisting seductive temptations, or varied challenges to prowess and the marks of achievement. All are extended to his son, Telemachus, who is the younger version of his illustrious father. Through him, we see the ideal that the son faithfully strives to fulfill. The setting of the action is at a time when there is "no law and no morality." It is a heroic age. Direct judgments are made; there are no compromises. There is no real code. Blame is laid, and punishment meted out.

Such principles of conduct in these myths, legends, fables, and poems are those we find taking shape in boyhood. Prowess and honor go together as compelling inspirations, much as failure and shame are persistent goads to restore self-esteem that must be earned. Its lors demands redemption.

This is in no way to suggest that the grandeur of the Homeric poems may be reduced to mere tales of boyish pranks. Nor does it make the poems less noble or their characters less significantly artistic to understand that the relationships of the dramatis personae illuminate for us today, as no doubt in antiquity, that boyhood is the first durable proving ground for masculinity.

Our literary heritage includes Proverbs, Ecclesiastes, and the other Wisdom books of the Bible as the source material for the instruction by the elders of the young. They are epitomized in the Wisdom of Solomon. According to R. B. Y. Scott's scholarly study of these two books of the Bible, they seem to have been composed not in Hebrew but in ancient Greek and teach "the four cardinal virtues of Plato and the Stoics: self-control, prudence, justice, and courage."[4] They are admonitions to the young and prescribe a way of life that may guide boys today as well as millennia ago when Qoheleth was supposed to have written them. They were not injunctions addressed to men so much as they were exhortations to the aspirations of boyhood and to what is expected of boys as they develop into maturity. These are the written records of the spoken word.

The surviving Egyptian Wisdom works have close points of similarity with Hebrew Wisdom as represented in the Old Testament. It comes to us as the father-to-son form of moral instruction exploring the problems of boyhood, its dilemmas with its virtues, and its vices."[5] It is offered in a collection of literary and folk maxims and fables for a son's guidance. For example, the Second Discourse in Proverbs is on the benefits of prudently curbing oneself against being perverse, impulsive sexually, and a lax follower.[6] The Third and Fourth Discourses urge discipline and fidelity, and not to accept or identify with the villainous readily, "not envy a ruffian or imitate any of his ways."[7] What boys have among themselves, either in word or deed, failed to promise in their camaraderie that they will heed:

> Proud eyes, a lying tongue
>   Hands that shed the blood of the innocent,
> A mind full of schemes,
>   Feet rung toward wrong,
> A false witness breathing out lies,
>   And one who stirs up quarrels among brothers.[8]

A millennium later, St. Augustine in his *Confessions*[9] writes of his boyhood cries, in broken accents so that "I might have my will." And what "miseries and mockeries" he experienced at school where he

> launched deeper into the stormy intercourse of human life. . . . We sinned in writing or reading or studying less than was exacted of us. . . . Our sole delight was play; and for this we were punished. . . . For I disobeyed, not from a better choice, but from a love of play, loving the pride of victory in my contests and to have my ears tickled with lying fables, that they might itch the more.[10]

> In boyhood itself, however (so much less dreaded for me than youth), I loved not study, and hated to be forced to it. . . . I was already, displeasing even such as myself; with unnumerable lies deceiving my tutor, my masters, my parents from love of play, eagerness to see vain shows and restlessness to imitate them! Thefts also I committed, from my parents' cellar and table, enslaved by greediness, or that I might have to give to boys, who sold me their play, which all the while they like no less than I. In this play, too, I often sought unfair conquests, conquered myself meanwhile by vain desire of preeminence.[11]

These are the recollections of a boyhood in Babylon. They are not meant to be objectively true so much as subjectively accurate.

Rebecca West's sharp-etched biographical essay of St. Augustine catches the boyish hatred of the drudgery of school that had him flee into reverie. "The chief cause of his resentment was certainly the humiliation it inflicted on his infant dignity; and he had that precocious insight into character which is as sand in the engine of any educational machine."[12] She also notes:

> he confesses to homosexual relationships in a sentence which, with characteristic insight, puts its finger on the real offence of homosexuality, by pointing out that it brings the confusion of passion into the domain where one ought to be able to practise calmly the art of friendship.[13]

Even modern writing on boyhood, seventeen hundred years after Augustine, fails often to make this conflict as plain as he did without the benefit of knowing its deeper dynamics. "No doubt there was a time when he was a horrid little boy, but there have been a lot of horrid little boys since the world began."[14] Rebecca West remarked on the breathtaking, penetrating analysis of the gratuitous character of boyish delinquency that St. Augustine calls to our attention. Our own Mark Twain cannot improve on the following words of St. Augustine:

> I lusted to thieve, and did it, compelled by no hunger, nor poverty, but through a cloyedness of welldoing, and a pamperedness of iniquity. For I stole that, of which I had enough, and much better. Nor cared I to enjoy what I stole, but joyed in the theft and sin itself. A pear tree there was near our vineyard, laden with fruit, tempting neither for colour nor taste. To shake and rob this, some lewd young fellows of us went, late one night (having according to our pestilent custom prolonged our sports in the streets until then,) and took huge loads, not for our eating, but to fling to the very hogs, having only tasted them. And this, but to do, what we liked only, because it was misliked.[15]

Augustine's confessional recollections of his boyhood show us what a compelling continuation of boyish adventures are in our legacy. Were not Gilgamesh and Enkidu bent on similar errands as Augustine's? The same sort of escapades, tests of endurance, trials of defiance, challenges to authority, and remorse at waywardness are always present. The boy Hermes was no less a culprit in defying Zeus than that young delinquent, Prometheus, whose interest was mischief more than charity to mankind. Augustine's reminiscences are like those we shall find in Mark Twain's Tom Sawyer and Huck Finn, what Bernard De Voto recognized as "The Phantasy of Boyhood."[16] De Voto's authoritative work on Mark Twain calls attention to *Adventures of Huckleberry Finn* and to *Tom Sawyer* as American masterpieces that have

> permanently enriched world literature, both are among common possessions of even unliterary readers everywhere, both have the simple but mysterious attribute of mythology that makes permanence sure, both are compacted of literary truth . . . boyhood is something more than realism, it is a distillation, a generalization, a myth.[17]

These works illuminate a psychology that we know exists yet we fail to perceive.

Whether as epic heroes, mythical or totemic characters and other larger-than-life figures, or by way of recollection or fiction, these are the durable forms that give expression to the gratification boys need in the identity they take for themselves and, in the last analysis, for their self-esteem. There are further accretions. By taking on those qualities embodied in heroes, ideals, totems, wearing the lion's skin or carrying the Golden Fleece or other mantles and badges of achievement, a boy and a man feel they transcend their anathema: their limitations. While transcendence is indeed the human aspiration, as we have observed, the fear of being limited has a unique emotional importance for a man. It commences in his earliest experiences and remains as a goad. This is not to suggest that we may reduce our literary and legendary estate to representing the psychology of boys in their boyhood period, but an understanding of this period of the development of masculinity illuminates the lasting, compelling force associated with it. In the universe of myths, legend, lore, and fiction, the chronicle of actual events is not what is significant in boyhood. It is the acts that are performed in relation to them that give the meaningful association to the acts and that in turn furnish importance to masculinity.

There is probably no better example of the importance of boyhood in later life as illustrated in literature than *Don Quixote*. In a short psychoanalytic paper, "Don Quixote and Don Quixotism," Helene Deutsch fused her rare refinement of clinical perception with an uncommon wit.[18] The result is more than an original, enlightening insight delightfully presented about one of the greatest characters in fiction. Her use of Cervantes's work focuses our attention on a character type of man. I hope to show that our understanding of *Don Quixote* may be deepened by the recognition that certain conflicts in boyhood constitute a central element in the adventures of the gentleman from La Mancha and his faithful squire, Sancho Panza.

Deutsch intended to show that in late middle age, men commonly experience disturbances of potency that may also bring on serious emotional disturbances. As a reaction, fantasy is inflamed. Deutsch leads us to grasp more of this phenomenon than she may have had in mind at the time or at least than she wrote about in her very condensed vignette of seven pages.

She begins by inquiring what happens when a man of about fifty years, Alonzo Quixada, a petty noble of La Mancha, becomes enamored of a peasant girl from Toboso. Our hero, she points out, is so overcome with apprehension and embarrassment by the demands he makes of his erotic wishes that any sort of acting on them is quite out of the question. This develops as his mind fills with "enchantments, quarrels, battles, challenges, wounds, wooings, loves, torments and other impossible nonsense" from having buried himself in days and nights of reading about such adventures.[19] He aspires to win eternal honor and renown by the "valour of his arm" in redressing grievances, turning wrongs to right, amending injuries, and correcting abuses.[20] (I would say displaced from his humbling site of impotence.) Of course, with cleansed armor and a mount sublimely named, he had only to find a lady, Cervantes tells us. To the "country Brunhilde" he chose, Don Quixote was no Siegfried, writes Deutsch, and Cervantes describes him as the chastest of lovers. From such ignominy, he has Alonzo Quixada emerge as Don Quixote, immortal. As all "the energies which bring the ego into contact with reality were withdrawn," says Deutsch, they come together within the self into a single narcissistic aim. From the various frustrations or

> deprivations which the external world on the one hand, and his inhibited masculinity on the other, had imposed on him . . . the severely humiliated and deflated ego succumbs in favor of a newly arisen ego ideal, does this so completely that the tension between ego and ego ideal which is necessary to self-criticism disappears. It is now possible for Don Quixote to enjoy the untrammeled possession of all powers and attributes which his ego ideal demands of him.[21]

We thus find this near-aging man is renewed by losing himself in the fantasies of boyhood. He makes of the brave heroes of that time his ideals.[22] However, the cost of that revival is not at the original level; now it is grossly inflated. The conflicts of boyhood are relieved by turning to meet the aspirations held by the ego-ideal. A boy's narcissism normally may be thus restored without sacrificing reality. But this is not the case in Don Quixote. He abandons the reality for boyhood fantasies rather than for an ego-ideal, that is, one that, while aspiring to fulfillment of an ideal, does not relinquish what reality demands. The opposite is the case with our hero. If we apply to Cervantes's Don Quixote what we have learned about certain types of men, Deutsch suggests, we find they are

> The "Donquixotesques" — to borrow a word from Unamuno — [who] see in Don Quixote the wondrous prototype of a hero striving for the fulfillment of his ideal. They attribute to him greatness and the truth which is so sadly lacking in the crude world of reality.

131

> This reality, under which they themselves suffer, seems to them shadowlike and grey, in comparison with the ego-ideal which they harbor within them.[23]

What has been overlooked, however, is that these seeming "idealists," the types Deutsch has in mind, demand of reality that it conform to their own overblown claims rather than the reverse. Their ego-ideal is one that properly belongs to a past period, boyhood, which has been retained unmodified and is thus anachronistic. Engagement in righteous causes, enterprises, and pursuits, in a man passing middle age, draws its impetus from the narcissistic ego of his boyhood. That ego-ideal, carried to middle age, then makes inordinate demands of the self. As middle-aged men stand small chance of meeting such charges, they tend to be concerned with grievances, discontents, and humiliations as expressions of narcissistic injury as though they were inflicted by reality. Its inappropriateness gets obscured until it meets the clinical eye. With it we may see the world enveloped in a turgidity no more cruel than reality is grim. And so much that we suffer is the toll our narcissism exacts of us in its resistance to the coercion of restraints.

We may only surmise what Cervantes may have understood as a writer of the deeper psychology of the gentry of La Mancha. If he had in mind to show us to what lengths the resistance to failed emotional powers may drive us, he succeeded. With the tedium of chivalric romance as a vehicle by which to redress the wrongs of the world and to engage in devising schemes for winning honor and to be acclaimed for service to humanity and thus gain immortality, Cervantes has furnished us an authentic biography of boyhood.

For our purposes, the boy's ego-ideal is a goad. Its narcissistic nature is not left behind but is continually carried forward in the service of the masculine self. Boyhood and youth are those periods of masculine development in which the concerns are what masculinity should be, what is truly the case, or what is even probable. Therein lie the ever-demanding trials of mascu-linity, waiting like dragons and giants; performance, mastery, and achievement must overcome them to save self-esteem. Instead of expectations for himself being brought within the bounds where success may be realized, reveries and day-dreams carry Don Quixote off. Such states are not confined to the intolerable decline of aging or impotence, rather they are in all our agonies on the realization of limitations. Who would not want to transcend them? Masculine narcissism, especially in boyhood, however, is uniquely vulnerable to being shackled at a time when its aim is emancipation.

It is interesting in this context to consider the views of boys and children that have been expressed in our heritage. As compared to the insights that we obtain from its perceptions of men, a description of "children" represents a digression that is characterized by a self-consciousness and an attempt to pro-vide models of behavior for children.

Children rarely are subjects of attention in primitive or prehistoric art. Where they are shown, they are as little adults. For millennia, they were hardly otherwise portrayed than mingled with a crowd. Although they were assigned a gender, there was no definition of the child as a creature with sexuality any more than were animals.[24]

The serious considerations of the nature of childhood begin to appear as the old dualism between mind and matter sharp-ened. The material and mental world had begun to be recog-nized for the first time, when not in the context of theology, as ruled by their own principles that were perhaps not divinely inspired. Despite the lessons to be handily learned about the human condition from legend, fable, myth, and such early writings of the ancients that I have cited previously here, the protagonists of freedom of thought and the essence of social existence began to come loose from the orthodoxy of opinion that resisted such propositions. The phenomenon of the mind and its ideas of reflection were of course not novelties. But the growing concern given to such considerations found expression among thinkers who were to have a profound influence in both philosophy and politics. From them, the Enlightenment emerged. While it was bound up with the spread of scientific knowledge and a reexamination of intellectual activity, the fact that it produced a reaction, Romanticism, has a direct bearing on our concern here. It was out of the Romantic movement that the reach for human emotional development, although out of grasp of scientific understanding, as its time had not yet come, went toward the preeminence of reason and the individual. Childhood had become a unique part of the Social Contract through Rousseau's earlier influence, just as a half century later Darwin made the child part of the study of evolution. He put psychology into the animal and evolutionary development into the human condition. Thus, until the turn of our century, the child's destiny was regarded either as a factor in society or as part of the biological chain. Its psychology was in the hands of the poets and the new writers, the novelists; the scientists were mute on the child. It is therefore not surprising from the growing movement of the need to know the self, the logical extension of Romanticism, that writers turned to look at childhood long before psychologists and analysts took it over as their special preserve. However, for the deepest scrutiny that brought it into science, they had to await Freud.

In the fifty years before Freud's discoveries about the role of childhood in human emotional development and experience, the child became well established as the province of writers. For them, childhood became a process of growth and development rather than simply a condition of immaturity. As it was also a state of great insecurity, regression, and fears, they gave it more mystery than illumination. What rapt attention was paid to a child's mind argued more for its "innocence" that society, with its impediments, would too soon corrupt. Wordsworth and Coleridge, like others back to Rousseau, wrote in unison that everyday life spoiled childhood, its innocence by experience, its wonder by reason, its purity by sin. However, even if the romance with childhood, portrayed for instance by

George Eliot, was that of a heedless time played out in a "daisied" field, some psychology of the boy began to emerge. A boy became a popular object of literary and social interest by mid-nineteenth century and a model of a boy, albeit from fiction, did appear. Between Dickens and Twain, boyhood was immortalized.

However lofty or penetrating the perceptions of the writers were, they held in common that a boy, like all creatures, was a product of his environment, subject to its vagaries, and thus was neither more nor less a subject of the natural world. They had fused Rousseau with Darwin in their poems and fiction. As father to the man, a boy reflected in his conduct the nature of his circumstances, often in reality trying and ruinous. Nostalgia was a refuge and the inner life of childhood was depicted as a longing for a lost Paradise. We now know that this was the real fiction. It was generally assumed, then as before, that a child was a little adult, and a boy, a sort of Lilliputian, who would soon enough grow to full manhood. By good management, more akin to conscientious animal husbandry than to an understanding of a boy's inner experience, he would be brought to maturity. It was nearly a century away from direct scientific studies before a child emerged from an object of unprecedented literary interest to an individual whose private experience often transcended the importance of his circumstances. This is a common lesson that still eludes many.

The real inkling we get that childhood contains two distinct sexes appears with the popularity of books. Why it is the case is beyond the scope of this work, but it may be sufficient to call attention to the middle decades of the nineteenth century in England, which was a period of factional strife among various religious denominations. Books written ostensibly for children were more vehicles for the conveyance of religious tracts and partisanship than they were for the satisfaction of a juvenile audience. As the Victorian age opened, the trickle of books written for children soon became a stream and were principally about boys. What came into view, according to Professor

Robert Lee Wolff, a leading authority and collector of Victorian fiction, were stories written for adults, for young people, and, surely soon to be identified, for boys.[25]

Before these, there was no book more read by children than Aesop's *Fables*. Aesop probably never wrote them down, but by the fourth century B.C., they were collected and written in Greek prose. From there on, various collections and countless editions have appeared. There were, of course, earlier books for children. That is, they were written in the expectation that the principles of proper conduct would affect them. They were known as courtesy books and were, in fact, intended for highborn children to "inculcate breeding and courtly etiquette along with religious piety and moral excellence, if not perfection."[26] There were short tales, moral ones and cautionary, where children are turned into donkeys or magpies and, for instance, Master Stephen Churl, a cur, and Master Anthony Greedy-Guts, into a pig, in *Vice in its proper shape: or the wonderful and melancholy transformation of several naughty masters and misses into those contemptible animals which they resemble in disposition.*[27] From such works, we may gather that childhood was considered a period of human passage that adults endured while they vigorously molded the human clay, which was obviously often resistant, into a suitable social shape that would make those who seemed to have utterly forgotten their own early experiences, more comfortable. Whatever else such writings show, they are convincing evidence of the human capacity for amnesia about one's childhood.

Although best left to those in other fields to discover the reasons, it is important here to observe that it was well into the nineteenth century, and by way of its writers rather than its scientists, that the nature of boys was depicted. The literary climate of the fifty years between Rousseau and Wordsworth brought the child into the scene. Whether it was the Rationalist school that preoccupied itself with the theory of education and not its practice, or the "cult of sensibility" associated with

Rousseau, the nature of the child was seldom considered. "Treated as a small adult, the child was to be trained out of his childish ways into the moral and rational perfection of regulated manhood."[28]

The whole approach to childhood is well illustrated in the fashion of dressing of a child as a little adult. Against all this was the Romantic reaction that brought with it deploring against moralizing and turning, as well, from the previous intellectual traditions of the Enlightenment. Blake was among the first to speak of the imaginative and spiritually sensitive child, his were the expression of intellectual sensibilities that were the stirrings of concern with the self. The close scrutiny of the nature of the child was still decades away. However, the beginning forays commenced with the discoveries that the nature of a man was not his reason so much as his instincts, his emotions, and his "sensibilities." Eventually, what was the case of a man began to be applied to the child. But it was another half century in arriving. The child was a poetic symbol before it was given a character. It was well into the nineteenth century before that took place.

Once cottage industry was swept away by the Industrial Revolution, the child was drawn deeper than ever into the labor force. With that, he became embroiled in its social conflicts. It was the novel that became the vehicle for the psychology of the child. There the child was described as the mute, helpless, innocent victim of social struggle and strife in whose behalf fiction spoke.

The imagery of the nineteenth-century psychology of childhood was a child deprived of joy, split off from wonder in urban squalor, dreaming of far-off islands, delighting in Nature as an unspoiled garden. All this was the agony of childhood, oppressed and socially deprived of a Paradise, thieved by the horrors Rousseau foretold. The novel brought the painful truth to light. The swirl of events tossed pathos and idealization and often squalor into a sentimental image of childhood experience sometimes pathetic as others were ecstatic. George Eliot, and

137

especially Dickens, were fated to leave legacies of ineradicable attitudes to childhood.[29]

While the novel was soon recognized as "a vehicle for psychological analysis rather than the recounting of events" to become the major literary form in the mid-nineteenth century, brought about principally by such works as *Oliver Twist, Jane Eyre, Wuthering Heights,* and *Dombey and Son,*[30] there was still lacking a discernible inner life to the characters. It was a life of existence, of experiences, reactions to their immediacy or reminiscences indelibly stamped that were a bottomless well to draw from. Self-reflection or scrutiny, however, is not a child's penchant. A child's scrutiny of others, which is often sharply discerning and penetrating, is only rarely turned on himself. The novelist was aware of the perceptions, and they were introduced in the case of childhood as the psychology of boyhood, much as Louisa May Alcott did for girlhood. The other side of perceptions, scrutiny, was not included. That phenomenon, which even adults are either unaware of or resist, is the beginning of self-analysis. That was to prove elusive, fragmented, and bound to a nostalgia of childhood behind some "golden gates" that reminiscences rarely passed through.[31]

There were many more influences, beyond the relevance of this work, that made the stream of books written for children into a torrent. Wolff notes that by 1860 children's literature was reported to be "increasing at a higher ratio than any other class." Children's books also commanded "the surest sale." He cites that *all* the Waverly novels, Harrison Ainsworth's *The Tower of London* and *Old St. Paul,* and *Westward Ho!* and others by Charles Kingsley were written for children much as Captain Frederick Marryat's writings for adults also had such stories as *Masterman Ready, The Settlers of Canada,* and *The Children of the New Forest* that were directly for children. These were books for boys.

The new literature was about boys to the extent that even if they were not the principal characters, they were within the substance of the body of fiction that was developing. Moreover, it soon became big business, with its sureness of sale. It was overwhelmingly an English-language affair. There were, to be sure, Italian, French, and German publications, tales of Swedish life, and the staples of the fairy tales by Andersen and those by the Grimm Brothers, and a large number of American books that children soon cherished. But the English and American books went into many translations relatively quickly. Their popularity in no way seemed to be diminished by the often wide cultural separation. If it seemed thus that English principles of "fair play" appeared always to triumph, and the stories appeared to be remarkably similar, it was not so much that a lack of originality stamped that fiction, although this was often the case, as it was that certain themes were timeless and place was, hence, anywhere. Girls easily and as readily identified themselves with boys in fiction, much as they did in everyday life.

The young hero emerged in popular literature more than one hundred years ago and has in this time not paled. Despite the passage of years in which his circumstances have seemed to have dramatically altered and in the course of which we have gained insight into human motivation with the exploration of our unconscious, the period of boyhood between early boyhood and youth remains more familiar to us from fiction than from direct study. We find the boy engaged in struggles of proving his prowess, governed by a self-correcting conscience, and, to that degree, loosened from parental guidance and ties, passionately devoted to his fellows and closely on them to his first love. The Victorian age of fiction gave way slowly to a tidal wave of stories; the age of comic books arrived.

The nature of boyhood as it is portrayed today in the flood of comic books is unaltered. The boy who appeared a century ago fearful of leaving home yet eager to get away, sure to encounter bullying, fearful of the schoolmaster, or tyrannized in shops where he worked, tempted to be lazy, to be attracted to vices, and loyal in adversity to first, real, deep friendships, is in countless tales and appears with the same fidelity in today's comics. These Homeric figures of boyhood are in no respect dimmed. They have turned in their chitons and spears for tights or capes and armed with technologically superior modern weapons, they are launched, as always before, to prove themselves. Just as the heroes are the same, so are the villains. All are brought up-to-date, woven into the fabric of a boy's emotional experience.

Where once the earth was stalked by giants, trolls, spirits, gods, and warriors, their kind has yielded to some seemingly new species. Where the Minotaur left off and Medusa menaced, the new era began. The nearly fifty years of comic books have presented the "Man of Bronze," "Bulletman," "Minute-Man," "Spy Smasher." Among others that followed were the costumed "Superman," "Captain Marvel," "Bat Man," and legions of others. Some are noble born, or rise out of obscurity and are orphaned and found by a couple — a shading off from the Mosaic legend — many champion the oppressed, are physical marvels, the avengers of evil that shrink villains to the "size of field mice," so that "death rises up before them in the guise of common garden snakes — a danger only to mice, small frogs, insects";[32] or a creature named Dr. Doom and the sinister "Red Skull" must be destroyed to save humanity.[33] There are monsters irresistibly turned out of men, who are compelled to drink potions that loosen them so that their temptations cannot be resisted. As the "Living Vampire, Morbius" is created, so is "Blade, the Vampire Slayer" to put an end to acts that victimize innocents.[34]

These modern versions of fantastic tales establish a continuity, even if only in vulgar form, with our oldest legends and most ancient myths. A common thread holds them together — their themes characterize a particular period of masculine development. The universality of the stories attests to more than their permanent popularity. They have a durability that culture and circumstances alter merely superficially. The recently deciphered myths of Babylon tell of the hero Marduk, who was a "precocious child, born virtually mature, like Heracles in

Greek myth, Moses in later Jewish legend, and Ullkummi in the Hittite story of the 'Monster Made of Stone.' "[35] From the Canaanites we learn of the battle of Baal against Yam. Baal had to be specially equipped with bludgeons made for him by the divine smith, Ptah. The Egyptian myths that recur related how Horus fought Set and was similarly provided with weapons forged by the artisan of the gods, or the Vedic myth when Indra opposes Vritra he needs be equipped with a "whizzing bolt" that could only be fashioned by the craftsman Tvashtri.[36] The extraordinary powers accorded heroes generally show two facts about masculinity. One is that the hero is limited and the other is that such limits may be transcended. However, they require some indispensable equipment. And by way of such adjuncts, the hero's remarkable powers are ensured. For example, there was Siegfried and his Tarnhelm, King Arthur and Excalibur, Perseus and his magic shield, Aaron and his rod. There are countless others lost in antiquity to the present crowd of comic book ones. All have a distinctly phallic character. The theme is timeless. The phallus either in fact or in symbol is an indispensable accouterment to performance, prowess, achievements, and heroics. Without it man is impotent, a victim, demeaned and likely to be vanquished.

Like the adventures, more familiar to us, of the *Odyssey* or the *Iliad*, these are tales of proving powers and prowess, and of secret temptations that produce conflicts. The importance of expressing the boyhood years in physical terms we all have long understood. However, this has yet to lead to our insight into the emotional problems of masculinity during them. Moreover, we are not brought to the realization that such particular conflicts, far from terminating with this period, extend through the masculine experience. Even in rare and great romantic classics — Robert Louis Stevenson's *Treasure Island*; the lesser but probably once as widely read stories for boys by Kipling; or, nearly a century later, *A Walker in the City* by Alfred Kazin,[37] a vivid autobiography of reminiscences, recollections, and descriptions of a boyhood — there is little or no suggestion, except what a psychoanalyst might cull to interpret as indicative, of a boy's inner life. A boy's experience of self is portrayed only as consisting of immediate reactions to his circumstances or their revival in recall. In short, only conditional responses are represented.

When there are lapses, as Kazin occasionally gives us a glimpse into nostalgia that consciously revives old and deep relations, the gap of painful separation is bridged in longing for a reunion. The alienation from the present carries us often to nostalgia where we were once among familiars. But, what in us lies beyond nostalgia seems not to be reached by mere recall or meticulous reminiscences when what they represent of inner life remains elusive, held in repression, and unconsciously is resistant to retrieval. The inner life for long has eluded the scrutiny of those who were intellectually so attentive to its caprice and who, without doubt, themselves had not escaped it. This need not be puzzling if we take into account the powerful reactions we know nostalgia lets loose. Freud's discoveries about them did not spring fully formed from his head. There was an intensified materialistic probing of the self as an intellectual curiosity before he discovered its immense clinical importance. Thus, from 1893 to after the first decade of our century, he virtually alone insisted that the unconscious was a universe in the human realm, that there was in it a ubiquitous infantile sexuality, and that there were conflicts that swirled about to produce profound effects on our behavior socially as well as sexually. Hence, frustratingly shunning exposure, beyond introspection, reflection, contemplation, and still judgmental and erotic, even fiction fails to shed more than prismatic light on it.

Jane Austen is believed to have said that one never does form just an idea — one takes up a notion and runs away with it. She could have had a boy's inquisitiveness in mind. "The riddles of sexual life" to him are prominent, even if unconsciously held away from awareness by the distraction of his physical exuberance. There are moments, times, occasions, periods and experiences of reflection, musings, reveries, dreams, and even occasional nightmares when his notions run away with him. Among them is his interest in his own genital. He does not fail to turn to himself as part of Creation, as we noted earlier. This is especially the case with respect to self-reference. Moreover, his wonder is held by his unique organ. He tends to anthropomorphize his phallus, unlike any other part of himself. It is one of the earliest expressions of his egocentricity that identifies him. It is a phenomenon of masculinity. It has neither a parallel nor any similarity in feminine psychology.

In *Lady Chatterley's Lover*, D. H. Lawrence's great literary talent makes plain what psychologists remain silent on. In the excerpt below, Lawrence shows us what deep reflections a man holds of himself that mirror his earlier wonder about his genital. Lawrence understood these were not new expressions but were actually old ones brought forward from boyhood to a lover's bed. We can see from this how imperishable is the boyhood fantasy of transcending limits.

> "So proud," she murmured, uneasy. "And so lordly! Now I know why men are so overbearing! But he's lovely, *really*. Like another being. A bit terrifying! But lovely really! And he comes to *me!*"
>
> The man looked down in silence at the tense phallus, that did not change. "Ay!" he said at last, in a little voice. 'Ay ma lad! tha'rt theer right enough. Yi, tha mun rear they head! Theer on thy own, eh? an ta'es no count o' nob'dy! Tha ma'es nowt o' me, John Thomas. Art boss? of me? Eh well, tha'rt more cocky then me, an' tha says less. John Thomas! Dost want *her?* Does want my Lady Jane? Tha's dipped me in again, tha hast. Ay, an tha comes up smilin' — Ax 'er then! Ax Lady Jane! Lift up your heads o' ye gates, that the king of glory may come in. Ay, th' cheek on thee! Cunt, that's what tha'rt after. Tell Lady Jane tha wants cunt. John Thomas, an' th' cunt o' Lady Jane!
>
> "Ay!" said the man, stretching his body almost painfully. "He's got his root in my soul, has that gentleman! An' sometimes I don' know what ter do wi him. Ay, he's got a will of his own, an its hard to suit him. Yet I wouldn't have him killed."[38]

What is a man to do with his penis that is rooted not in his groin but in his ego? There it is a measure, evidence, proof, even a voucher of himself. Can less be said of a boy, when indeed he is father of the man? It is no mere whim or creative stroke that prompts Lawrence to reveal the masculine character in "John Thomas" as having a "will of his own, an' it's hard to suit him." As an aggressor a phallus typifies and comes to personify masculinity. The boy in boyhood identifies himself with his phallus as the expression of its association with aggression. And hence, for himself it is the talisman of triumph and transcendence over his fears of passivity, over his identification with a woman, to help to quell his dread of the limitations he entertains and those he foresees.

We may not expect from fiction or perhaps even autobiography an exposition of the intimate details of boyhood's private daydreams, dreams during sleep, reveries, or masturbatory fantasies. These elements of mental life are subject to repression; some of the elements are consciously dismissed as anxiety-provoking and unwelcome and are censored. It is difficult even for the clinician who is determined to unearth them as necessary to his therapeutic efforts. Some approximation of the "inner life" revealed is portrayed by an adolescent youth, Holden Caulfield in J. D. Salinger's *Catcher in the Rye*.[39] Holden Caulfield tells us at the very outset that if we want to know about his earlier private life,

> I don't feel like going into it, if you want to know the truth. In the first place, my parents would have about two hemorrhages apiece if I told anything pretty personal about them. They're quite touchy about anything like that, especially my father.[40]

Of course, he omits to say that *he* is "touchy." And he says he prefers to begin his story the day he left "Pencey Prep." Salinger then proceeds to give us an action-packed first-person narrative of the adolescent's misadventures in youthful sexual experiments and curiosity; the overt acts are typically banal because they fail to reveal the depth of the boy's character. In being so typical, his escapades, mischief, conflicts over his

144

powers and prowess draw a heavy curtain that leaves us only with the illusion that we have glimpsed his inner life. We have a sense of his bravado but not what is behind it. The ribaldry of this period of a youth's life is genuinely portrayed but we are given no clue to the fantasies associated with the inner sexual life. Admittedly, this has only been acknowledged in recent decades in science or fiction as a normal physical element of everyday life in even the very young. But the emotional content of such an important part of boyhood's everyday existence, if only limited to fantasy, is lacking. Even more removed are those fantasies associated with active sexuality that would reveal their unconscious significance.

Fiction about boyhood is at best a reconstruction. That is to say, it comes out of adult life as a painted memory of boyhood. As in another context Don Quixote may have said, boyhood is shown not as it is but as it should have been. Fiction falls short of penetrating the opacity of boyhood beyond the competitive striving for performance and prowess. And analysts euphemistically, conventionally categorized it by its "drives," of an aggressive and sexual nature. Our understanding of boyhood masculinity hence is left at best to a confined perspective that does not reveal that its actual aim is to satisfy the unremitting demands of a boy's narcissism.

Chapter 7

THE RISEN PHOENIX
IS BOYHOOD

"LATENCY," THE PERIOD DESIGNATED by Freud as beginning about at the end of a child's fifth year and lasting until the first manifestations of puberty, has been assumed by psychoanalysts to be a fallow time of relative freedom from conflict following the denouement of the Oedipus complex. Insofar as the little-boyish aspirations come to no real fruition during this period, it has long been supposed that they are therefore abandoned and expunged from awareness by repression and amnesia. In fact, during this period, which I prefer to call "boyhood," an active phase is launched in earnest. It is a time of notoriously aggressive pursuits that have as their chief, unconscious aim the reconditioning of the battered ego of failed wishes and painful limitations from the earlier phase. It is here that the characteristics of greening boyhood most familiar to us represent the activation of the aggressive pursuit to restore the masculine ego.

Like the mythical phoenix, the masculine ego must arise from the embers of its threatened extinction in the oedipal struggle. This task for the boy is not eased either by guidance or instruction in masculinity. Because of the unique vulnerability of his self-esteem, a boy endlessly revives the reactions of this period to restore his loss. His ruling passion is not merely to be gratified, as it was for the younger child. It is now a boy's quest and active chase to achieve self-esteem through his own prowess, and by that prowess to achieve a sense of power that only accrues from self-esteem. He can put aside the "lame and impotent conclusion," that he came to about himself in the oedipal phase. From this discrepancy between his aims and his achievements, we may observe the processes of recovery from disillusionment, from envy that mirrors discontent, and from the humiliation a boy's narcissism is predisposed to suffer. When achievement serves principally as a vehicle for redeeming oneself, its tight links to performance remain; we may trace performance in adult life to this period. In such a life course, achievement, paradoxically, does not accumulate. The drive to perform and to use its results compels the boy to exhibit them. Rages and aggressive defenses are brought on by defined circumstances, conditions, and social forces, all of which threaten to impose real or imagined limits. These reactions bring self-recriminations, self-destructive ideas, impulses, and unconsciously derived defiant acts as confirmation that limitations to wishes are imposed and resisted.

Throughout the period of boyhood, the conflicts previously confined to the family now undergo important change. Progressively liberated from the immediate family circle, with its intimate rivalries, its seductive dependency, and its erotic conflicts, by a spreading, unconscious amnesia that increasingly blankets the earlier years, a small boy is thus prepared to begin to form his next, wider, and necessary social relationships. This is not to say that he quits his family for them, but, rather, that he has the added impetus to loosen his ties, which he had heretofore neither considered nor been obliged to attempt.

Boys begin to enjoy a new loyalty with their fellows, held fast in a mutual pursuit of masculinity. Now, more than ever, the deep concern with performance is heightened as it serves the ends of prowess that the oedipal experience denigrated and also no less the new, social, emotional need by way of it to win comradeship. Even a small boy has a fundamental concern with his performance. He acquired it through the expectations of those who care for him and rapidly incorporates them as his own. They develop as the expression of his masculinity in eroticism, expectations, and ambition. All this is no less true in finding with comrades their approbation and a shared experience in prowess and self-esteem.

The chief explanation for our until recent ignorance of the period is that the underlying emotional life of the boy is normally more firmly gripped in repression than it was earlier or will be at any later time. He is much less articulate about himself when his attention, aims, and purposes appear to be so concentrated on his relationships with his fellows, among whom he is bent on proving himself. Naturally, he is very resistant to revealing himself to reflection on his emotional emergence from the immediacy or proximity of his family ties. Perhaps this may explain why in the voluminous literature of psychoanalysis analysts have had the least to say about "latency," or boyhood, and why they have made no distinction between a girl's "latency" and a boy's.

As I have shown, we have no real basis for supposing that the longings, aspirations, and emotional needs of small boys will be abandoned when they are persuaded that their high expectations and even dimly perceived wishes are not to be realized. Indeed, experience shows the opposite to be true. However, most psychologists or analysts still hold that latency is emotionally a fallow period. Such suppositions are doubtless founded on the difficulty and virtual absence to the present of explorations of the psychology of the period between latency and puberty.

It is no accident that folklore, myths, and fairy tales give us timeless and countless episodes of desperate struggles that dramatize those adventures that test mettle and prove worth. They all have roots in this period. Unlike the later adventures of a youth, the encounters in boyhood depend for success on high-mindedness, worthiness, prowess showing great skill and mastery, and, above all, the triumph over those adversaries, foreign to the boy's own band, who would, lacking principle, subvert a strict conscience. What is denied in such enterprises or ventures and is omitted from psychological studies of this phase is that the launching of campaigns toward great achievement follow from ignominious beginnings. The colossal libidinal failure of the oedipal period is a narcissistic injury of major proportions to a small boy. It results in an enormous impetus to restitution. Boyhood is therefore a time of active engagement, by way of becoming socially valued. It is unconsciously a rehabilitation of masculinity.

A boy's private life, not directly reflected in his behavior, is masked. It is not an aspect of himself at this time he is either likely or ready to reveal even to his fellows — unlike the adolescent, who solicits and pines for an intimate relationship that includes sharing inner experience. Boyhood, as we shall find, in this and in other respects differs from youth.

*   *   *

A young boy's attachment to his parents and especially to his mother becomes attenuated as his boyhood emerges from the immediacy of the family circle. In the everyday psychology of boyhood, a boy's wishes are determined by the prevailing winds. Some boys follow the newly emerging, stricter conscience expressed by idealizing men and longing for identification with those of heroic stature. These boys feel that a relationship is sentimental when it is not wrapped in fears, mysteries, and power. Along with such sources of conflict are still other fantasies of cruelties toward phantom enemies no less formidable than and remarkably resembling the heroes. As if this were not enough, boys feel deep but shifting loyalties to boys like themselves or to ones with envied qualities. Typically, devotion and hostility alternate and give rise to conflicts that bluster and buffet this period. No less than any other time, this period is one of bondage to lust, as well as to the strictest self-injunctions. Yet, there is no aspect of the human emotional condition that has had less study.

In his last work, Freud described latency as a "lull" in sexual life or its development,[1] which lasted to the first manifestations of puberty in which "shame, disgust, and morality" become so well developed that "they rise like dams to oppose the later activity of the sexual instincts."[2] Freud suggested that it was a period in which ethical restraints developed by way of blocking sexuality, and that, as a consequence, these barriers divert development into our great social, religious, legal, and ethical institutions, which form our civic life.[3] He admitted that much of what he reflected on about this period was hypothetical, but there were symptoms produced. As he said, "It is a great pity that no one has as yet collected them [symptoms of latency] and systematically analyzed them. Being the earliest products of neurosis they should best be able to shed light on the mechanisms employed in its symptom formation."[4] Since his early writing on this period shortly after the turn of the century, those who have followed him seem to have taken him at his word that we should regard this time of development as one long period that delays sexual development until puberty;[5] modern psychology seems to believe that "latency" in human experience is not only a lull but must also be dull.

The work of Berta Bornstein is an exception. Her direct clinical study of "latency," reported in 1949, even though it is not addressed to the aspects that apply to boyhood, does tell us what is typical in a boy of this age: "the full grandeur of his world of fantasy."[6] Her work demonstrated boys' wishes for omnipotence, highly narcissistic aggrandizement, and a dread of passivity, against which they defend themselves with aggressive fantasies.

The following case is noteworthy as an illustration of this fear of passivity in boyhood and the aggressive response to such a fear. While Seth was compulsively orderly and appeared to be neurotically concerned with the future, he was always a good pupil and a favorite among other boys. He did, however, make mischief at school and was repeatedly punished for minor infractions. Because he seemed endlessly involved in mischief, he created the impression that he was incorrigible and was, from the school's point of view, just short of being delinquent. The school authorities were unable to effect any change in his behavior and asked for help. The parents virtually stood aside, not participating in the problem beyond expressing their willingness to comply with the school's wishes. They had no complaints and, in fact, argued at first that at home the boy was no trouble.

Seth was an accomplished athlete. He led other boys in sports as well as in school. His parents were working class and intelligent, but uneducated and ill-informed. The father was a salesman, hard-driving and demanding. The mother was an obsessional house-cleaner who had never been employed outside the home. The boy had two sisters, one younger and the other eight years older. He was the favorite child and the older sister's "baby."

A tall, athletic-looking boy, nearly nine years old, Seth sulked a bit because he saw no need or reason to be given psychiatric attention. However, his reluctance was not enough to keep him away. What quickly became evident was his protest against "rules." He would only complain that they were a "pain in the ass." The period of treatment began with his complaints against "rules." He expressed his anger and his feeling that he "had to get around them." After the excuses of what people did, citing public or political figures and the "cops" — in short, people in authority — he demanded reasons why he should not do the same. He bridled at being a mere boy and at the fact that men were not subject to rules as he was. At home, he admitted, no one knew how he hated rules, especially those his mother laid down; she ran the house by "rules for everything." He, on the other hand, wanted to get around them. In this vein are certain comic book heroes who secretly change to superboys — who leave rules behind and are free to pursue their wishes. It was hard for him to see that flouting "rules" as he did had some relation to his concern with the future; that his wanting to be free, that is, to be without rules, made for unpredictable conditions that were uncomfortable for him.

The first suggestion that there were deeper conflicts that represented more than a reaction to circumstance came with rules about masturbation. He could not say where he learned that "you are not supposed to do it." He took it to mean you are not supposed to use your penis. The prohibitions were more directly about what his older sister would react to rather than his mother, should he have sexual "ideas about her." Usually he was contemptuous of girls and this brought out his feeling that even though he would want to do something sexual with a girl, it would have to be with a stranger where the familiar rules would not be known. He "would be free, like a disguise." Then he could do as he wished. All the trouble with rules was actually not so much with them as with interference with *wishes* that he equated with freedom denied him by rules.

The fantasies of relations with girls were a contest from which he emerged the star. He wanted an older girl. (He was unconscious of its being his sister that he wanted, because he insisted the girl should be a stranger with whom he would take unlimited liberties.) He would not have to do much. And he would be an athlete in sex as he was in games. He had notions that he would be outside the law, "off-limits." "I can't stand handcuffs, it's not fair." He did not, at this point, appreciate what he said about masturbation when he wanted the free unfettered use of his hands. He complained that only outlaws enjoy freedom. He knew about "putting a penis in a vagina. But it's like going in a cave. You could get trapped, hurt." Nevertheless, he wanted to be daring, to do something (meaning something sexual) that is forbidden, to engage in a venture and by it to defy danger. Defy the rules. He would thus have stood the test and proved himself. The "older girl" was no more than the vehicle to convey him to manhood. By transcending the limits, the "rules," he unconsciously advanced his masculinity.

He long insisted and at times argued, while we played at cards or other games, that experiencing limits everywhere and even thinking of them in privacy as "rules" and prohibitions made him angry. He was denied his "rights," deprived of the fulfillment of his wishes, and it amounted to being rendered poorer. He was not merely fancying himself beyond social constraints. On the contrary, it will be recalled, he was not delinquent. He had no real grievance or inclination to act that way toward school, others, or his family. He did, however, believe that to attain distinction he had to get beyond the imposed barriers. He was also convinced that this was the only way to succeed. He was not to be put off by fearing to scale these barriers. The encounters at school — less to be dreaded than the sexual ones he fantasied — or adversaries, who were never identified more precisely, to be overcome were what he expected. He often rather charmingly cited the comic books that all his contemporaries read as showing — admittedly they were just stories and of course not true — that what one had to do to be a man was more than just go to school and play around home.

The aim of the school was to persuade this so-called incorrigible boy to accept the "rules" he resisted, to comply with authorities he defied, and thus to help him conform to their expectations. However, the problem was not that he lacked a sufficiently developed conscience or superego, which is what his conduct suggested. Closer scrutiny showed that he felt himself to be in need of testing and proving and of being assured by his own efforts of an earned self-esteem. His doubts about it arose from the fears associated with compliance. His restless resistance to "rules" asserted his defiance of the dreaded passivity that was typical of his mother, who in her obsessional way lived by rules. The boy could not risk being identified through them with her; his conduct was his "masculine" protest. There were also wishes to be like his mother and his sister, but these were disquieting, unconscious ones that were only implied and not directly acknowledged.

153

My help for Seth was dictated by his need to find assurance in himself that his masculinity was not compromised except when he fancied himself an "outlaw," that the need for "rules" did not require him to be passive, and that an adaptation to social conditions did not compel a surrender to authority.

Bornstein has called attention to the lack of uniformity in this phase. However, as first Freud and as others later confirmed, there is the boy's need for strict adherence to self-rule and the demand for severe punishments for the slightest infractions. In the name of righteous indignation and justice, the exercise of sadomasochistic fantasies is indulged not infrequently with masturbatory fantasies. Against all such eruptions of sexual and aggressive fantasies, sometimes expressed in play or only in daydreams, self-reproaches are common. They may not satisfy the unconscious self-accusations, so it is common for boys to resort to compulsive, nagging quarrelsomeness, thereby provoking censure. Play for mastery, prowess, and skill provides relief from these conflicts. Further relief is provided by daydreams in which the boy fancies himself in heroic roles.[7]

During the past twenty-five years, there has begun to develop some recognition that the "latency" period is not lacking in sexual urges and pursuits, as evidenced by the confirmed commonality of masturbatory, voyeuristic, and exhibitionistic activities that boys carry on both alone and together. There is a tendency nevertheless to pay more attention to a boy's warding off his inner sexual demands, thus making available so-called energies for character development, than to those he embraces and from which he is gratified.[8] Analytic writing in the last two decades on the same period of development emphasizes that the boy's sexual life is under a growing and hence more developed self-control, some of which is unconscious, and that it is a time of sexual inhibition. In place of sexuality, a sense of self-esteem emerges from "achievements and mastery" that are thought of as particular to this phase in the service of earning social merit.[9] Some writers have called attention to the

154

fact that the difficult social conduct, often typical of this period, is related to the guilty, private sexual behavior, such as masturbatory activities, for which the censure of adults is sought through such displaced forms as obnoxious manners.

There is a great impetus in boyhood to join other boys who themselves flee their unconscious wishes. The typical rages of the early phases of the period are unconsciously aimed, as the examples cited here illustrate, at the feeling of limitations. The direct effect is to intensify wishes rather than lessen them. The boy's narcissistic aims run parallel to his wishes. Self-regard is for a boy precariously maintained when it rests so much on prowess and as he emerges from his oedipal struggles where he was notably lacking success.

I had as a patient a twelve-year-old boy Frank, who was easily provoked by trifling circumstances. In his rages, he clung more than otherwise to the company of the boys with whom he played and with whom he often quarreled. He was disgruntled for days on end, neglected to take care of himself, and expressed the feeling that he was abused. In fact, his mother was indulgent of him, but the more she tolerated his demands, complaints, and fury, the greater was his contempt at her submission. In this respect, he was like his father, a powerful man with whom he very strongly identified.

In masturbatory fantasies this boy had images of a strange woman who was bound and helpless and whom he sexually used. He could not be very explicit as to what he wanted to do with her except to perform some sexual act that demeaned her. But he also had ideas of rescuing her.

The boy had a good relationship with his father, but he was resistant to take over some of the chores about the house that were his father's. On the one hand, he wanted to be in his father's place, and, at the same time, he rejected doing anything suggestive of it. The source of most of his rage was jealousy of his sister, who curried his father's favor. The father enjoyed the attention his daughter gave him, and the boy wanted to be in her place. It was she whom he envied.

Unconsciously, he was threatened by the possibility of having an intimate relationship with his father like his sister's. When he was not holding himself aloof, actively playing away from home with his friends or happily engaged in his own pursuits, he was angry, aggressive, provoking, and forcing restraints from each of his parents.

It is not illuminating for us to reduce Frank's struggles to adapt himself as simply indicative of an unresolved Oedipus complex, and that, inasmuch as he did not abandon it at least five years before, when he was about six years old, he was continuing his infantile sexual conflicts. We have long known that the Oedipus complex comes to some resolution at that time of emotional development. However, this reasoning has carried with it the supposition that the Oedipus complex normally terminates then. That being the case, it is thought to explain that the great surge of social development, i.e., the ego or adaptive functions of skills and achievement, follow in the years after until adolescence appears with its new turn of events. The evidence in everyday life does not support this.

Frank strongly identified with his father with whom he had, in many respects, a good relationship. To that extent he was well adapted socially and functioning normally. Little imagination is necessary to see that his sexual fantasies about a strange woman whom he would demean in a sexual act represented his conception of the sexual relations of his parents. In it, the woman was subject to the man's will. She yielded to it and, although in fantasy he, too, wanted that submission, the woman was demeaned in the "dirty" act. As we have learned, he was also jealous of the intimacy that he wanted. In his irritating, provoking behavior, he got the punishment he "earned" and often perhaps a bit more, which made him cry out that he was abused. He manifestly wanted the affection that his father lavished on his sister; on a more unconscious level, he would take his mother's place. These are old conflicts. They were revived from another period of boyhood that would not be subject to repression unconsciously by a more developed superego or stricter conscience, and, as a result, will be displaced onto women. Like a stranger who would have no immediate recognition as associated with mother or sister, his fantasies had a looser rein. As an extended reaction to the same conflict, the wish to assert his masculinity brought Frank to intensify his masculine strivings. They were expressed through prowess and achievement, socially through work or school, and in fantasy of high adventure and fantastic achievement.

During boyhood, both eroticism and ambition are given up within the home, and, to this extent, the analysts are correct. However these emotional needs begin to be carried on outside the immediate family with a passion that previously appeared not to be present. The heroic exploits engaged in through fantasy, and their success, although in the company of others, one's companions, are unconsciously still also aimed to please a woman. The narrow limits of the family circle are crossed, and, although there may be no immediate mother to win, the wish is displaced to a surrogate or some fantasied figure unconsciously associated with her. The vaulting ambitions, so typical of a small boy, are also not altogether given up with the disillusionment of the oedipal aims. On the contrary, during boyhood, the boy fires that ambition. We learn that joint enterprises with other boys are developed in which mutual fantasies are acted out. They have the staple of power, prowess, achievement, and a heroic stature obscuring the old oedipal rivalry which is now newly clothed and removed from recognition. Manifest erotic wishes associated with a woman are inhibited, repressed, and thus withdrawn from awareness, leaving the boy to join his companions with a freedom he longs to enjoy. Together the boys form a band of adventurers and engage in exploits and combine to acquire a mastery over chance through skill. It matters little which field is used to play out these aims — herding goats through the Atlas Mountains, chasing seals in the Arctic, or playing stickball with gangs in New York City — the nature of the period of boyhood is not altered. Manifestly, women, girls, mothers, sisters are repudiated. Repression obedient to these ends frees the boy to promote his masculinity less encumbered by a conscious audience of women and girls his family provides.

He wants to leave home because it is the scene of envy, frustration, disappointment, and rivalry. As a result of these feelings, he gains an enormous incentive to restore himself, which he will commence on the playing fields with his friends. This is a time when strong emotional fences need to be built. The lonely and isolated boy will try to achieve the same ends, but his journey will take him more through daydreams and fantasies than by way of encounters with his fellows.

In the throes of such aspirations that typically are immodest, a boy is distressed when his muscular development has as yet not met his wishes, so that his shape seems to him more like a girl's than a boy's. He is comparing himself unfavorably with a longed-for physical ideal. The only sign that betrays his concern is no more conscious than refusing to wear a particular shirt that clings close to his skin. His chest appears to him not to be muscular, i.e., as masculine as he wishes himself to appear. He becomes excessively modest with this and similar convictions in which he questions his masculinity. Not all of them are conscious. He refuses to wear the shirt. His vehemence about it is inexplicable to his parents. They explain it away as some absurd notion of the boy's being sensitive about his appearance, without realizing that an important issue is at the root of his distemper. Moreover, he is afraid his peers would notice his "deficiency." His anxiety gets unwittingly displaced to the size of his penis. Once more, it becomes a source of distress as it once was when he was a little boy. The conflicts that are thus aroused revive old, troubled periods of competitive anguish, measuring himself with his mind's eye and finding the same, sad conclusion he felt long ago — when he had "not enough." Whether the boy resolves to find release from his dilemma by increased activity or by a retreat to passivity will be a choice influenced, as he may have been previously, by the circumstances of his life. The boy in the following case was pulled in both directions.

Ron was a very capable nine-year-old who began to give his teachers some concern when it became evident that he was falsely claiming illness. He obviously wanted to avoid schoolwork, and he complained that he was too tired to engage in play with other boys. This young boy came from a coastal village and was an avid sailor who learned quickly from his father to become a skillful navigator of a small craft. He loved boats and especially testing himself with his boat, as if it were an extension of himself, against the elements. He often had to be admonished and even disciplined because of his insistence on taking risks that frightened his family. He had no notion that his fearless conduct had a deeper significance.

The boy's relationship with his father was nearly an exclusive one, for he was favored over a somewhat younger brother and a sister who was younger by three years. The father was an exacting, hard-driving, perfectionistic teacher, determined on his son's achievement. For each nautical knot the boy learned he was exhorted to do another and still another. When Ron was not consciously striving to please and to win his father's praise, he was in fear that he would fail. The seriousness of his performance for him was not limited to sailing. School took on a similar importance; he goaded himself there as he had earlier when his father taught him knots. In his encounters with other boys, he soon felt compelled to outdo them. But, fearing to alienate them in his zeal to elevate himself over them — which he often succeeded in doing — he became anxious to please his friends but also convinced that he would not be liked. His eagerness to acquire a skill or master something as a secret triumph caused him often to abandon what he might achieve to quiet his fears of the hostility he felt success would bring. He gave illness as an excuse, or he found a pretext to explain his fatigue.

To excel meant to bring on anxiety; underlying this was the

notion that to achieve meant to triumph over others' weakness, to be relieved of fears of his own by the pleasure of proving himself over others. It was a hostile competition in which he won the qualities of masculinity, all of which were sources of fears. As is typical of boys this age, his direct sexual fantasies were inhibited; however, they were easily revealed in his avid reading and fantasies associated with comic books. In these fantasies, he was especially engaged with curiosity and conviction of the relations between men and women. These relationships were exercises in brutality. His notions about women were that they were not altogether feminine, by which he meant that they had male qualities; although somewhat less powerful than men, they were violent or could be violent. By the exercise of mysterious powers, which compensated for their difference from men, they could render men weak and helpless, and somehow men were reduced to being less than women. The boy's sympathies were with the efforts that men must exert in their own defense against cruel encounters with other men and with rapacious women who could not be appeased.

The appeal of "superboy" from the comic books was that he could outdo others; he needed to rely on no one; he overcame obstacles that others put in his way. Although this boy wished to be entirely self-reliant, he was not without friends who nearly matched his abilities. He was not exactly loved, but he was pleasing, and felt that others should pay special attention to him, because he won by combat, proving he was smarter than others and thus capable of triumphing over them. They therefore had to submit to him and his authority. This was all a role strictly for men or boys like himself, not for women and certainly not for girls.

As we have described earlier, a three-year-old boy has much the same idea about his role. Now, in this older boy, the more sophisticated expression is given to the threatened masculinity that needs to reassert itself, prove its mettle, and thus secure his masculine narcissism. This boy was strongly influenced to action by his father, and his mother wished to defer to her husband and enjoyed his aggressiveness. While she did not herself want to be associated with it, she could realize its fruits through her son.

A ten-year-old boy, Henry, was having difficulty at school and angered both his teachers and his classmates. He was very capable intellectually, but he employed his abilities both in school and on the playground so that others were demeaned. He was querulous with his teachers and earned everyone's dislike. As a result of these problems, the school advised his parents that help was imperative for him.

Henry had two older brothers with whom he bickered fairly regularly. Both parents took this to be expectable behavior from three boys close of an age in a family. The parents were busy with their own affairs: the father worked regularly at a clerical job, and the mother also worked at a part-time occupation to supplement their income. She was the more forceful and demanding of the two parents, and she ran the household much as she wanted. Although she was not deeply concerned about her son's conduct, she was aware that he was and always had been a "poor loser." She also felt that he was not so skilled physically as his brothers were, and she knew this troubled him. Although she placed emphasis on his superior academic achievements, she was disturbed that his relations with others were often unpleasant. The father kept himself at a distance, so that it was not possible to learn much about him. This in itself was telling, inasmuch as it was also Henry's experience of his father. He was a well-developed, stalwart boy who looked his age. At first, he appeared timid, and it was not evident that he created such animosity in others. Soon, however, he became free enough to make obvious to me how aggressive he was and what great ambitions he entertained for himself.

After many hours of therapeutic effort, in which competitiveness with virtually everyone appeared to have no limits, he began to reveal guardedly his masturbatory activities. They were at first associated with the fun of perfunctory and somewhat hilarious games with other boys, such as pissing in toilets together while joking about their powers in the streams and making coarse comments about the breast development of girls a grade or two above theirs in school. Otherwise, little of a personal self-conscious sexual nature was exchanged with his friends. This is not at all unusual, as boys in this period are comrades. But unlike girls this age they are not confidants.

Henry's masturbatory fantasies were reluctantly disclosed. They were the images of himself as a celebrity seduced by an older woman. It was important that she took the initiative. He was not required to do anything. She undressed him, she was excited merely by his appearance, she "ran the whole show." No less important, however, was that he was in control even if he was not obliged to do anything and felt some sense of victory. All that took place was for him. She adored him and he "sat there beautiful." It was his penis that she really admired. It stood for strength, so she admired what he had. There was no consideration of her. He was himself excited that he could bring her to want him. He imagined that perhaps he would perform some sexual feat, some "great act," but he had no notion of just what that would be. He was afraid to be actively seductive. What he was to do was a sex act that was measured by his great erection. The mere sight of it was, he liked to think, enough to bring her to immense passion. As soon as she removed his clothes, the great erection appeared and the woman was immediately enchanted with what she saw. His sexual ability was determined by what just looking at him created. However, there were also fears and anger that he might not measure up, at first to her expectations, but then more fundamentally to his own great expectations.

There was no pleasure in the sexual act, which was never really defined. What remained most important was that he had a controlling influence because of what the woman needed from him sexually. There were many ideas about the powerful need for sexual gratification that drives women. It made a *man*, like his father, who was not thought of as forceful, yet who was in command because he had what a woman wanted. There were no explicit notions of the relations between his parents. They were too repressed to be brought out.

His father, he said, would want him to be sexually served. It would prove he was a man. His father would like that. He was afraid to be naked before his father, because he feared that his father would be disappointed in how small he was. This soon showed itself to be his own disappointment at comparing himself with his father. The comparison was embarrassing to him. The size of his own penis reminded him that he was only a boy. The comparison with his father's genital made him feel "puny."

He knew that his mother wanted him to have a big penis. This had been on his mind ever since an older cousin developed breasts, and the mother remarked how pleased she and the girl's mother were to see that occur. His fantasy was that she would be even more pleased when he had a big penis. He rejected any notion of a direct connection between his sexual wishes and what his mother wanted for him. Moreover, he was frightened by the idea of what she would like for him. He feared he might not "measure up" to her wishes. Even with this association, he could not bring himself to acknowledge openly that he had said this about the woman in his masturbatory daydreams. He admitted that he tried to please his fantasy woman in other ways. He wanted to be what she would admire, and he wondered what an older woman would want. He feared that he would not be adequate to what she wished, and he got angry at that thought. His most exciting fantasy was a penis she could not resist. This put him in control.

Central to the boy's private sexual life was the notion that the phallus is the important implement of ways and means. Its mere existence, uncovered, dictates its own course. The sheer possession of it and its gross proportions made it all the more evident that the importance given the penis was governing both in the boy's mind and what by his own projection he attributed to the "older woman." His fantasied success lay in

163

acquiring, by way of his admired phallus, the ruling control over a woman. In these encounters, the "older woman" had all the initiative. It was not that the boy was passive by nature or character, but rather that the sexual aims, at engaging a woman, brought him close to the strictest taboo. Hence, to project onto her what he wanted, he arrived at the solution to the conflict unconsciously, with the least guilt. Women, he thought, are satisfied by possession.

There are a host of anecdotal stories that have made the rounds for generations among boys this age. They express a woman's sexual zeal in which the man is a simple instrument to satisfy it. For example, that couples were found who could not be "peeled apart"; the woman had so locked herself "somehow" to the man that an "operation" was needed to separate them. In another story, there are supposed to be some foreign women who conceal blades in their vaginas for the purpose of hacking off a penis.

In contrast with the younger boy's sexual wishes that made him like an understudy who dreaded to act a wished-for part, we now find a solitary performer who lacks competition. Although this boy removed competition in his fantasy, we saw some of it in connection with his father and brothers in fantasy and overtly in rivalry with his brothers that extended to his companions at school. The main act of this drama was a performance. The woman was no partner. In the literal sense, she was an object, and his success with her was as a performer. He, however, was inclined to withdraw and to fantasize about great achievements and feats he felt too puny to begin to undertake. Notably, the demands of his narcissism brought him far short of realizing them when he was tortured with feeling inadequate to the task of fulfilling his great and urgent needs.

In both instances, it was in the boy's narcissism from which demands issued and in which his deepest motivations were imbedded. The conventional psychoanalytic wisdom supposes that we are witnessing "drives," i.e., instincts, that are dictating his behavior. In the one case, the theory is that these drives are too strong, and in the other, they are the complete opposite. Both draw a narrow theory of motivation in boyhood.

The theory fails to account for the importance of a boy's narcissism as a powerful continuing motivation whose gratification is never abandoned or satisfied. We have noted that it plays a great and critical role in his earlier years. Its course gets lost to sight in this period now woven into the fabric of the boy's environment, much as it previously was in his immediate family. What in his relationships in this period draws his mettle as it had before, when he was in the bosom of his family? The boy who was cross and aggressive and given to outbursts of temper was not expressing it solely out of frustration. He was also taking his father's role, as he unconsciously regarded it, in which he was contemptuous of women and his sisters.

We know the beginning of this from our familiarity with an aspect of a young boy's emotional development. Now, in this period of development, in which the identification with men and with an ideal of a man is more defined as masculinity than previously, when the mere possession of the phallus was the criterion, the display of masculine attributes is no longer merely confined to an exhibition. The shift is toward achievement, prowess, and mastery. The previously even-tempered, curious, intellectually stimulated boy of eight or ten years of age becomes, a few years later, tyrannical in his demands of his mother; he is critical of her domestic work, even at times abusive toward her and even more so of his sisters, toward whom, on the least pretext, he is openly hostile. He allows no show of affection at times, permits no sharing of his wishes. He looks to his fellows.

An eight-year-old boy, Andy, whose teacher had become very fond of him — "he is such an appealing, bright little boy" — found that he began to fail his schoolwork, which he had previously accomplished easily. He was given to daydreaming excessively and, when asked, denied that he had anything in particular that held his attention away from his school subjects. His relationship with other boys seemed to be good and had in no way changed recently. He willingly came to see me because the discrepancy between his ability and his performance had created an obstacle to his learning. After many visits and months, he revealed with his daydreams his masturbatory fantasies. Although they were commonplace enough in my professional experience, they were a source of deep attention to him. He knew that among his friends masturbating was common, but he neither questioned nor was questioned by them what he had in mind with this act. There were some exchanges among the boys about "fucking." Such remarks were chiefly in the way of admissions of curiosity and interest in the act of intercourse; they were also hardly more than perfunctory references.

He, in a halting fashion, revealed that since he became aware that his teacher especially liked him, masturbation took on an importance that it previously did not have. He had become for the first time very fond of a woman outside of the family. Her being outside the family and "not like an aunt" was important to him. He would think about her getting undressed and often would stop at that point and recall other women with as little clothing, as at a swimming pool. He would imagine that if he were the lifeguard he would find the teacher attractive, as he had noticed at the pool how the guards' attention was given to women bathing there. He would look at the teacher's breasts as if they were unclothed, and even that seemed not to feel safe. He would not look at other parts of her body. He would then think of her having sex with a man. "They get into bed." I asked, "Like you saw your parents get ready for bed?" He replied that he did not think of them but of the teacher and a man. He admitted he did not know what they actually did, although he was watching the scene in his mind. "The man was on top, he forces himself into her." She was described as willing, submitting to the man's power. This seemed to be the whole importance of the act to him. What the woman did or was engaged in doing had little content to it. The

166

actual details of the sexual act were not known to him nor did they seem important when the issue was that the man must assert his will. The boy's attention shifted from observing the man, the lifeguard, a muscular type, to the woman's breasts. He looked away from seeing, that is, thinking of, her other parts or her organs. Instead, his attention was riveted on the man, his strength and power, and he fantasized about what he could do with it. The woman was only vaguely regarded and, in fact, he wanted to avoid her; she was important only in serving the man. Andy was very reluctant to disclose how much he was attracted to the man. The teacher's devotion to him was recognized as exciting, but at that point he got anxious and was concerned with the woman who was sexually submissive to the man. The boy's excitement was as a witness, who took the role first of one partner, then of the other. His chief interest was in his identification with the man and even when he reluctantly admitted his part in being a woman in relation to the man, it was to admire the man all the more. It was a dangerous feeling, but so was it associated with risk to have a woman admire a man and to have his teacher like him. He feared his own expectations: would he live up to them or be humiliated should he fail?

This was a relatively brief period of being preoccupied at school with his fantasies, excited by his teacher's interest in him. In his fantasies he revealed how important it was for a boy to think in terms of being domineering in a sexual experience and also to exercise control that is no less important to observe. Underlying is the problem posed before, as for all boys: the incestuous wishes that now again are manifest; as previously, their resolution must once more be brought to moderation.

What fails to be fully or adequately understood and is central to the psychology of masculinity is that the association with being an aggressor and identifying oneself with aggressive conduct and with the corollary, the horror of passivity, are not some instinctive behavior of people or the "human condition." These two associations reflect the idea that masculinity carries a psychological sense of peril. The prevalence of the identification with the aggressor in boys and men is explained by the desire to offset the dangers associated with masculinity. Paradoxically, women, the so-called weaker sex, seem not to be so threatened. We do not find this defense so universally in them as in men. This is not to suggest that passivity in women is without its component conflicts. Passivity does not, however, constitute the same emotional menace for them as it usually does for men.

Identifying oneself with the aggressor is a defensive role, as demonstrated at its discovery by Freud in 1920[10] and elaborated more than twenty years later by Anna Freud, who showed it merely as a means of a child's mastering feelings of weakness, helplessness, and even dependence by assuming in play a stature of strength. "By impersonating the aggressor, assuming his attributes, or imitating his aggression, the child transforms himself from the person threatened into one who makes the threat."[11] In thus overcoming the anxiety about actual past experiences or the dreaded ones in fantasy or in dreams, success over anticipated events may be assured or the lingering burden of menace, mitigated. In Freud's work and in that of other analysts, this phenomenon remains one to be plainly observed primarily in childhood. From our examples here, this is indeed the case. Because the emphasis is mostly circumstantial, to account for this important means of defense we have too often overlooked the large role that lifelong identification with the aggressor plays in masculinity. This role may be traced to a boy's notion where early it becomes integrated with the development of his character, that sustaining masculinity is associated with risk. As a consequence, aggression is regarded simplistically as a reaction to conditions of everyday life. Its part in the lifelong defense of masculine narcissism necessarily gets neglected, except for those flagrantly extreme circumstances in which aggression is then attributed to an exceedingly vulnerable character disorder.

The defense of the self by way of identification with the aggressor, real or imagined, because it is usually far removed from consciousness, is regarded merely as an act of aggression in response to conditions. Such analytic and popular notions about aggression are heedless of it as a powerful defense against the masculine fears of passivity, of being a victim, and as having a role in the recovery and surmounting threats and injuries to narcissism. In forming narcissistic defenses, in achieving mastery, and thus in adapting to the environment, aggression performs a critical role in the major aspects of masculine life. Aggression is indispensable in the restitution of male narcissism, which the conditions of everyday life inevitably tend to erode. When aggression fails, masculine narcissism suffers.[12]

Many psychoanalysts, whose studies concentrate on a child's pursuits, lead us to suppose that there is little else than libido of significant magnitude to engage children.[13] This discussion is not to suggest that libidinal pursuits are at any time excluded, but, rather, to affirm that there are, as well, other important tasks.

For some boys, the display of prowess becomes so fused with achievement, which is equated with masculinity, that restoring self-esteem by way of it remains the only goal of emotional development in relation to others. When it remains chiefly egocentric in its benefits, the result is merely to become gregarious and not social. This is commonly seen in bullying other boys and provoking fights in which severe rages are related to unconscious, deeper issues rather than the trivial ones used as excuses for demonstrating and asserting triumph over a feared ignominy. In games normally involving other boys, these boys practice alone, for instance, with a ball for long periods of time, not to achieve proficiency as it may appear and as may often secondarily occur, but in order to acquire a domination over others. For these boys, the games are of relatively little importance; the source of satisfaction is in having the upper hand. It is not surprising that losing is virtually intolerable and leads to arguments over rules, to cheating, and to laying blame.

A young woman brought to me her nearly six-year-old son. George, who, she confessed right off, was "spoiled." The immediate reason for her coming for help was that the boy had become "unbearably demanding and uncontrolled." From approximately the time that she and her husband had begun divorce proceedings, eighteen months previously, she and her son had lived alone. After her husband moved out, her son often shared her bed, demanded to kiss her on the mouth, and took to declaring that he was the "boss" and that "maybe only Santa Claus was more in charge." When she claimed certain authority over her son, which he regularly resisted, he often reminded his mother that she was "only a girl." When they went to market, he was the "most strong-willed, persistent person in what he wants that I know." When he got angry, he threatened to pull out her eyes. He wanted to see her sad and crying. This frequently took place and was a scene that he had witnessed between his parents. He insisted that he was grown-up and accountable only to "Santa Claus." (I never discovered what special authority he recognized in this figure except for his great magical powers.) He took the name of a popular television entertainer and regularly refused to answer to his own name.

George was a well-developed, bright, alert boy who looked his age. He strode into the playroom and picked up a toy telephone, into which he announced as his name that of the man whose name he had taken. He ignored my inquiries about his identity. He went on to declare that he was a fireman driving a fire truck and continued to play with other trucks, usually taking the part of the driver. Any suggestion on my part that he be other than the driver—a passenger, a helper, or some other role —brought out no willingness to alter the choice that he had firmly elected. This play went on unchanged from one visit to the next, repeated with a monotony that showed his determination to hold to his wishes.

His play on many subsequent occasions demonstrated his continued preoccupation with denying who he was. He insisted that he was not a boy but a man; when I made references to his being a boy he became angry. I therefore observed that he hated being a boy. He would not admit this directly, but revealed in his play what being a boy meant to him. In the context of depicting fights among toy animals, a frequent, exciting source of play, the little ones stood aside. They were the ones who don't fight. They are afraid, he told me. His reply to a question about whether he had fears was "I hit my father, too." He reported that sometimes, when his father spanked him, he hit back. While he was recalling this, as he pitted animals against each other in serious, merciless struggles, he said that he hit his mother when she sometimes brought him the "wrong juice." He imitated the scene spontaneously by shouting the juice he wanted and using dolls to characterize himself and her as she failed to do what he wished. The mother's reports corroborated all that the boy played out with fidelity to the details of such scenes at home. He let loose a stream of shouts, "orange juice shit." With more curses at his mother, he shouted that he was a cowboy with a gun, designated dolls as his mother and father, and shot them, proclaiming that he was bad. The fracas ended with his saying, "Cowboys don't have fathers and mothers, just cowgirls have them." He went back to the telephone and spoke into it, mimicking the voice of the man whose identity he had taken and shouting that he was "boss." He terminated this visit with the declared intention of going to market to buy his own juice and the candy he preferred.

By the time George was seven years old, subsequent hours of therapy-play disclosed a persistent need, one that he would not relinquish, to make his own rules, to win in the games that he invented or that were formal, popular ones, and always to be associated with superhumans who had no need for parents. (This follows closely on the theme of the comic book character Superman.) He denied his dependence, being a young boy,

having limitations, or losing at a game. In short, any suggestion of limitation or passivity aroused his fury and excited an
intolerance of himself. Many therapy hours were required for
him to understand and accept conditionally that his fears of
being abandoned, as his parents abandoned each other, were
not realistic; he had to learn that he would not be abandoned
and that denying his trepidation or having contempt for danger
would not bring security.

It takes little speculation to realize that this boy's open
conflicts with his mother were connected with his father's
departure from the household. Left alone with his mother, he
naturally fancied himself in his father's place, as in fact he
often was when sharing his mother's bed. He was all too
acutely aware of how inadequate he was to his wishes when he
declared that he was no boy, took the name and thus adopted
the identity of a man, was answerable only to a superman
(Santa Claus), and designated his mother a girl over whom he
asserted his authority. These frank oedipal struggles ordinarily
would have been modified and attenuated by this age. In this
case, however, the absence of his father and his mother's
surrender to his demands, which had a seductive importance,
gave an added impetus and further extended, rather than
helped bring to an end, the normal oedipal conflicts.

A boy's oedipal wishes and the conflicts that issue from them
are as familiar to us as are the aggressive activities with which
they are associated. However, there are also present deep and
broad implications neglected by most who study the subject
when the focus is held to the sexual and aggressive conduct of
the boy. The problems of self-esteem, as this boy typifies them,
lie in the need to prove oneself a match for one's extravagant
wishes, which make their appearance, as we have observed,
long before and long after the oedipal ones. If we take the
Oedipus complex as the boyhood culmination of a long series of
trials and ordeals, we may then more fully appreciate that it is
a landmark in a boy's development — not only of his sexual life
but also of his narcissistic development. Later periods, though

less dramatic, are inevitably built on this one, as latency with renewed perils, trials, errors, and successes. None is final.

The enormous importance of turning apprehensions of performing into the gratifying display of prowess and mastery always commands attention. However, the question of what the process is that carries such significance has tended to create a division among those who have made a study of it. The influential, voluminous works of Jean Piaget are emphatic in explaining the acquisition and exercise of the cognitive functions of children as laying the foundation for these achievements.[14] The Freudians have put their attention on the role that libidinal aspects play toward these ends. Such views in the last half century have been the great preoccupation of many analysts and psychologists. The gap between the two schools of experience remains. In their concern with the phenomenon as reflecting the human condition, neither one has given sufficient attention to the powerful influence of masculine narcissism. Nor, for that matter, has studious consideration been given to how similar and different is the influence of femininity on the process.

While it is known that structural and aggressive activities are common to boys and occasional to girls, they tend to be attributed to what the boy is encouraged or expected to pursue. To give this fact no more importance than merely observing that it persists and reflects a certain cultural influence is to give a meaningless answer to a searching, repeated question.

To what extent a small boy's play directly reflects his interest in his own person must remain a matter of speculation. As we have observed, however, George is not unaware for long that he is the bearer of an organ having unique properties, not the least of which is that it contains his identity as masculine. Despite a boy's intellectual understanding that the absence of a penis in girls represents not a loss but a difference, it appears that in certain important respects ignorance prevails. The boy's anxiety associated with the loss or absence of a penis is impervious to superior knowledge and is a notion that many men never altogether give up. Many social and cultural mores support their emotional convictions. It should be small wonder to us that a boy is irresistibly drawn to wishing for magical powers, the exploits of a "superboy," and has aspirations to become a superman. With a belief in tests of power, which he translates as masculinity, in which he may prove his invincibility forever after, a boy strives thus to hobble his fears. Together with the incalculable value that masculinity seemingly holds for his mother, and his father's defense of it, a boy's narcissistic estimation of his genital organ is assured. His expectations of himself are directly magnified. Because of this and because of the unconscious disillusionment associated with it, the boy emerges from the oedipal period preparing all the more to prove his masculinity; like that mythical creature the phoenix, it is seen by him as rising from the ashes, palpably. In all his masturbatory activities, he, like a chastened, wiser investor, will engage in diversified enterprises.

Despite the emotional rigors of being a small boy, the importance of the long-held theory of a boy's "phallic worship" has largely been dropped by analysts. It is as though, having reached the zenith of "phallic worship" in the Oedipus complex, where he found himself wanting, the boy quits his focused interest and belief in his penis and with his rush of activity ushers in the "latency" period, albeit without continuing to carry the burden of his penis into it with him.

However, even though Freud and other analysts have since employed similar case material (like the case of Little Hans) to show the fears that boys normally suffer, no one has amplified their significance and effect on boyhood. Nor of course, is the lasting effect on masculinity revealed.

By the age of three (as a rule) a boy has become convinced that to be without a penis is a perilous state. He has himself in mind as a model. A small boy, we have long known, need not actually be threatened with mutilation in order to be perceptibly frightened of it. Because even as young children an effective, lasting source of dread develops in us all. It is that the fate of others might well become our own. This is self-reference. It is especially characteristic of young children to take what is plausible for the reality. In boys it inflames the mere fantasy of mutilation at the sight of females to give it a terrible reality. It is a living proof, as it were, that the penis can be "lost" and makes vividly real these fears and influences the boy's fantasies about mutilation. As we may anticipate, such a repugnant fate will be relegated to repression. However, conditions, circumstances, and experiences may always make what is repressed return to awareness and with it a corresponding reaction. The reaction is often a replication of the original one. While we all fear injury and mutilation, it is a particular, even if a mostly repressed, fright of boys and men. Among boys one commonplace reaction to this inner anxiety is seen in their being prone to exhibitionism with their genitals and playing games of performing with the penis. Manifestly, they are earnestly engaged in prowess. For example, they match their urinary streams with each other as they unspokenly do their penises and pursue other similar private sexual contests. These feats are unconscious narcissistic expressions of prowess that girls obviously do not engage in. One of the chief underlying aims is the infantile gratification in what one may claim; and, it is to see what others possess in concealment. It is unconsciously also intended to confirm that something is not lacking in oneself. All serves to reaffirm what the boy himself has that he prizes.

The boyhood interest in examining a girl is not only to be excited by the experience, or titillated by it, but also, no less important, to be unconsciously gratified by the anatomical or genital difference in which the advantage is his. A further source of his interest is an underlying question that he has held since he learned to know the differences: does she have a hidden penis? It would be very reassuring to him if that were the case.

This conflict occurs in childhood. But it is then found commonly to persist unconsciously into manhood. A little boy develops the — to him, catastrophic — notion that a girl has no penis or, to offset such a dire conclusion, that she has one too small to be seen, that it is somehow hidden, or that with time she will acquire one, which is to say, it will grow. He certainly is not instructed in these ideas. He makes and holds to his own explanations and conclusions. He draws them from his observations of himself, of others, or of animals, as we may recall how Little Hans at the zoo confirmed his beliefs from what he observed of the creatures there as well as those he saw on the streets. A boy's notion that a girl will be properly restored is not so much charity toward her as protection from her irremedial fate and limitation becoming his own. He finds her state intolerable. What's to prevent its becoming his? He imagines it could happen. When he spares a girl such a fate by persuading himself she has a genital like his, even though it may not be evident, he is in some measure relieved.

The idea of a woman with a penis appears not to be expunged emotionally in boys or men. The notion of its absence in women remains a persistent unconscious dread that appears later in life in the dreams of adult men. For instance, the return of this repressed idea may occur to a man dreaming who, "in a state of nocturnal excitation, will throw a woman down, strip her and prepare for intercourse — then, in place of female genitals, he beholds a well-developed penis and breaks off the dream and the excitation."[15]

My own clinical experience provides corroboration. I had a patient, a man nearing middle age, who reported the following dream: "I woke up from a nightmare. I was taken with shock! I saw my wife, as she was getting undressed for intercourse; she had a penis. It was mine! The idea of making love to a man would frighten the hell out of me — making love to another man is shocking. And my wife now has no vagina. Should I fondle or kiss the penis she has? Am I her? Is she me? . . . She's a man in the dream, not a woman. And it's my penis. Does she have mine? I remember wondering: Is mine gone?

"I woke up at this point. Is she the man? And I am not? That's what was so awful. . . . I don't want to think her a woman with a vagina! It's shocking. . . . She has a penis! It's awful. She's the one without a penis. And in the dream she has mine. . . . *I am the one without one! She's the man in control.* The one with the penis controls. She's the man. She's the man in our marriage, I think sometimes. Sometimes, I think she is masculine. It's that she insists on her way. She wants to direct.

"It's like my mother directed my father. He never amounted to much. I didn't like to see that as a boy. I don't like it now. It's why I prefer to do things alone and not with my wife. It gives her control and it makes me feel feminine. But that's like my father. It's like they say, my mother wore the pants. I'm deathly afraid of winding up like my father.

"I could never stand it that my father was weak. Would I have to be? I have proved my strength, my masculinity. He didn't. He couldn't cope with my mother. I am out to prove I can do what he couldn't do. A wife that leads devastates. She deprives masculinity. I had to prove — and did — that I am better than my father, who was feminine to my masculine mother. My wife has to break me down by finding fault. And it's then a flaw and demeans my masculinity. I am deathly afraid not to be masculine. Yet, I hang a penis on my wife. My penis! I'm overridden by that."

In the return of the repressed impressions and fantasies that make up the dream, boyhood fear is plain. This man dreads the possibility of his having his father's fate and surrendering to a dominating wife. How close his convictions are to the actualities of his boyhood is not so important as what he believes. He fears he himself is in exactly the situation in which he had seen his father. In his vivid dream he is feminine to a masculine woman. Further, he declares that he cannot tolerate a woman's femininity, her willingness, her vagina, her lack of a penis. Her possession of his gives her "control" and deprives him of his.

He most feared to sacrifice his masculinity and to yield it to a woman who wanted it from him. Yet he gave his penis to her.

Was he not expressing an unconscious wish that she carry the penis? It was consciously an alarming idea. It shocked him even to dream it. This was his nightmare: that he was the victim, the one without the power, the control. Willingly giving up his penis contradicted his worst conscious fear. He had all the more to prove that he wanted his penis, his power, his masculinity. And, above all, he was not to fall into his father's ignominious role. However, in the dream he appeared to choose to do that. He so frightened himself that he put an end to the episode by awakening.

It would be psychologically naive to oversimplify the nightmare by interpreting it as an unconscious return of a long-repressed oedipal scene from boyhood, as if in his dream he had taken his father's place with a wife like his "phallic" mother. While this interpretation is correct, as confirmed and amplified in the course of many other analytic hours, there are additional considerations to the overtly stated self-castrating fears.

This man came for treatment in his despair caused by the struggle with his wife. He was unaware that both he and his wife each needed to be the more masculine and that neither one could abide femininity. Their mutual problem, however, was not identical. The wife's feelings of deprivation are important to us here insofar as they reenforced in her husband how precariously his masculinity was held. His need to secure that masculinity was overdetermined, the more so by her demands born of her own discontent with herself as a woman. Her efforts were to solve her plight by "directing," "controlling," and resisting his masculine needs. He feared that what proof of masculinity he had acquired would be insufficient to the challenges his wife had laid down and that he would be required to be tested over and over by both his wife and himself for proof of his masculinity, which was neither conclusively not irrefutably established. Not to be overlooked is the deepest source of his anxiety and conflict: that what he most prized he would unintentionally give to his wife, that he would demean himself to femininity like his discredited father. The menace to his masculinity was not from his wife. She was but the *agent provocateur*. The real menace was within him. He wanted unconsciously to be identified with the more masculine figure, which in his experience was his mother. Here the unconscious logic contradicted the rational.

This man was inclined to take flight from his wife into excesses of work, where he "proved" himself with renewed zeal. He avoided their intimate relations, which brought about reactions of despair from the underlying, unconscious wishes. On the other hand, he was just as eager for intercourse to prove his masculinity. His wife, for her own dictates, often refused or resisted his wishes. She unwittingly denied him the opportunity he needed to affirm his prowess. He could not leave her for a more "willing," "feminine" partner "with a vagina," someone less masculine-seeming than his wife. Despite all his conflicts, he genuinely loved his wife. One central element in his devotion, of which he was unaware, was that she was the feminine counterpart of himself. It would be no great risk of speculation to surmise that he was also hers. He had wondered whether the dream suggested a desire for a homosexual relationship, but this notion brought on panic at the idea of passivity to another man. The implications were unbearable, and there were floods of fears of having a feminine role (although there is an unconscious homosexual aim in the desire to be with a masculine woman).

The clinical problem was finally resolved by the couple's pleasurably sharing in this man's masculinity. His success depended upon his finding that his masculinity was firmly established once it was not threatened by the repressed fears held over from early boyhood. His ability to share his masculinity with his wife without threat of its loss because of her need was what brought about the final resolution. However, because the couple's newfound compatibility was based on an unconscious homosexual rapport or harmony, there were no prospects of their having children in the near future.

Thus, the idea of a woman with a penis may continue and, as

we have seen, even become a fixed (albeit unconscious) belief. Not only may it appear in dreams as nightmares, but the underlying conflicts that give rise to such dreams or ideas become part of the psychology of a man's everyday life. They are not confined merely to the occasionally alarming and bizarre material of dreams. As we shall find later, when the boy develops as a youth he may require a penis of his sexual partner, much as this man did. In some instances, he may be drawn by means of it into homosexuality or to girls who are not too "feminine." "Real" women may remain impossible sexual objects because "they lack the essential sexual attraction."[16] Jan Morris's autobiographical account, described in Chapter V, makes this preeminently clear. We saw in him that the small boy's anxiety associated with the absence of the penis remains. In his case he divests himself of it and requires it in his sexual partner. A further variation on the same theme is one in which a man finds the "tomboy" an irresistible partner with whom he is most compatible and whom he marries.

We know that a boy's play, like his questions, betrays his normally continuing, restless concern with assessing his performance, gauging his prowess, and testing his powers in the service of securing elusive self-esteem. Before boyhood, these pursuits were solitary.

With the development of the superego, the monitor of the self and its conscience, the barriers of the previous phase are altered. A strict, severe rigidity of the further-formed conscience of boyhood emerges and quickly envelops in amnesia any conflicts with it. Thus disposed of by repression that unconsciously sets in, more firmly than before, to remove from awareness those wishes, intentions, and acts that would violate the dictates of the superego, the inevitable, natural result is a scanning self-consciousness. This period of boyhood is characterized more by action, and, unlike the previous period, when activity was more often independent-minded, now it is important to share it with others. The period of solitary contemplation or reflection comes later, but now self-consciousness is associated with the press of activity, the expectations of performance, and the inventive ferment of enterprise.

With the growing force of repression on his unconscious conflicts, the boy is committed more freely to engage in those conscious aims that he enjoys: an adversarial role in arguments, occupation with contests, siding with rectitude, and gaining mastery that proves his worth, and identifying with those characters of fantasy and fiction who act out his wishes again and again, at their peril, to affirm masculinity.

Chapter 8

THE THIRST OF YOUTH

SELF-INTEREST IS the outstanding quality of a group of boys. Regardless of how this is expressed — whether in acts of heroism, self-sacrifice, or petty or vicious delinquency — the group demands from each member a contribution to its self-esteem. As with any group, its formation and stability rest on each member's relinquishing an egocentric need for the sake of all. This makes it appear that the members feel loyalty toward one another (and, in some measure, this is the case, as demonstrated by occasional exhibitions of selflessness). Popular fiction, as well as myths and legends, has fostered group loyalty as an ideal of boyhood.

In fact, the structure of a band of fellows is inherently unstable. The band's formation is largely an emotional response to its members' common, but individual, conflicts that result from the oppressiveness of their family circles, from the social opportunities to escape them, and from the ineradicable longing to prove their mettle. Although individual boys are highly egocentric in boyhood, the age is characterized by an intensely shared, but not intimate, social experience. The readiness of a boy to join others in sharing his dreams, fantasies, and heroic exploits or adventures is well known. Mark Twain, perhaps our best popular source for the psychology of boyhood, gave us no hint, however, of the period that follows it, that of "youth."

When they are in the boyhood phase during the years of about six to twelve, some boys are leaders and others are followers. How they sort themselves out for such roles will depend on the skills they have acquired, the mastery employed, and the nature of the relationships that are sought after from the identifications developed in the earlier periods. The satisfaction of masculine narcissism will be central in governing the experience of the group. The demand for self-esteem in boyhood brings the group together, and the narcissism of adolescence will break it up.

As we become more intimately familiar with the comrades separately, we find that their masculine narcissism is held up as a looking-glass for a shared experience. In it, each boy sees the exploits in which he has engaged with others either in fantasy or in fact. These are the vehicles that convey the masculine narcissism to be proved. Alone, each felt weak, helpless, and dependent; in the company of one another, each has found some escape to redeem himself. When the boys are identified together as part of a band and invest their prowess and aggression in each other, each boy transcends his fears, apprehensions, and weaknesses, to embody them in a titular leader, who is envied and admired. His position is held in jeopardy from the narcissistic begrudging of it by the others. As the narcissism of the group elevates, so does the envy. It is not a period of altruism, self-sacrifice, or heroics on behalf of another. The narcissism of boyhood yields only to a group, but it soon begins to pall: its gratification gets worn thin; it can no longer be sustained in a diffusely shared experience. With the boy's development, narcissistic demands for a more individual, intimate relationship increase. Prowess, mastery, and achievement are still critical to masculinity, but now the search is for more intimacy. The question of whether it will be with another youth or with a girl opens this new phase, which, in either case, will be a period of individual exploit.

Thomas Hughes captured some sense of this change in expectations when Tom Brown reflects on what he wants to leave behind him in his passing school days. Tom is actually also looking ahead. " 'What I want to leave behind me,' said Tom, speaking slow and looking much moved, '[is] the name of a fellow who never bullied a little boy, or turned his back on a big one.'"[1] Conrad, better than anyone, conveys the fervor with which the youth looks to the future when he wrote, "O youth! The strength of it, the faith of it, the imagination of it . . . the test, the trial of life."[2]

These are the spirits of youth caught like rare flies in the clear amber of fiction more than a century ago. Since then, it has steadily come into clearer view. The deeper psychology of it has remained with the poets, the dramatists, and the novelists. Modern writers, such as Stendahl, Melville, Joyce, and Faulkner, showed us that youth was a time of a man's development. In our century of modern psychology, however, youth has been clinically narrowed to juvenility. It has been given no rose to carry.

Scarcely more than a decade ago, serious scientific writers and popular essayists together claimed that the problems of young people rested in their persistent and often frustrated search, remarkably like Don Quixote's, for their "identity." It was assumed that somehow the dynamics of economic and social change, which at times naturally made for greater or lesser stability, most affected "youth." Their pursuit of an elusive "identity" that too regularly escaped their hold was taken to signify that their unrealized aspirations created their conflicts. Because their personal and social roles failed to be seen for their egocentric character, and seemed to lead more to dilemmas than to definitions, youths' place in the social order tended to be less than satisfying. Their anxious striving for a more certain future raised more doubts than assurances. This placed them in a quandary and left them there, skewered in their perspectives.

The solution was believed to lie in "searching" for a suitable self-realization. The emphasis from social engineering was on a need for an assigned or acquired role. It was further assumed that the vagaries of circumstance might effectively thwart the wish to extend the wandering, restless groping. There was no accounting for the resistance or rebellion common in youth that worked against the discovery or development of this self-realization.

In the 1960s, when youth was being explored, there had been no distinction made as to gender.[3] Clearly the youth of a female must be different in kind and concern. We will so treat it here.

The boy's view of the world commences with the conviction that physical powers bring prestige as well as success, and that "the body is very much the instrument of the self." Rather than diminishing with time, this view is reinforced by the conspicuous changes that occur as advances in the development of the body during youth.

> The athletically-built boy not only tends to dominate his fellows before puberty, but also by getting an early start he is in a good position to continue that domination. The unathletic, lanky boy, unable perhaps, to hold his own in the pre-adolescent rough and tumble, gets still further pushed to the wall at adolescence, as he sees others shoot up while he remains nearly stationary in growth.[4]

The masculine ego-ideal, stamped with the need for performance, prowess, and mastery, makes a boy's Oedipus complex the apogee of unconscious boyish aspirations and also marks its *commencement de la fin*. Girls are spared these conflicts that require a boy to prove himself so early and yet doom him not to succeed. The masculine ego-ideal is hardly some abstraction to be passively claimed and enjoyed with the emergence of youth. "Performance," while having its acknowledged social merit, has a particular, ever-present, critical audience:

the boy himself. What is expressed, in concert with what the environment requires, is no more or less than the inner need of satisfying a tyrannizing masculine ego-ideal. The social and cultural demands are significant, but only insofar as they coincide with what the boy feels he should be as a man and what he aspires to be. If the fulfillment of these demands seems to be an unlimited obsession, the boy is more narcissistic and thus more neurotic. The rewards of his prowess are then not what he has done but what he will do next. The social and cultural milieu in which the private drama of prowess and mastery is expressed are secondary to the boy's compulsion in which he disregards what he has done and fixes on what he will do to prove himself. Devoutly wishing the end of these conflicts, the boy is left with an unconscious, passionate severity of self-criticism and a heightened superego that demands more of performance and prowess than he previously charged himself with. When he played it out as part of a group with whom he shared his efforts, the burden of his narcissistic demands was distributed. But as a youth, who must prove himself to his own, individual self-image, he is under his own mandate, even though he may appear to merge it with his fellows in their aggressive activities or pursuits.

Analysts have assumed that the aggressiveness characteristically associated with the activity of boys and men was somehow a natural expression of endowment that became incorporated into the ego-ideal of masculinity. Prowess as a dynamic essential has been neglected. From its earliest forms in a small boy to its most advanced expression, prowess supports the ego-ideal in masculinity. It is simple-minded to suppose that most achievements of men may be reduced to "penis pride" because performance once was rooted in it. On the other hand, however, it would be no less ingenuous to suppose that a man's exploits fail to carry their implications to him (even if only unconsciously) of meeting his masculine ideal to its beginning, or that he has in some measure fulfilled the expected masculine ideal others have or have had of him.

Beginning in early youth with the maturational push of biological events of puberty, a boy's aspirations cast him into his society, which begins to absorb him as one of its ripening members. At the same time he sheds many conscious family dependencies and further loosens infantile ties. This is critical to his becoming associated with and a part of the adult world. New loyalties are formed, and intimacies and identifications with people other than the family are unconsciously shaped. While some of the family conflicts are naturally acted out with others, some are left within the family. The boy is permitted a greater freedom as the inhibitions within the family are attenuated outside its limits. These developments also bring a sharper end to a bisexual orientation that was tolerated within certain limits in the family because of the split identification that a boy experienced. In his youth, the boy begins to resist the split, because he wants to consolidate his masculine identity.[5]

Homosexual wishes, dreams or impulses, and fantasies, which are inevitably activated in the close relation that being part of a pack of boys brings, are heightened at puberty. Physical maturation manifestly gives them an impetus. They are usually resisted, sometimes only perfunctorily engaged in, and even wholly rejected with violent resistance. The youth who is gratified by passive homosexual relations as a rule seeks them with an older companion or a man, not with his peers. This is because the feminine identification has not been relinquished from the earlier period, and the boy's gratification in that role will not come from sexual intimacy with another boy like himself. The more normal course, as a reaction to the homosexual tendencies, is a flight to a relationship with a girl. This is the more desirable, as it serves to reinforce the denial of disturbing homosexual aims that the boy associates with aspects of femininity.

The role a youth ordinarily desires for himself, as we might anticipate, is an active one. Some of what it may entail brings on fantasies of wishing to be intimate with a bold girl, who is or seems to be "boyish." He admires her for it and feels that her activity would somehow mitigate his apprehensions and guilt about his being sexually active. Moreover, a "tomboy" as a sexual object and participant is often just sufficiently removed from the unconscious homosexuality that needs to be warded off so that she becomes very desirable. Of course, he is unconscious of the narcissistic gratification that comes from the fact that the "tomboy" is close to being an image of himself. This period of masculine development is characteristically the most narcissistic one. It is therefore not surprising that the wish to "find" oneself has as its object to find oneself in another.

The boy's fears for himself issue, as they did before, from his tendency to have extravagant expectations of prowess. Now, however, these expectations are extended to include sexual exploits, which are perceived on a scale bigger than life. Such notions further the awareness of his limitations. The ever-present specter of failure deepens disappointment and is a harbinger of despair, passivity, and often depression, which commonly has its clinical beginnings during this period. Such fears may also galvanize activity intended to overcome them.

> To try to find out how to influence, control and effect the environ-
> ment in our favor is not entirely a rational endeavor. Each of us
> knows that our limitations create a gap between our wishes and
> their fulfillment which we strive to bridge and that our failure is
> not ordained. It is in ourselves generated by our exorbitant wishes
> we are resistant to recant. As if to do so would be a self-inflicted
> narcissistic injury. It is one we are the most loathe to administer.[6]

This central conflict that men carry with them is only briefly resolved in youth. Later development and experience are necessary to engage the fears more effectively.

A psychoanalytic study of a young boy, Ben, beginning high school showed that he worked compulsively hard at his studies. His efforts succeeded in earning him the highest praise. Enlightened attention to his performance failed to recognize the intensity of his obsessions with achievement. His motives for driving himself to excel were simply understood as a conscientious reaction to social demands and an appreciation of the real competition that confronted him. Ben was driven to prove himself not defective, limited, ugly, and he dreaded the certain fate he believed was in store for him should he in the least relinquish his inordinate efforts. He was tortured by aspirations that he feared would elude him. His extravagant demands were neurotic; they revealed an unconscious conviction of being inadequate that could only possibly be overcome through the compelling effort to achieve. Although he earned the high praise he won, each new occasion required him to prove himself once again as though he had never before done so. This example shows the fusion of the excessive demands of his ego-ideal and the unbounded narcissism that drove his perfectionistic zeal. But for his excessive, uncompromising, uncontrolled self-demands that he must have the "edge" or else he would lose all he gained, he might not have spilled out such anxiety that his family and teachers, who could no longer help him moderate his obsessions, enabled him to receive psychoanalytic treatment.

Ben was possessed by a compulsion for performance, prowess, mastery, and achievement. These were not scholastic aims; they were the fulfillment of masculine goals. It was a tyranny of a masculine ego-ideal that had become a narcissistic, insatiable aim. He appeared to be zealously ambitious and inordinately aggressive and in a frenzy to destroy all threats of competition. His leadership during boyhood was hardly challenged, but in his youth, his narcissism would tolerate no close friendship.

Only after much reluctance and effort was this boy able to reveal how vulnerable he felt sexually. Despite his record at school and with his fellows, he was uneasy and fearful that he would fail to prove himself with a girl. This was his secret agony, and his growing interest in girls gave him his deeper despair. This unknown and unaccountable symptom was contradicted by his outstanding activities in the rest of his life and led to his being sent for clinical help. In relation to girls, he began to be troubled that they were more mature than he. He fantasied about a girl in whom he had an interest that she would coax him by her sexual interest in him. Under these conditions he would be willing to follow her attention and direction. He asked of himself privately, "What's expected? How far should I go? What should I do? I watch myself. As I sat with a girl at school, I watch her and feel there must be a right way." These ruminations about his conduct are not over proprieties, as may superficially appear.

When I proposed that his concern had a further importance to him rather than to the girl, he replied in a humorous vein that at the same time was gravely serious, "I have a big secret, I pretend I have an 'S' on my undershirt. It stands for 'Stud-Man.' I want to be Stud-Man or Stunt-Man. He would know what to do, what controls to use. He has lots of sex. And he is fearless."

Ben's associations were to his father who he recalled bragged to him about his exploits with girls as a youth on the occasion he observed his son's interest in them. His father encouraged him. The boy reflected, "I feel he can't wait for me to grow up; I can't wait for my body to catch up to what I want." He reluctantly admitted that he believed his penis was too small compared to the rest of him. He was actually comparing his with his father's genital. His private, but not unconscious, idea was that he was in training for sex, much as he was in athletics. As "Stud-Man" or "Stunt-Man," he would be a sexual athlete, he hoped. His fear of girls reflected his concern for himself rather than with them. He feared that girls would ridicule his penis as too weak or too small. "She would expect a much larger one. I want an orgasm like a geyser!" He focused on what he should expect. "What's it like to be a man?" His reflections were to identify himself with his father, actually with his father's alleged prowess that Ben envied. The unconscious, incestuous wishes behind the prowess are evident, although they were elicited much later in therapy.

As we got further knowledge of his fears, he described the vagina as like a "mine shaft, it's dark, black." If he played with a girl sexually, the more excited she became and the more willing she seemed to be to have intercourse with him, the less passionate he was. He feared, "I was not up to her. My penis would get swallowed up. She wants it. She could be a Venus's-flytrap. I want a girl more like me. It wouldn't be so dangerous. Sex has to be quick. I would have to get in and get out so as not to get caught. The real thing is dangerous. I'd have to trust the girl." The idea of being naked with a girl was embarrassing and even more so was to look at her "dark patch." He remarked that a girl who is "too young for [pubic] hair" scared him. She looked "deformed." While he admitted this was a ridiculous notion, "I thought of it more than once." His image of a woman sitting to urinate was an "idea I can't take. I'd feel safer if I knew a girl was not so lacking."

This youth's approaching manhood brought on a palpable reality that previously was confined to fantasies of masculine activity. Performance in what he thought it meant to undertake sexual relations was to be an index of his masculine worth. As he became sexually active with a girl, and thus went beyond the experience of his masturbatory fantasies to testing himself in reality, his need to prove himself became more pressing than ever. What youthful love he experienced and however enthralled he conceived himself to be, he focused principally on the deeper conflicts issuing from achievement as a mirror of himself and the masculine values it reflected. He would of course bring all his previous conflicts associated with masculinity to his first real sexual experiences with a girl. With her, his youthful masculinity would have its major challenge.

A youth's masculinity carries him beyond the circle of boyhood camaraderie and the contests of the playground but not altogether away from those unconscious sexual conflicts of boyhood from which his companions provided some respite. As we have just noted, some of his earliest fears were revived. A girl who seductively teased a seventeen-year-old student who was away from home at college, excited him to want to get into her bed. The fact that she was a virtual stranger to him was all the more enticing. But he was also fearful. To be sexually active and venturing beyond masturbating seemed to him a risk. Sexual intimacy was a defiant act. Considering all that it previously meant to him, he acknowledged rather conscientiously, "You take on a big male power and the girl is not a buddy!"

His relations with girls before he had left home for college were more like those with his friends. He enjoyed the familiarity of sexual play that stopped short of intercourse. Those of his friends who had actual experience were eager to display the experience as prowess, masculine over feminine. It was no shared exploit, but a rite of passage to the masculinity of manhood. Now, however, to be chosen by a girl for sex brought on fantasies both flattering and frightening. It gave him a new sense of freedom about sex, but he asked himself, "What will I do with it? Somehow, I can't allow it. How do I compare? Maybe I won't do as well." He was not aware that he was comparing himself with his own fantasies carried over from early boyhood, regressive notions of his humiliating comparison with men, his father, and all with whom he had admiringly identified himself and envied. He revealed that his solution was to prefer a girl who had no previous experience to compare him with another. His assumption, of course, was that he would compare unfavorably. It was an old, invidious comparison resurrected from early boyhood. This is a common wish that men express in wanting a young girl and a virgin as a sexual partner. She would then from her innocence bring no uncharitable confrontation, and the persistent boyhood anxiety of being inadequate to the performance would be avoided. "I want to be told what to do; I want the girl's approval, not her criticism. I don't care what she wants," this youth blurted out in his anxiety. He was reminded of frightening family scenes when one of his sisters was discovered to be occasionally sleeping with a young man.

His related thoughts were, "Sex is a tool a yard long; how will I do it? It's a loss of control. My sister got hell for that." His masturbatory scenes were images of violent rapes. He projected himself into tough movie characters who sexually dominated women. Moreover, sex with anyone was exciting, he claimed, so long as it had no other involvement. It was also explosive. "Sometimes, I like to imagine I'd like to be a cop and ask a rape victim what's it like?" In this case, he was the voyeur, inquiring "what's it like?" It was much as when, among his friends, he vicariously enjoyed their telling about their exploits with girls. Whether they were real or fictional mattered far less than the opportunity to identify with the sexually active, aggressive storyteller.

These ideas also brought with them alarming fantasies of being in the woman's place and the object of a sexual assault. These were vivid scenes in which he pictured himself in his sister's place. He could not imagine his mother as sexually active; his interest in her was deeply repressed. His further ideas about his sister brought to mind associations of the weakness in women, yielding to their sexual impulses. These thoughts were confirmed by the accusations that arose in the family scenes in which his sister was accused of letting her sexual impulsiveness rule her. He thought of women having menses and taking men into themselves. The identification with the sister produced a reaction of the menace to be like her. His thoughts of masturbating came with the idea that his penis in his own hand was safer.

Another youth, Paul, since early puberty had a seemingly endless series of sexual experiences with girls and only on one occasion mutual masturbation with another boy. He had been depressed, and, during the residual effects of excessive smoking of "dope," he attempted suicide, by lacerating his wrists. This self-destructive act brought him into treatment.

This boy's active sexual life began with a brutal relationship toward a brother less than three years younger than himself. His parents tolerated his open physical assaults with a remarkable degree of permissiveness. These assaults were rationalized as the normal "rough-and-tumble to be expected between brothers so close in age." The parents interfered only to prevent some actual injury to the younger brother. There was not much remonstrance and little appeal to moral authority or injunction. The boys were separated more as one would wrestlers who had to be kept within rules.

The hostile relationship continued. The younger brother avoided the older one, but he seemed to accept his lot. There was no history of his vigorously defending himself, nor did it appear that he was encouraged to defend himself. The extent of Paul's private fantasies against his brother were revealed reluctantly in the course of the treatment of the depression. He principally felt guilt over his conduct as he grew older, but he displaced the guilt to his mother. He blamed her for having the younger one, and his hostility toward his brother was meant more for her. The brother was the scapegoat. The father was exonerated inasmuch as he was himself a very aggressive man who interfered the least in the struggle of the boys with each other.

Paul's identification with his father as a model fitted his purposes. The further unconscious significance, however, of these assaults was associated with the younger brother's being regarded as feminine, and the attacks were as though on a passive, feminine man or girl. The boy promoted his identification with his father in treating his brother like a girl. It was a displacement to him easily arrived at from sexual fantasies about the mother. The aggressive mother, an unwitting party to the "fighting" between her sons, was in the midst of their struggle. During analysis, it was uncovered that at the root of the older brother's fear was that of being in a woman's place, the brother's, and being sexually assaulted. His wholly gratifying, sadistic sexual life was functioning as a defense against himself being like his brother and a homosexual object to his father.

The father teased and belittled his wife, venting his rage on

194

her as my patient observed the scenes between them from the time when he was a small boy. Although an aggressive woman, the mother seemed to her older son to accept her lot as an object of abuse by both her husband and her son.

Referring to countless sexual exploits, this late adolescent revealed, "It is exciting to feel you're dominating a woman. She takes it in the ass." These were associations to his recollections of playfully mounting his brother from behind, when they were ostensibly wrestling. He was then perhaps seven or eight years old. These ideas occurred with the scenes of "buggering" his brother. They were thought of in recalling intercourse with girls. He had an abhorrence of anal intercourse and had no such experiences. "There are certain girls who appeal to me. I want to have them admire me. If I don't get it quick, I get vindictive. I want the kind that says, 'Take me! take me!' Those who like to be captive. I'd never want it myself. If I did really want it bad, I'd be fucking myself. Is that killing myself? My father didn't say it but he taught me the best way to be a man is to put a woman down. I carry out his mission. I'm doing it to men, too. I feel I'm the fucker. I'm the humiliator! Sometimes, I'm afraid I won't live up to it. I might get it in the ass!"

On occasions when he spoke of playing tennis, "or any game, I begin like I'm a loser. I can only win from behind. It's a great weakness to be a loser. So I start to win, I write shit all over the other guy. I don't really say it, but I think it. I like to play with a guy who can't stand to lose. Winning is like killing. The guy who loses gets killed. If I don't beat the guy, I'm giving in like a woman. If I don't go after being a man, I'm a woman who sucks cock! I'm an asshole! A cripple!"

He recounted fearful dreams that were fully disclosed unconsciously to be homosexual episodes in which he was the object of sexual assault. There were conscious injunctions. "I have to be a man. And I think, no! Maybe being a woman would be easier. I'd be a mother's boy. I have to hide that. She wants me weak and says I don't have to worry about success. My mother is a big loser. I felt like that when I tried to kill myself. I could

195

not stand that feeling. When I can't feel like a winner, I'm put down. Is my cock too small? I can't leave myself alone when I feel like that. I've got to be like my father and show off my manhood and think where do I stick it! That proves I'm no woman. A woman is cockless! I like it best when I think a piece of ass has a cock on it. I can't think a woman is cockless! She's got one like a hidden needle. It's revolting not to have one. Waste them, I think. Fuck their brains out. Sometimes I'm afraid I'll be like them, the walking wounded. I might lose it in a cunt. I'd get damaged. A man's got to be a fucker. If not, I can't stand myself. I feel like hurting myself. I felt like that. I wanted to die."

There were many hours of other preoccupations. They revealed quite the opposite side of the same conflicts. There were circumstances and fantasies of being forced into situations in which he himself could not inflict himself on others. He also experienced situations in daily life in which compromises had to be made, satisfaction had to be put off, and disappointment was certain. These experiences evoked such expression as: "When I can't get it to work the way I intended, I hate it. I feel like I have to give up. My father would never say give up. I say I can't and I hate myself. If I wished it and it fails, I get sore. I feel it's my strength that's gone. It's like being a captive. I feel I'm a victim. Like my manhood is gone. I feel scared. And if I get bossed by somebody when I'm like that, I feel 'cunty.' There's a tremendous anger, I'm afraid. That's when I turn on myself! Why not turn on myself? Didn't I fuck myself? I remember, I tried to kill myself!"

The vignettes of these youths show that, despite their individual differences and their diversified experiences, particular conflicts are held in common because of their masculinity. One of the principal problems in studying youths is that their private experiences are characteristically kaleidoscopic: they exhibit constantly changing, highly colored conduct. This is to say that their anxieties, conflicts, relationships with others, and feelings about themselves carry them from the peaks of elation to the depths of despair. Their quickly embraced enthusiasms give way as rapidly to repudiations. In the wake of such burning excitements, chilling hopelessness may follow,

> or at other times sterile — intellectual and philosophical preoccupations, yearning for freedom, the sense of loneliness, the feeling of oppression by parents, the impotent rages or active hates directed against the adult world, the erotic crushes — whether homosexually or heterosexually directed — the suicidal fantasies. [7]

These are elusive states that by their very nature resist being revived consciously and tend to be avoided even with an analyst. Moreover, the youth is reluctant to scrutinize what he may readily, passionately experience; its implications are frequently alarming to him, that is, he fears his masculinity is compromised. He takes refuge in their transience, or he is fearful that their significance is lasting. He fears homosexuality. He repudiates it by a rich variety of emotional defenses that may effectively obscure his fears. This means that the analytic treatment may be felt by the youth as a hazardous venture. Thus, the analyst meets obstacles to his efforts that are far more formidable than are those encountered either in young children who are not so troubled or in adults to whom some intellectual appeal may be made to tide over the anxiety a youth often finds alarming.

The youth encounters particular difficulties with the analyst because of a narcissistic urgency in his need for reassurance, an intolerance of frustration, and "the tendency to treat whatever relationship evolves as a vehicle for wish fulfillment and not as a source of insight and enlightenment." [8] The period of youth, by definition a departure from the earlier, relatively peaceful phase of development, is characterized by a variety of emotional disturbances that reflect dynamic, unconscious changes taking place. It is, therefore, not surprising that behavior may "come close to symptom formation of the neurotic, psychotic, or dissocial order and merge almost imperceptibly into borderline states, initial, frustrated or fully fledged

197

forms of almost all the mental illnesses."⁹ Drawing the line then between normality and pathology is only done with difficulty.

Each of the boys discussed here was productively engaged in school, employed otherwise at times, came of average, conventional, middle- and working-class families. They were typical in their relations with their contemporaries and in the fact that there were no uniquely influential or traumatic events in their experience. Thus our deeper understanding of necessity would come from the revealing comments they each make about themselves.

For instance, we noted that the accomplished, athletic boy who wanted the exercise of sexuality to be a "stunt" and to prove him a "stud" was fearful of women. His masculine narcissism was in jeopardy when the very organ he would employ to prove himself a man was, he believed, the object of envy. The imagery was as vivid and authentic to him as it was old and familiar to us. He was not ignorant of the nature of sexual relationships, but as an adolescent youth his masculine ambitions had now entered into actual sexual conduct with a girl and left the tissue of fantasy in which it had been previously enveloped. He brought to it all that his previous masculine aims carried. His penis, as we have observed before, had to be a performing organ, used in the service of masculinity. It was not merely an excremental organ or one for lovemaking. Power, force, and prowess were synonymous with it. His fear of ridicule from the girl, that his penis was too small for the task in mind, referred to the immense, unconscious significance that he gave to the undertaking, rather than to the real dimensions of his genital or its functions.

The second boy elaborated on the same theme. He wanted to defend his efforts at accomplishment or prowess by force through identifying himself with a "cop," and his fantasies were fired by the violent scenes at home. However, they were not the cause of his associating himself with violence — we find identical fantasies in boys from the most tranquil families. The sexually experienced boy enjoyed the most sadistic fantasies about sexual exploits with girls, but in his case, the unconscious homosexual encounters were clearly an extension of heterosexual relations with women. This pointed to homosexual relations having a secondary disposition, rather than, as some have supposed, primary. I shall refer to this later in the discussion of homosexuality.

In the instances cited here and in the enormous literature on adolescence, the sadistic elements in sexuality as well as in other conduct in youth have long been observed and variously attributed. But analysts have explained it as an inability to "neutralize" aggression. That is, to find some other socially acceptable expression of it. Others have restated the case as an arrest of development in infantile sexuality, because anal and sadistic behavior, expressed during early development, are associated often with rages and are part of the psychology of early childhood. These phenomena are well recognized. The explanation of the so-called arrest of development or the failure to harness or direct "energies," i.e., the sexual and aggressive drives, as a continuation of an infantile state seems not to have advanced our understanding of its appearance in youth, where it plays such a large role if not always a manifest one.[12]

Although the manifestation of aggression constitutes one of the most formidable and dramatic aspects of male adolescent behavior, it has not been satisfactorily traced within the adolescent process. As soon as the first strivings of puberty increase drive pressure and upset the balance between the ego and the id that prevailed during the latency period, the preadolescent boy turns away from the opposite sex. The aggressive drive becomes pervasively dominant and finds expression in fantasy, play activity, acting out, or in delinquent behavior.

You will recognize this kind of boy . . . playing with, drawing, or impersonating battleships and bomber planes, accompanying their attacks with gunfire of onomatopeotic noises in endless repitition. He loves gadgets and mechanical devices, he is motorically restless and jumpy, usually eager to complain about unfairness of his teacher, assuring us that the lady is out to kill him. In his behavior, language and fantasies, the resurgence of pregenitality is recognized.[11]

As we have observed, the older youth retains the substance of the fantasies of the "preadolescent" years much as he continues to carry, that is to retain, many "pregenital" (i.e., infantile) conflicts. While these are ordinarily repressed, given proper conditions they are easily evoked. A college student, for example, entertained two alternate sexual fantasies from early puberty. One was to be stroked on the genital by an older woman who was dressed and who sat beside him. She was the active one, while he, naked and lying down, was passively receptive. In the other, a more voyeuristic one, but in which he was hardly more active, he was loved and admired by a very beautiful, highly intelligent girl who possessed firm protruding breasts.[12]

The commonplace dread that men have of passivity tends to be attributed to their continuing identification, although repressed, from infancy, with a woman personified as weak and passive compared with men. As we have seen in examples cited earlier, small boys are intractable in the conviction of their fantasies of a mother and of women that they must submit to a man's sexual aggression and hence superiority. The identification with the man is compelling. Yet, so much induces a boy to be like his mother. Unconscious conflicts of interest result. The alarm at being like her issues from them. It resists being mitigated except by abandoning the manifest sexual aims that involve her or surrogates for her. Only the next period of development, "latency," offers a refuge. This phase, typically centered on a pack of boys together, supporting one another in exploits of prowess and mastery, offers a respite from the direct challenges of the sexual wishes that being within the limits of the family circle evoked.

Should this phase, boyhood, become prolonged, cronying or

boon companionism develops. And may remain fixed. The effect is to compromise the development of youth and early manhood. Many socially acceptable forms of this phase, in which the company of women is shunned or an exclusive relationship with a woman is at best shallow, promote an institutionalized and ritualized existence among men. We find this advanced "boyhood" in their work, sports, and in aspects of their social life. Underlying is the unconscious flight from active heterosexuality to the seeming less demanding unconscious homosexual company. In it physical prowess, performance, and achievement lose little of their earlier boyhood importance, significance, and gratification and offer escape from the conflicts intimacy with a woman may entail.

In fact, there is one set of fears of passivity in relation to men, and there is another and different complex of fears of passivity in relation to women. What is more, the mere condition of passivity is not what men fear, as we have been led to think. What evokes fears of women being witchlike, devouring, or otherwise menacing and even mutilating, are neither uncovered nor removed by the knowledge or the experience that a woman surrenders to a man through a sexual encounter and that he appears thus to prove his superiority by virtue of his physical power that she enjoys. There is a tendency to overlook that these persistent conflicts are associated with certain problems inherent to masculine narcissism.

A first-year college student, Tom, at seventeen younger than most, had been admitted because his previous exceptional scholastic record merited that consideration. During the second semester, he became so depressed that he was unable to do much work, and he felt somewhat, but not seriously, behind. More important to him, however, was his alarm that what was once an easy achievement, his schoolwork, from which he drew much pride, now was so heavy a burden that he feared he would be unbearably embarrassed at his grades. In fact, some few grades were just below excellent, but he summarily dismissed reassurances from his family and teachers.

He came from a large family that had great expectations for him. Physically, he most resembled his mother, according to him, feature for feature. His identification with her in many other respects carried deep implications for him. She was a housewife, and she enjoyed a private, reticent life in her family. The father was a successful businessman. He held himself, as did his wife, to be a model father and patriarch. He presided over a large family of collateral relatives who treated him as the *pater familias* that he was.

Tom worked conscientiously at school. "I tried more than the other kids to please my parents. I work for their approval. I feel I don't work enough even if I do more than anyone else. It feels like it is not enough. In a way I know it is, from what everybody tells me. But I have to placate my father. It's not that he gets angry. I never do anything that does. But I feel I don't please him. I used to compare myself to other kids when I was five or six and I just didn't feel safe. I had the idea even when my father praised me. I still can't take it. He must be kidding. I get scared. I felt helpless. The only one who could really protect me was my father, so I had to be sure of his good will." The source of the menace escaped him entirely; he had no clue that his own hostility toward his resented father, on whom he so heavily depended, fed him an unconscious, continuing ration of hate.

"The reason I work so hard is that it makes up for feeling I have no abilities. Of course, I have them. But I feel I don't. At least by work I'll get praise. I really want to be different from the others in my family. And be somebody. I am never satisfied. So I can like myself, I have to be better. I can only be by hard work. I have no hope what I'll do that'll be valued. It's foolish only to have these terms. But I can't let go. It's to get my father's favor. He has me programmed. I am a 'rat.' Rewards and punishments will train me."

There were recollections without end of his father's authority that required achievement as the only route to being valued. The father and others in the large family of admiring relatives

pointed to his success earned through tireless work. By implication the mother was a mere housebound creature. Hers was a
life of devotion, work, and waiting for the father's praise. This
youth was like his mother. He was also her confidant. He felt he
had no choice. "I can't be like him. And I can't accept myself as
nothing. She is that. When I'm being like my mother, it's a low
form of life. No one respects me. How can they. I don't! All my
life she was intimidated, easily upset, worried. And she has
told me that. So we have to depend on my father all the more.
He's the only one who's great.

"I used to think when I did so well in school that would help
this feeling. But it didn't. I still felt I have to depend on my
father. So I do what others want. It's womanish. My father
doesn't do that. Only to worry at pleasing others is what my
mother does. No one wants to know who I am. Why should
they?

"I believe my father wished I was a girl. I could win him if I
was my sister. He wouldn't like me on a higher plane than
himself. He wants me to think he is a hero. All that he does is
great. It's a sick competition. My mother and I are together. He
never listens to her any more than he would to me. I hate
myself. I am like my mother. I fear the violence in myself. I
have to control it with being quiet. I can't argue. As a kid there
was all this harping on greatness. I wanted it. But I keep
looking at myself. And I'm missing it. I failed to be like my
father. I'm a woman. What makes me think that? I am my
father's slave. Mother has to be his slave. There's nothing that
says so. But he expects it. Like her, what I do or want is not
important.

"I have a secret handicap. Under the surface, I'm like my
mother. I sound like her. It's what she would say. I hate myself
for something. I know I didn't really do anything wrong. But I
wonder, will I be punished for something? I feel like a criminal
and don't know what I've done. Is being my mother's favorite
wrong? I'm always on trial. Couldn't I do what my mother does
and just worship the great man? It makes me into a nothing to

think that. I am totally no one, then. It's like my father has a monopoly on masculinity. I want to be in his place. It gets me anxious. And to be in my mother's place is depressing.

"Some of this shows with my girl friend. I have to do what she wants. She flaunts relations with other guys. She denies me intimacy when I want it. She competes with me. I hate her for it. Maybe she'd like me better if I was mean. But I can't be. She decides. I'm angry, resentful. I'm at her mercy. I hate it.

"I write a poem. I'm suffering. She decides its worth. I can't declare it. I see it in dreams. I'm being dominated. I lack sufficient masculinity. What do I despise about myself. My mother marked me for greatness. But I say no. Sex is a little war. The conquered submits. This happens with my girl friend. She's only happy when she's on top. There's something wrong about that. I end up guilty. I force myself into submission. I really hate it. I can't help thinking of my father. It extends to my roommate. I'd rather feel the failure than the anger. The angrier I get, the weaker I am. I'm helpless with rage. I want to hurt myself! To throw my penis away."

In Tom, we see the agony of being identified with his mother. But in his instance, it had become a defense against the rage at feeling fury at his domineering father. The identification with his mother was reinforced through her unwitting need for her attachment to her son and her suffering, which to him was so seductive. His father gave him no place for his masculinity by retaining it, at least in the youth's eyes, for himself; the mother's seductiveness caused him to identify himself with her plight; and his girl friend deprived him of his masculinity for herself. He was left in despair, stripped of his masculinity, weak, dependent, passive, and furious at his humiliation. Rather than turn it on his father, whom he deeply envied, he would spare him; rather than deny his mother's part in fostering his identification with her, he put himself in her place; and his girl friend embodied both parents to him. She dominated and competed with his masculine wishes, taking that role for herself, while at the same time seducing him into acting as if only he were masculine. He was aware only of his hateful fate, the guilt against those with whom he was so deeply involved and who had impoverished his life. He felt he had no recourse but to attack himself rather than destroy them. By being everyone's victim, he unconsciously exonerated himself from his murderous aims. The price was prohibitive—his masculinity. He could not afford it. He was obliged therefore to repudiate his mother, but at the cost of his needed, dependent relationship with her. He was in a dilemma from which he could not alone extricate himself. One effort in that direction was to want for himself, guiltily, the enormous hostility, domination, and overbearing character that he attributed to his father. He was unconsciously identified with his image of his father.

We learned of the beginnings of this process from small boys who identified themselves with the aggressor. While this continued to be the case here, the youth also hated himself for these aims, especially when he acted them out with women. When we found this phenomenon in small boys, their strict conscience had as yet not fully developed. This youth's reaction, now conscience-ridden, took the part of servility and self-abnegation. It showed in his slavish denigrating of himself with a series of masculine girls who were best satisfied when they mounted him. He then entertained passive homosexual fantasies of being used and obedient, and he had reminiscences of being a good boy. It resulted in helpless rages. He lived, he said, like a laboratory rat. By that he meant he was caged by the goads and rewards of his father's conditions. It was as though he were in a maze, incapable of finding a course except as he was prodded into one or another confined route along which he then ran. What aggressiveness he felt made him "ratlike." It frightened him that he found he wanted to turn, being cornered, against his father. To avoid doing it, he turned his fury on himself. A self-mutilating rage haunted him often during the day in fantasies of injuries and accidents and frequently in his dreams in which he was victimized. Thus he unconsciously spared others. And of course, especially his father.

A remarkable parallel suggests itself in Kafka's *Metamorphosis*.[13] A son, Gregor longed to be loose from an oppressive relationship with his father. After much self-reproach for such insubordinate wishes, he began to relate that a hideous "metamorphosis" had taken place in him. It was as no despised, desperate rat, but in his case it was a transformation into a verminous insect — cockroach. His reference to the "self" led to guilt-ridden reflections that he "was so tormented by conscience as to be driven out of his mind and was actually incapable of leaving his bed."[14]

We observe a scolding criticism issues from some anonymous authority. His thoughts are that he is demented and in a helpless condition with regard to his father. His mother and sister were compassionately distraught by his plight. But his father was fierce, pitiless, and would savagely drive him away as a loathsome creature. No entreaty availed. None was understood. To his mother and sister, "Gregor was a member of the family, despite his present, unfortunate and repulsive shape and ought not be treated as an enemy."[15] But his father was "mulish" and grim visaged. We are to suppose he wanted only that his son accept the dutiful role he meted him. In it Gregor feels demeaned. He is unmanned. Thus he is rendered repugnant. Was it his father's doing? Or like our youths, was Gregor perhaps metamorphosed by his own notions? To submit to an implacable father is perilous. It is to be in a "rat" world or Gregor's, a verminous one. It is that condition where masculine narcissism yields to ignominy. The effect is loathsome to the "self."

Among the problems uniquely in the wake of a boy's puberty are the meanings he invariably assigns to sexual excitation, to genital sensations, erections, and ejaculations. He associates them all with fantasies and reveries of prowess, power, and achievement. All are both long familiar and important to him from his past. But now the musings begin to carry the real burden of the possible actual exercise of sexual powers, meaning, that is, exploits over women. As such adventures provoke the anxiety of failure, a displacement from them to activities and enterprise that manifestly may seem unrelated to sexuality offers relief. Only closer scrutiny reveals their roots are inextricably in it. As the fruits are similar and spare anxiety, the incentive to enjoy the sublimation thus found is often irresistible and actual sexual encounters get deferred. But the active sexual fantasies are not dampened.

Together with the omnipresent importance of action, a youth often gets lost in his reveries of passive sexual aims. When they appear, they are secondary or derived. The penis is no passive organ either in its nature or in fantasy. And by extension, in the minds of boys and men, a girl's or a woman's genital is assigned an active and, what is more, even an aggressive role. Given that this is thought to be its characteristics, it allows no sanctuary, offers the penis no refuge. Hence, unconsciously it must be subdued; the encounter with it calls for penetration as though it were a fort. The penis as the agent of the man thus proves itself and him with honors. Myths, legends, and even present-day folklore bear this out. The overwhelming role that sadism plays in the mentality of boys and youths, with the penis as its executive, has been amply demonstrated.

In later youth, when the intensity of egocentric attachment excites homosexual or passive wishes, the sudden termination of friendships begins to occur. This period of development comes at a time when older male adolescents will "fall in love (often only in fleeting fantasy) with every male peer or male adult whose mental and physical faculties are momentarily envied."[16] Such experiences are expressive of the search for an idealized image of oneself which seems to be suddenly recognized in some quality observed in another. Of course, as soon as a blemish in the character appears, the mirror is cracked and the passionate interest is lost, faster than it was found.

For instance, as a youth makes forays from the company of

his familiar group to find a needed, more individually exclusive relationship with one like himself, a girl may be in his sights. On his way, however, he may discover that a boy satisfies his pressing, unconscious, narcissistic longing. He is apt to be drawn unconsciously to him as one like himself, or as one whom he would like to be, and with whom he can speak miraculously easily and express himself eloquently. There seems to be an unspoken, immediate, mutual understanding. The same effect may come from finding a boyish girl. Such intense, enthusiastic relationships give voice to a frequent refrain in a joy of kindred spirits that find each other, reflected in one another, searching and being rewarded with finding one's soul, to one's amazement, in a being with an essence having "a distinction without a difference" from oneself. Such encounters confirm the narcissistic craving of this period of masculinity. It is a time that, because of the intensity of its self-absorption, promotes a flowering of transient, unconscious homosexuality, even as the partner is the "boyish girl."

The remarkable incidence of homosexuality appearing in youth, commencing its appearance in early adolescence, is well recognized since at least antiquity. But a scientific explanation for it has only begun with the modern understanding of this phenomenon in men from Freud's studies.[17] He referred to it variously as representing inhibited or arrested development or "sexual infantilism." There was a difficulty, he explained, in drawing a sharp definition about homosexuality between its appearance in normal and abnormal sexual life. His view was that only when normal heterosexual life is excluded by a homosexual choice did he consider it pathological. He was not here referring to sublimated forms of homosexual relationships.

Shortly after psychoanalytic studies began to appear early in this century, an enormous literature started to burgeon. It was mainly focused, inconclusively, on the origins of homosexuality. Theories about biological processes and those that lead to genetic gender differentiation have been put together with some psychoanalytic theory about bisexuality to emphasize that the formation of sexual identity all comes together during the early nursery years. Some are led to believe that homosexuality more specifically is finally set in the oedipal period.[18] Some analysts hold the opinion that sexual identity develops and is set early in infancy, where the mother is given the singular role in its determination. If she is inclined to cultivate a close, dominating partnership with her son at that time, she is held to be central to the development of homosexuality. This supposition has not led to further illumination of the dynamics involved. Perhaps more significant is that a homosexual element, regardless of its possible origins, exists as a persistent, unconscious conflict in masculinity throughout all its phases of development and remains a part of a man's everyday psychology. As a component in all the phases of a boy's development and a presence in neuroses and psychotic states whether latent or manifest, homosexuality normally in men is a source of dread in their masculinity. Nowhere in masculine development is this more plain than in its commonplace appearance during youth.

For example, Chris, a young student, presented a shy, passive demeanor that belied his private, excessive aggressiveness. He complained at the student health service that he knew he was unaccountably fearful, which made him unable to do his work. He worried that it would lead to failure and probable dismissal from college.

After a few consultations, it soon became evident that his meek, pleasing ways masked an intense, grudgingly confessed competitiveness. His secret wish was to triumph over other boys through proving himself the "smartest." By that feat, he would beat the others, so to speak, into submission. These were his principal fantasies. It followed, not surprisingly, that he feared that the other boys were no less ambitious, and that they equally wished to destroy him. Explorations into his unconscious aims brought his admission that he wanted to see them as victims. Still deeper in that role, he thought of their being compelled to perform fellatio.

These images were associated with his father's exhortations to set aside his timidity. The issue had come up often in the past. He viewed these urgings as contempt for his reticence. Now in his first year away from home at college, Chris took this contempt to apply to his fear of girls. It was his own wish to be a sexual athlete. This was related to his idea of sexual relations with a girl as a feat — but one that he did not dare initiate. He thought girls would scorn his efforts, and he was therefore inclined to abandon the entire enterprise as a failure. He would not go out with them.

As his mother was closer to him, he interpreted her encouragement to overcome his shyness as her being seductive. "She wants me to try to please her." He next became enraged and blamed her for his failure. This was associated with a sexual reverie that he wanted to do nothing actively sexual. On this theme, Chris later admitted he wanted the girl to undress him; he would just stand before her naked and she would admire him. He was not thinking of her or feeling other than to be worshipped. He was utterly unaware until much later in his treatment that this fantasy was a more up-to-date version of one he had about his mother years ago. "I least want to admit I want to be worshipped. My mother always said that I should just try to do better no matter what I did." It was soon evident that it was not certain to him whether it was her ambition or his that was being promoted. Since the two were not separable, the conflict was intensified. He really wanted to be a "bully, humiliate other boys" and the homosexual fantasy that appeared at this point was to control things, which was what his mother tended to do. "She was always ready to put others down, to criticize, set rules so no one else would be able to do it." He would himself feel safer, he knew, when he set the rules. But with a girl he was often furious in a way that made him wonder what enraged him. His thoughts were that he hated a girl like himself. "It's her weakness I can't stand. There is something wrong with it. The vagina is scary. It's not decent. I can't place all the parts. It's like a jungle, dark, and a man groveling in that wet place. I can't identify with [women]. They are not like myself. They are different. I can trust somebody I like, somebody like myself would be better, a man. I must be part woman, to think that. But I have to turn to someone like myself.

"I don't really admire myself even after I've done well. I am not really good enough. I look for what I'd like for myself in other men. If I could get into them, be like them, I'd blame myself less. It's like to be the greatest is for my mother. All for her! If I was a girl, it would be easier. I want girls as friends. A girl might hurt me. But another guy won't. I let one get hold of my balls, and it didn't scare me the way it would if a girl did it. With a girl it's a job to do. But with a guy I don't have to be so dominating. We can do things together, like a merger. We share and think alike and I want to feel the same thing he does." There were associations to feeling close to his father, "looking up to him." There were shared experiences with him, and thoughts about another with whom he found he had much in common, "like he's the same person." He referred to his best friend with whom he had masturbated, enjoyed looking at, admiring him as he would himself and taking an inventory of his friend's qualities, i.e., his muscles, penis, strength, hair; feeling like "twins" was appealing. He was attracted "to all friends who are boys"; their strength and the qualities that make them masculine, with which he associated himself, were reassuring. He recognized he was "making love to myself." "It's irresistible. But with a girl it's a commitment to her and I lose myself, I won't do that. My friend is like what I want to be. Everything comes easy to him. I would do anything with him, join him, that's what is so special about him, and I get excited thinking of wanting to be with him and upset if he ignores me when I want to be with him."

In the previous period of development, we do not find such

211

longing to be with one's ideal image of oneself. The boys in that phase resisted singling out one for another. They most admired being joined, as a group of adventurers, in exploits, feats, and tests of prowess and performance. The favorite friend or exclusive individual experience was not sought after until the vanity of adolescent youth gathered its momentum from the turn toward oneself that before was sufficiently satisfied by being simply a member of a real or imagined exclusive group. So long as physical activity with others was focused on gathering together and pooling of prowess, performance, and achievement, the narcissism of the group was dispersed among them. As we have observed earlier here, groups are notoriously unstable. They fail to satisfy the individual narcissism, especially at a time when in youth it flourishes and resists being bounded.

There have been many friendships like this one just described. They get to a point when constant attention is demanded from the friend, anything but praise is taken to be criticism. There is a sense of longing to be the other, and, thus, any inadvertent, critical remark from the friend has the effect of separating one from the ideal that is longed for. Often a boy is aware that his wishes are "selfish," that is, narcissistic. They are expressions of being self-absorbed and lead to feeling depressed and self-critical. He would ask a favor, and if it was not immediately granted, he would take this as a rebuff. He would be quickly enraged with hurt that he "was not at the center of everything." He was eager to act selflessly, but also he would test the other's willingness to put him first.

Chris was fearful of women. He dreaded their scorn of his masculine pretensions. In regard to them, his unconscious associations led to his critical and seductive mother. Thoughts of her brought out fantasies and reveries that were near to consciousness. They showed that his early boyhood fears of women had persisted. His desires were dangerous to harbor. His relationship to his father seemed the lesser risk so long as he was submissive, obedient, and was not disturbed by the repugnance of his own hostile impulses. When they occurred, he became alarmed. For long, he was unaware that his frequent nightmares of being pursued, threatened with assault, and menaced by men who aimed to do him in were projections of his own fury that had been repressed during the day but during sleep escaped the barriers of the unconscious to frighten him. He was appalled to learn the variety of ways his rage found expression. He hated the authority of his teachers and expected their scorn and criticism. He was naturally more comfortable with his mother and found the explanation for it in their having so much in common. What he was unaware of was that they shared a parallel or at times even identical relationship with his father.

On the other hand, his masculine aspirations were self-defined more than they were related to an ideal. They took the form of searching for a "twin." That is, someone with whom he would have the most in common, not as he spoke of it about his mother, which was repressed, but rather one who would be like himself. The companionship and camaraderie he sought was to discover in another his own qualities, interests, and especially a hostility toward authority he could share. It was an exercise in making love to himself of which he was entirely unaware. These are homosexual relations that are not acted out literally sexually. But they, nonetheless, had deeper erotic significance. His homosexual relations parallel those with girls. On close scrutiny, it can be seen that his search to gratify his masculine narcissism was served in one aspect by sexual experiences with a girl and another aspect of the same pursuit is satisfied by relations with a boy.

These youths all illustrate emotional problems typical of their period of development. Their conscious distressing fears and anxieties characteristically cover deeper conflicts. As a rule, through sheer diligent efforts in physical activity, a holdover from an earlier time of boyhood when restless pursuits often took over under stress, and through added hours of study that renewed a sense of performance and achievement, a respite was found from the oppressiveness of their difficulties. In recent years, drugs, alcohol, and other distractions in often adventurous circumstances are used in order to bring respite from the more immediate distress. However, these effects fail to restore the sense of mastery and masculinity is compromised. The boy may repress the long-standing problems nevertheless, but there is no assurance that they will remain repressed. On the other hand, so far as the youths are concerned, when repression succeeds, which is indicated by the subsiding of acute distress, they seemingly are recovered. They have a feeling of the entire experience being transitory. This may be further helped by an absence from school for a semester, which in actuality is an avoidance of the requirement for performance. A temporary lapse of performance can come about by an illness or physical disorder that remains elusive to diagnosis and eventually dissipates. As an effective flight from the blow to masculine self-esteem, the escape is a welcome relief.

As often happens in such instances, the conflicts are relegated to amnesia. There the painful experience is stored. This is not to suggest that its effects remain there inert. On the contrary, they require that emotional defenses against the underlying conflicts be maintained. They are subject to being breeched; the barriers unconsciously erected against them are prone to be unpredictably penetrated by the unforeseen nature of relationships and events. As a result, a repetition of the earlier disturbances may reappear either in similar or related forms.

A youth is not ordinarily a willing subject for self-scrutiny and examination, despite his absorption. The two, although opposed, are frequently thought to be the same. In the instances illustrated here, the respite the youths needed was not soon enough forthcoming to permit escape from despair, and the intensity of the fears of irreversible consequences being sufficiently alarming, the problems persisted and led to treatment. The deeper issues were thus uncovered. Instead of being brought into the shelter of repression, they were exposed so they might be resolved.

As we have observed, each phase of masculine development demands reaffirmation. What is increasingly evident, as we study masculinity in each of its periods, is that what was proof-positive of masculinity established in one phase seems only ephemeral for the coming one. With each development of masculinity, new criteria are set, new experiences must be mastered, and new evidence gathered that one's masculinity is indeed irrefutable. What is exasperating in this seeming litany is that masculinity, which characteristically bears fruit for its fulfillment, must do so for each of its seasons. Convincingly productive as one phase or period of masculinity may be, it fails to establish itself permanently.

In this respect, perhaps the most trying period of masculinity is youth. It is the time of greatest self-absorption, self-consciousness, and self-criticism. It is generally thus the most narcissistic time of conflict. We may recall this was said to be true of infancy — that it was the most narcissistic time of life. But, unlike youth, the narcissism of infancy is not its central conflict. Youth is the opposite. It is normally filled with both narcissism and the conflicts heavily associated with it. The search in adolescence is for an intimate, exclusive relationship that is more emotionally suited to the emerging development that puberty heralds. And youths bring to their quest what previously acquired masculine narcissism they now want further gratified. But masculine narcissism is not a stable condition. It remains precariously held. This is derived from the fact that the identification with a woman, despite the depth and magnitude of the conflict it engenders, is repeatedly reinforced just as it is even more vigorously resisted. Paradoxically, the lifelong need for a relationship with a woman on the one hand enhances and promotes masculine development and its narcissism, while on the other it threatens it, requires it to perform and make good its claim.

Even the small boy repudiated femininity, which was the

215

outcome of the incestuous wishes during the oedipal period, and often remnants of them thereafter. Forceful protests against women and girls were made and flight was taken into the close company of other boys; when this was given up sufficiently for an active sexual relationship with a girl, the fear of being identified with her, the underlying wish to be her, and the ambivalent lust to be a feminine partner to another boy or man was revived again. When this came to a point of consciousness, it often brought shattering panic. The identification with a woman seems to mean the abandonment of masculinity. The earliest cases here have demonstrated this dread. As we have observed when in later years the compelling need was to quit masculinity for femininity, the problem lay more as Hobson's choice to abandon masculinity for some role that an irresistible self-abnegation could not satisfy.[19]

Each assertion of masculinity entails the risk of sacrificing some of it. Moreover, once achieved, masculinity is not an impervious identity, in contradiction of popular notion that identity, once found and established, is merely lived out as a role defined by genetics, affected by circumstance, and influenced by social institutions. The latter view makes of existence a mere part played, with greater or lesser talent and satisfaction, in the individual's history.[20] Such notions naively remove masculine identity from being a dynamically continuing, narcissistic conflict of the everyday life of men and boys.

Chapter 9

MANLY DEEDS

WE, LIKE THE immortal gods, prize a man's zeal for his work. His capacity for work and his readiness to put his sweat ahead of virtue are seen as signs of emotional well-being. Some classes of men, privileged either by culture, position, or other conditions, are exempt from the necessity of labor for survival, but even among these exceptions, pursuits of one sort or another acquire an importance that parallels that of work.

We find, too, that the qualities — performance, prowess, mastery, and achievement — so important throughout masculine development are applied with equal vigor by a man in his work, whether to support professional or private pursuits. The emotional investment in work is self-assessed in accordance with the cardinal signs and merits that satisfy masculine aspirations.

Moreover, work is a phenomenon of adult life, because with a man's emerging maturity come demands that require his relinquishing the egocentrism of childhood. Social living, from the outset, compels the self to yield its egoism for the sake of another. Therefore, it is in adulthood that the familiar, developed criteria for masculinity are brought to bear in work.

If there is any time in which libidinal pleasure and gratification in work coincide most intimately, it is during early manhood. When such a fusion of the two persists and is not divisible, work takes on a highly erotic (albeit not necessarily manifest or even conscious) importance. Prowess and achievement become the focused, narcissistic aims of manhood. The most obvious examples are in the performing arts, television sporting events, and whatever pursuits that lend themselves to an ever-widening stage. There are, however, less conspicuous examples in everyday life that are no less significant. Or, perhaps they are more so because they are not publicly exhibited.

For example, a young husband and father, Adams, was obliged to complete some requirements in his work in order to get a promotion. What real satisfaction he enjoyed as a man with his wife and child was clouded by the elusive gratification he sought in what he had to do in order to get ahead in his job. His efforts seemed to him trivial. He procrastinated, he became anxious, he was certain of failure, and, finally, he could not arouse himself from a lethargic depression. He continued to work, but the weight of his expectations was a deterrent rather than an incentive. It was at this point that he came for help.

His field was a popular one, and he had many ways to choose to meet the requirements. He no sooner began to review his efforts than he told of his feeling that his attempts were puny and not a basis from which to launch a new career. As we began to scrutinize what he was after, the impediment to his efforts became clear. The unconscious stream of ideas that were revealing began with, "It's a weapon I'm fashioning, for combat to beat all the competition. So there will be no claims. First of all, it's got to be big. The top in this field. It would be easier if it was more modest. But it has to be big!"

When I inquired as to why he felt this when it was not what was being asked of him and was entirely unnecessary, he went on to say, "What I want to do with it is prove my greatness. I get the notion I want to demolish others in the department. Even if it doesn't do that, I'd like to feel it will at least hold them in terror. It may not work, and the thing will explode in my face. It's a foolish weapon that I'll turn on myself. People will laugh at me; I'll not be taken seriously. I always wanted greatness. I have, ever since I can remember, worked my balls off for it. And still I'm afraid I'll fail, even though I never have."

In these expressed ideas lies the malignant nucleus of what we have known since Freud's work in the first decade of this century. Freud discovered that hostility employed to satisfy one's ego will, in the course of demeaning others, be turned on oneself. He discovered this phenomenon about severe melancholic states, but he was not aware that the same sequence of inner emotional events may take place in neurotic ones, as shown by this young man. Such hostility brings on the same fears, anxiety, and despair with its suicidal wishes that often fail to appear consciously. While in this case there is a low risk to life, the suffering self-abnegation is similar. We see this in the fear of becoming the object of ridicule. With such self-denigration, depression follows.

This man had a dread of limitations. He felt that the fruits of achievement were likely to be lost, as they were beyond reach. In this vein, Adams reluctantly admitted, "I refuse to accept limits. To live or tolerate limits is a reminder of feeling self-destructive. I want to defy them. I only want to think myself an exception, even when I know I'm not. I don't want to be limited by my wife, by what I do or even eat! It's not just being great versus small. It's great against self-destruct. I'll get too big and pay for greatness. It's not reality that's killing me. I know that. It's the notion to be the exception. Being without limits, like above the law. My work has got to prove my greatness. I am afraid it won't. So I can't do my work."

The conventional observation of this man's aims is to take them at their face value as the most puerile of ambitions. However, his fantasies revealed their unconscious, exhibitionistic qualities fixed on performance and power. His preoccupation with masculinity was clear, but it was not directly related

219

to his wife. It was not she but, he believed, his occupation that would ensure it. Ordinarily there would be a temptation to suggest that he had displaced from her to his work the proof of his masculinity. But here, prowess and achievement are aims and ends that precede his relationship with his wife. In point of fact, she was sexually more like one of his accomplishments than an intimate partner sharing his masculinity.

He said that he always lived by comparison, that he never worked on his own for himself but in relation to what others were doing, and he endlessly compared himself to them. He was compelled to do this and feared he would not be best or win. He was self-absorbed in proving his masculinity, and we see that he was solitary in it. Neither being a husband nor a father served to satisfy masculinity. Work was a threatening challenge to it.

Further analysis showed the depth of his relationship to his mother. The father was excluded. The mother needed her son, as a boy and later as a man, to verify and personify her ideal of herself. Through him, she would reify herself. Her obsession with his masculinity helped to make it an objective to be endlessly demonstrated, although not directly sexually. As we have seen in earlier-cited instances, this is the taboo. Very likely, this made his marriage possible. Sexually, he belonged to his wife, but his masculinity remained his mother's.

The fact that he was an only son among four children increased his mother's attention on him, or at least to the extent that she had no similar investment in her daughters. There is ample evidence that his father was not so ambitious as his mother, nor was the son living out his father's life, as he was his mother's. While masculinity was of special importance to her, we cannot say it was less so to his father, but it was different. She made many demands on her son's masculinity, while the father, by comparison, made far fewer. His chief injunction to his son was to obey his mother. The son's masculine narcissism was committed to satisfying a mother's unconsciously masculine ideal. We saw this scene earlier through the eyes of mothers in their zeal to realize their masculine wishes. In this instance, we may observe some of the unconscious effects it may have on her son as a man. We see how his self-esteem was bound to his mother's aspirations for herself; she unconsciously hoped to realize through her son's performance and achievement the masculinity denied her. When he failed or feared he would fail his ideal, which was unconsciously his mother's that he made into his own, he was in despair.

As with our other cases, this young man demonstrated that a coercion existed from which he did not escape. It was the maxim of his narcissism. There is nothing to be accomplished by searching here for its origins. To do so would be to repeat what has been done countless times. It would merely bring us to the most common beginnings of it where we are all our most egocentric: in infancy. However, what is more important for our purposes is the role that circumstance and relationships reveal of the process of development of a man's narcissism.

Modern scientific psychoanalytic literature rarely illustrates a character type in which this challenged narcissism and its effects can be readily seen. However, Helene Deutsch, in a brief, clinically sharp vignette, showed the loss of self-esteem and the resulting onset of severe depression through the character of Conrad's Lord Jim. She cites Conrad's words about Jim:

> He passed the days on the verandah, buried in a long chair, and coming out of his place of sepulture only late at night, when he wandered on the streets by himself, detached from his surroundings, irresolute and silent — like a ghost without a house to haunt.[1]

It is a "state of broken-down self-regard." From her short communication, we understand what Conrad brings to light: no one is safe from a narcissistic loss. While this is the human condition, masculine narcissism is especially vulnerable. Conrad makes this clear.

221

Conrad's Jim was a young man of twenty-four years, thrust by the circumstance of an emergency to save his life, which cost him his honor. He had a "kind of dogged self-assertion which had nothing aggressive in it."[2] It was a necessity directed as much at himself as at anybody else. Aboard ship, he was very smart aloft and looked as though he was destined to shine in the "midst of dangers."

> He saw himself saving people from sinking ships, cutting away masts in a hurricane, swimming through a surf with a line; or as a lonely castaway, barefooted and half-naked, walking on uncovered reefs in search of shellfish to stave off starvation. He confronted savages on tropical shores, quelled mutinies on high seas, and in a small boat upon the ocean kept up the hearts of despairing men — always an example of devotion to duty, and an unflinching as a hero in a book.[3]

These were his secret pretenses. They had never been tested at sea. He took a berth as chief mate of the *Patna*. During his idle moments on board,

> his thoughts would be full of valorous deeds: he loved these dreams and the success of his imaginary achievements. They were the best part of life, its secret truth, its hidden reality. They had a gorgeous virility, the charm of vagueness, they passed before him with a heroic tread; they carried his soul away with them and made it drunk with the divine philtre of an unbounded confidence in itself. There was nothing he could not face.[4]

The crew were raffish scum; they were men who "did not belong to the world of heroic adventure."[5]

Conrad thus sets the stage with a young ship's officer entertaining the highest aspirations for himself; his daydreams embraced their fulfillment with an impatient, vaulting ambition. His self-esteem shone in the reflection of the realization he had met his ego-ideal. And the setting is further sharpened in that he is among a crew who are so lacking in dignity that they hardly think enough of what they are supposed to be. The catastrophe occurs. The *Patna,* with its innocent, helpless, crowded cargo of Moslem pilgrims, sinks. Jim, to save himself, abandons the doomed ship with its mob of passengers. The aftermath is predictable. Jim defends himself with angry justification. Anticipating criticism, humiliating insults, he is alternatively depressed and convinced that he is blameless. Forgiveness is denied him in his self-condemnation; he is the object of severe censure that he both expects and feels he deserves.

It is not only what he did that turns all to ashes, but in the loss in self-esteem, he is thrown from the pinnacle his day-dreams had taken him. With his aspirations gone, his lofty distinction from the crew erased, and, not ever understanding quite "his own artful dodges to escape from the grim shadow of self knowledge," he is left with a "far away look of fierce yearning after that missed distinction" of a heroic role. Instead, he suffers nightmares of being a victim. When he leaped from the ship, he "jumped into a well — into an everlasting hold . . . from a height he could never scale again." Jim had "loved to imagine himself a glorious racehorse, and now he was con-demned to toil without honour like a costermonger's donkey. He did it very well."[6] His torment was more from his loss than what he actually had done.

Marlow, the narrator, takes us to witness Jim's redemption, i.e., his honor, on a remote island of a Pacific archipelago. It was among an alien people for whom he had no past and was thus anonymous, where, in Jim's words

> existence is necessary — you see, absolutely necessary — to anoth-er person. I am made to feel that . . . it is a trust. . . . I believe I am equal to it. . . . If you ask them who is brave — who is true — who is just — who is it they would trust with their lives — they would say, Tuan Jim. . . . They can never know the real truth.[7]

Conrad's novel is not a clinical study, but, through his narrator's words, we are reminded that a man's self-esteem demands "putting out of sight all reminders of our folly, of our weakness, of our morality; all that makes against our efficiency — the memory of our failures, the hints of our undying fears, the bodies of our dead friends."[8]

Lord Jim shows masculinity's narcissism is precariously perched. As Conrad wrote, you must be able at times to "fling away your daily bread so as to get your hands free for a grapple with a ghost."[9] To do otherwise is to become a victim. The loss is in self-esteem; the suffering is in ignominy.

* * *

We have seen that the emotional conflicts that men develop in boyhood and associate with masculinity are carried through youth to maturity. A popular fiction and an unverified scientific supposition is that men, especially the ones who have won distinction, as though by consent, yield to the dictates of their limitations and thus they gain an earned relief from its discontents. However, we have no evidence that this is the case. We have observed that men, contrary to received belief, do not accept their limitations. In fact, the reach for self-esteem exceeds its grasp. Is achievement sufficiently sustaining to a man that his appetite for its fruits is glutted? And does he no longer need thus to be nourished?

We find that, in his more sophisticated years, when the marks of mastery have accrued and the signs of success are evident, a man uses his achievement as critical buttresses to the structure of masculinity and displays them, sometimes consciously in boyish pride. With a youthful exuberance, he makes of these accomplishments patents of achievement that resist being put aside in the years of manhood. The adult years, given to the acquisition of both experience and practical knowledge or finished skill and technology, do not put aside the egoism associated with prowess or performance conveyed from the earlier ones.

Masculinity is thus an alloy of self-esteem and performance or achievement that performance is turned to. Unique properties evolve from this composition, which is maintained but never completed. While masculinity develops and matures, it is prone to relapse into its previous states. Self-esteem that no longer continues to be earned through performance or achievement, or is impoverished of accomplishment, affects the bond, and it can fail. Self-esteem has unstable properties. Without continuing performance, either in fact or in fantasy, self-esteem diminishes, and periods of emotional depression invariably occur. The keystone to depression is the withdrawal, diminution, or impairment of self-esteem; when that occurs in men, their masculinity is threatened and can result in depressions that are often of clinical proportions.

Men with past triumphs or who have surmounted recognizable difficulties are not spared this fate. Winning honors or wearing badges as testimonials are not without significance but their lasting effect becomes superficial or cosmetic in masculine narcissism. Insufficient to sustain self-esteem, like all ornamentation or embellishment, a renewal and thus a real (more than a wished-for or supposed) achievement dispels discontent with the self that is otherwise inescapably revived. Relief from lowered self-esteem becomes pressing. Either it serves as an engine of change to further performance or achievement, or else deliverance may be found in fantasy. In one case above, reality may be sacrificed for the needed balm to self-esteem. The lives of small boys, as we have observed here, are filled with great expectations. The limitations that they feel compel them to the future. The more private aspects of men show that the same thirst for accomplishment and self-esteem is not slaked by mere wishes, nor satisfied for long.

The continuing need to furnish proof of masculinity, especially to oneself, remains. It has long been assumed that its object is only to demonstrate it to others. The egocentric need to gain that affirmation and thus exhibit it for oneself has been neglected. The periods of masculine development give proof of its variation. What is appropriate or possible for one phase is not fitted for another, just as the culture, changes in the role of circumstance, or custom add to the vicissitudes of what constitutes evidence of masculinity. Regardless of these considerations, the need to prove it remains.

A young, married teacher, Barnes, had easily and successfully earned an advanced academic degree. Without much delay, he obtained an untenured college appointment where he was regarded as a promising member of the faculty. Nevertheless, he seemed not to overcome the disconcerting conviction that his scholastic achievement was founded on some indulgent oversight of his teachers and the college trustees more than a measure of his real success. Yet, he was fully aware that his diligence, coupled with his ability, had truly been rewarded. Because of his unshakable discontent, which periods of well-being could not dispel for long, he came for treatment.

Slight events with disappointing outcomes gave rise to inappropriate reactions of despair; their recurrence gave him the sense that he was a victim, not, however, only of circumstance, which he had long thought, but, rather, of some inner, disquieting, elusive flaw or limitation. This brought to light an old conviction that he could not expect to do so well as a somewhat older brother whom he always envied for being capable with the least effort, as it seemed to him. In actuality, this was not the case: the brother was simply modestly settled into a routine administrative job that gave him steady increments of pay and security. Our man, however, had endlessly compared himself unfavorably from the time that he was a youth, unaware that it was envy. He spent countless hours in despair and self-pity, fantasizing about running away from home, when he was a child, and now, running from his wife and children.

These periods came on with disappointments following fragmentarily unconscious fantasies of expectations of grand achievements. His apprehensions increased. They also came from omens he read into his work. Just as in games in which, as a boy, he did not sufficiently distinguish himself according to his ambitions, so in his present tasks, if he were less than he judged to be excellent, he became morose.

A searching psychoanalytic exploration of the earlier times showed that all such self-deprecation was related to his dismay at the extent to which he was being like his mother. As a schoolboy, he had perceived challenges in his lessons or with his friends as contests in which he expected to lose, and efforts at self-assertion were precluded, because he was certain that they would lead to further humiliation in defeat. He associated such ideas with his mother when he compared her with his father, and himself, as compared to his brother. He only imitated other boys, whose exploits he sometimes dared to engage in. His air of bravado masked his privately held fears that he was insufficiently masculine. At college, he was no different. There he was fearful that he would not perform well academically, and there was a sexual parallel: he was afraid of being impotent. He found some relief from the self-denigration in fantasies that he would join men with large penises, and they would rape a girl. It was not simply the ideas connected with brutality that gave him some respite from his inhibitions. He thought himself an observer, but in the scenes of a "great" performance, he was a participant.

During intercourse with his wife, Barnes sustained his sexual excitement with these images and fantasies. They actually replaced his wife much as they had in his earlier, premarital sexual experiences. He would thus feel less pressure to perform and lower his anxiety, distracting himself by retreating into the fantasies, which were not deliberately invoked but came with sexual arousal. Through these fantasies, he was able to feel that he was an effective sexual partner to his wife. He attributed it to some lucky accident that he performed successfully during intercourse, just as he had previously done when he received a good grade at school. This way he avoided the recognition of any deliberate intention on his part. Inwardly, he gloated, but the fears that next time

227

would again test him remained, waiting for the occasion. Sexuality was defined as an adventitious action rather than expressive of a relationship.

There were fleeting moments of a loving experience. He was eager to hold on to them, but they were elusive. As he could not sustain them, he despaired. He felt closest to his wife when it was as though she were a counterpart of himself, the feminine part. It brought out the compelling need to display prowess and made giving a masculine performance more pressing. He believed that he would gladly have traded for a passive feminine role were it not so abhorrent to the prized masculinity he pursued.

Psychologically, he resembled another young man, Wilson, who was not married and who had numerous sexual exploits with a variety of women. This man was never in love, nor actually intimate with any of these women. It was only important that they appeared to others to be intimate. That would create the impression of conquests and thus achievement. Some of the women were his own age, others were a bit older, some were married, which represented a private triumph over the anonymous husband; and a number of them wanted to marry him. All of these experiences glutted his masculine narcissism.

At a time when he needed some "relief" from driving himself in work, which, to him, was tantamount to proving himself, i.e., his masculinity, he found it in the company of a contemporary whom he admired. He even idealized him as a model. The intensity of their mutual interest in each other soon led to a homosexual relationship in which he was the passive, feminine partner. It lasted several months. His passionate interest in the other man was as if he were peering constantly into a mirror that reflected his own, idealized image of himself. He neither actually perceived the other man nor understood him as separate from himself. The more he idealized the other man, the less, on reflection, was he himself masculine. He became so alarmed that he was near panic and he abruptly broke off the relationship. He sought treatment to be "rid" of his homosexual "temptations."

His early expressed notion was that he merely needed rules of conduct instilled in him. By following these rules he would be spared his dread of "feminine weakness." He regarded his "neat, careful ways," his "lacking being robust," at times a "weak will" and "little power," his sensitivity to physical pain and a readiness to show emotions all betray "feminine qualities." He abhorred them, was at a loss how to escape them; they often found appeal in relations with women. He was consciously unaware that these qualities he attributed to women degraded them. He only discovered in treatment that he had retained such ideas since boyhood. More startling to him was the disclosure of his unconscious identification with women, especially when he thought of himself in critical terms. His urgent incentive toward "perfection" revealed that he was "no better than a woman," "being like a woman, an imperfect man." The near-panic that drove him into treatment was approached as such inescapable self-abasing comparisons flooded him.

Wilson secretly admired men who were "violent, reckless, amoral," as he characterized the man with whom he had the brief homosexual experience, his ego-ideal. It was a clear demonstration of how much the homosexual relationship consists of an engagement with oneself, looking into one's own eyes and seeing in them the idealized image of the self. His fantasies about the man he would wish to be were expressed in the following way: "A man knows what to do, does what he knows, that's what I hope to get here, get rid of my feminine quality. Even more contemptible is a man who would like to be a woman. It's worse than being a woman. They can't help it. But not to want to be a man is to need to humiliate yourself so that you don't perform! To choose to be less of a man is to give up. What would be worse?

"It's the power connected with where the performance

comes in. It's not just having power. It's using it that I want. . . . With women I want, I give no mercy, be hard. Maybe I'm like that because I'm feminine in a masculine role. It's not to be cruel to women that I'm thinking of as it is being masculine. Without that, I'm asking to be a man without masculinity."

I asked him whether he wished himself to be in a woman's place. He responded, "The idea of being feminine, as we both found, when it's not so frightening, is in a way liberating. I'd like being taken care of. It's a hard life being a man. As a wife, it's simple. Just lie there and need only accept. Do nothing. The penis is something to worry about. I remember as an adolescent I'd look at it. I stared at it in the mirror, and I'd wonder, will it tell me what to do? I knew what I wanted to do with it to girls, but I'd worry, will it do its job? I used to think maybe it's easier to give up being a male, but it doesn't do anything for masculinity to be 'gay.' The 'gays' don't really want to be men; and they can't be women. As I said before, can you really be a man and not masculine?"

Barnes remained unreconciled until treated, despite his real achievements in a good marriage and success in his profession. As a boy, he was rankled by his limitations. He was often captured by daydreams of running away from home to where secret wishes for adventure and the realization of a boy's masculine aspirations would be found. They would far exceed what seemed possible in the narrow limits that everyday life imposed. Where great achievements would be realized, nonentity would be lost. What he had in fact gained and won remained flawed. The strength of his identification with his mother and then his wife were the unconscious obstacles that barred his way to an ideal of masculinity purified of femininity by deeds. That cleansing, however, was more like a purge or an atonement for feminine wishes he required to realize the masculine ego-ideal that eluded him. He was saying, in effect, that if there were no feminine identification, a man's masculinity would be liberated.

The same could be the words of Wilson, whose feminine part of himself remained actively wishing to be gratified. In both men it created, as it always had, a course of unreconciled conflict. It was the unconscious similarity of conflicts about masculinity through which skeins of femininity are naturally woven that makes these men so alike in spite of their obvious differences. Each carried from boyhood the ego-ideal of masculinity as expressed in prowess and demanding its engagement in proved performance. For each one, masculinity requires endless reaffirmation as though it might outshout the feminine voice that resists and is not to be stilled.

Ordinarily, the fantasy of being a woman, which sometimes occurs in daydreams or in dreams during sleep, may be associated with the greatest alarm. When that is the consequence, it may proceed from arousing every shade of disquiet protest to extremes of panic of occasionally psychotic proportions or sheer nightmare not readily dispelled on awakening. The wish to be a woman is both longed-for and protested against in every phase of masculine experience. Hence, in each period of masculine development and perils it must be brought to some resolution. However, as by the quirks of circumstance it may be at any time unraveled, the same conflict again and again may have to be laid to rest. The interment is not permanent. To see one's wife as a counterpart of one's masculine self is to be drawn once more to the boyish view of a woman and into the conflicts in its wake. The tendency is to regard her benignly as merely receptive, simply passive. And, with that view, a man may expect to be spared his "burden" of performing.

Incidentally, all women could not possibly be so uniformly patterned, but these men do not identify themselves with the images of women who are aggressive, powerful, or even evil or gorgonlike. The general readiness of men to identify themselves with the aggressor has its exception here. The explanation most likely is that such women represent a menace to masculinity and the wish to be identified with a woman would not be best served by her personifying malevolence. It is important that she be quite the opposite. This is not to suggest that a man may not identify himself with hostile and aggressive women, but that is not his motive in choosing her. For both the men just cited, the wish to be identified with a woman indicates their deep-seated conflicts that they cannot solve as problems of their masculinity. They would not be better off through identification with an aggressive woman; and thus to be gorgonlike, which is unconsciously monstrous. At their work, they are in fact successful, but emotionally their real achievements leave them wanting. They take flight from their discontent into wishes to be feminine. Their predicament remains unresolved so long as they are impaled on its horns.

A man's lifelong, unconscious conception of himself contains a paradoxical inequity. On the one hand, he conceives of his masculinity as an advantage that begins with his awareness of his maleness; and on the other hand, a "burden," because he is obliged to perform. This, too, is both instilled very early in his psychology and is compounded by his self-representation in which he sees himself in terms of a little boy's devotion to prowess. However, from his unconsciously sought-after identification with his mother, it offers a respite from the ordeal of masculinity. The image of a secure, assured, stable masculinity is a wish, a fantasy, an aspiration that reality mocks all too often. The early years of boyhood are notoriously ones in which masculinity lacks certainty. That is one of its powerful engines toward prowess and mastery. The periods of older boyhood and youth give promise that the fulfillment of masculinity brings manhood. Without end, in varying degrees of awareness, this process goes on. This is not to suggest that a woman is an unconsciously present image before whom a man must knowingly or not display his capabilities. That is often the case, but perhaps even more so is the masculine self-representation that must be satisfied and is another engine to provide fulfillment for the demands of masculinity.

Masculinity has a task that is carried from boyhood. Among

his fellows, a boy must prove himself in the band of his companions that was formed, among other motives, to escape women. But the need to perform and display prowess is not eluded with them, nor is it given up later. Masculinity must also be a capability that other men admire. Hence, the need to perform, to give the impression of it, and its banefulness as a property cannot be overstated. For instance, many men who reach so-called retirement age and are economically secure, maintain an "office." It may provide scarcely more than a stage where a man may daily appear, but it is sufficient to support the necessary illusion that he is still among his fellows working or pursuing his interests that hold his attention, and in which he performs his rounds of achievement. He is often deaf to his wife's pleas to remain at home. She is in effect unwittingly addressing him as Shakespeare's Fool does Lear: "Now thou art an O without a figure."

Perhaps no comment on the case is more rueful than Mark Twain's. Given to inventive play on biblical themes, he found the commandment "Thou shalt not commit adultery" especially galling to masculine prowess and a wry, irremedial inequity. In *Letters from the Earth*, Mark Twain wrote that the law of God

quite plainly expressed in woman's construction, is this: There shall be no limit put on your intercourse with the other sex sexually, at any time of life. [For the man, however,] God's law is this: During your entire life you shall be under inflexible limits and restrictions, sexually. . . . From the time a woman is seven years old until she dies of old age, she is ready for action, and *competent*. As competent as the candlestick to receive the candle. Competent every day, every night. Also, she *wants* that candle — yearns for it, longs for it, hankers after it, as commanded by the law of God in her heart.

But man is only briefly competent from the age of sixteen or seventeen thence forward for thirty-five years. After fifty, his performance is of poor quality, the intervals between are wide, and its satisfaction of no great value to either party; whereas his great-grandmother is as good as new. There is nothing the matter with her plant. Her candlestick is as firm as ever, whereas his candle is increasingly softened and weakened by the weather of age, as the years go by, until at last it can no longer stand, and is mournfully laid to rest in the hope of a blessed resurrection which is never to come.[10]

The demand for masculine competence is not so narrowly limited as Mark Twain lampooned it. The imperative, however, for masculine capability dictates far in advance of a boy's adolescence, even before he is remotely capable, and the sharp pinch for its evidence abates neither as the "candle" weathers nor as it wanes.

The reaffirming proof of masculine competence a man requires may indeed be found in his conjugal bed, where a fruitful performance there gives him the assurance of masculine success that may tenuously extend to the marketplace. Nevertheless, he also carries with him, in his everyday struggles with little tasks that frequently are erratic, often brittle, and that, through circumstance, commonly escape control, the germinating seeds of discontent with his masculine ego. The gap from the ideal tends quickly to widen. As a result, painful reminiscences, always easily revived, are brought forth and evoke repressive denials of the long experience with the elusiveness of mastery, the self-demands for performance, and the slowly developed sense of competence. These are deeply set conflicts in men. They furnish the early-acquired sense that the need for greatness, superior achievement, or triumph over adversaries are like mirages and are beyond grasp. The disquieting apprehension of being easily gulled tends to be associated in men with hopelessness and fears of passivity. These feelings are expressed sexually in fears of impotence and the prophecy seems notoriously often to be fulfilled.

Relief is sought through the creation of inner demands. These may come either in a choice of a feminine role that is not overt, in which passivity is rationalized as compelled by circumstance, a feminine role that is not threatening to masculine aspirations, or a feminine role by way of unconsciously finding the company of a man and thus to place even greater demands on oneself for evidence to parallel such conjured-up masculine adequacy. The underlying doubt, however, is not expunged. For instance, as in the so-called macho syndrome, the dread of feminine identification is acted out in often exaggerated, stereotyped reactions of conduct that the culture and style attribute and caricature to be masculine. This is as common a practice in the folkways of New Guinea as of New York. The masculine conflicts are the same, only the forms are somewhat different. The issue remains unresolved. The flight into femininity unconsciously continues to be pressing. It is often associated consciously with the further sacrifice of masculinity in wished-for pleasures from a man. Such desires bring with them a decline in one's masculine narcissism. As a reaction, a heightened need for self-esteem occurs. Paradoxically, the more pressing the need, the greater the vulnerability to injury, and the "slings and arrow of outrageous Fortune" seem to find their mark more easily.

As we have observed, in each of the earlier phases of masculine development, it is in the relationship to men, at times even more than it is in the company of women, where the conflicts of the masculine ego are brought nearest to an equilibrium and closest to one of its most serious disorders. The most intensely dramatic are to be observed in the homosexual panic in which homicidal mania is not rare. The desperate terror that unconscious homosexual wishes may create, masked by intense anxiety, often goes unrecognized clinically. In various forms these fears are common to men and virtually unparalleled, clinically, in women. Homosexual fears are clinically unknown in very young girls and are ordinary in boys. Further, homosexual panic states are clinically common in men and rare in women.

Psychoanalytic theory holds almost universally that it is a mother's excessive intimacy with her son that is the root of his homosexual development. The evidence that supports it is consistently convincing. There are occasionally other factors as well, but they do not contradict this theory. According to the succinct and authoritative comment by Socarides, "These mothers exert a binding influence through preferential treatment and seductiveness on the one hand and inhibiting, over-controlling attitudes on the other. In many instances the son was the most significant individual in their lives."[11]

It is generally found that the son feels he has usurped his father's place and bears, as a result, an inordinate, but often not conscious, sense of guilt for it. When such a relationship with a mother develops, it gives a boy's incestuous fantasies real substance. His conflicts are plainly predictable. Commonly, they are that he should find ways to terminate his mother's preference for him. Also present is his desire neither to yield to nor to forgo his mother's choice. He is firmly set in doubts. Whether he will dislodge himself and, if so, how he will go about it profoundly affect his growing masculinity.

The boy's conflict creates ambivalence toward his mother that may be expressed by an unwarranted hostility over some trifling encounter to declare his freedom, or by the opposite reaction of being overly solicitous of her wishes to indicate his close attachment. Neither the protests nor the provocations necessarily lead to independence. They may merely create the sense of a defense against his wishes to submit to his mother's aims. Because of the importance of the relationship, it is not to be expunged but only its value may be affected. That is to say, when the experience is limited by devaluing it as fruitless, it can be given up. We quit what is profitless. But when a mother's needs for her son fail to allow this to take place, the mother and son retain deep-seated conflicts, often in spite of the appearance of compatibility. These conflicts tend to further the son's homosexuality.

Because of the position the boy is put in by his mother, he develops extravagant egoistic fantasies he is loath to abandon. The narcissistic appetite increases. In the fantasies that feed it, the son raises himself above his father, who he prefers to believe is weak and hardly a fit consort for his mother, whom he tends to idealize. In identifying with his father, the boy expects his father to be angry at being displaced. Here, too, the boy is of two minds. He would like to appease his father. It would relieve him of his guilt and anxiety. One unconscious solution is to be in his mother's place and thus admired for her qualities, especially the ones he idealizes and boyishly conceives of as feminine. They are often no more than a boy's caricature of femininity that parallel his "Superman" traits that he believes are required of him as he replaces his father. Three-quarters of a century after Freud's case of "Little Hans," it still remains the most objective example of the dynamic significance of a boy's early relationship with his mother where the beginning homosexual development may be observed. It will be recalled that Freud, having given this unique demonstration of a small boy's oedipal conflicts, concluded that what he found in "Little Hans" simply confirmed what he had long before discovered to be normally present in the early psychosexual history of men.

It is the outcome of these conflicts that is not so deterministically fixed as analysts have tended to believe. The importance of a boy's early attachment to his mother is in no way extraordinary. However, it is its unmodified persistence, in which there is a lasting identification with her beyond early boyhood, that has its profound effects in his masculine development. As we have seen, conflicts resulting from a continuing identification may intensify the drive toward masculinity. It thus successfully represses and brings relief from the burden he must otherwise carry. When this drive fails to develop, a lasting identification with one's mother may set a boy on a course of masculinity where homosexuality is the outcome. We have also observed that the most secure solution to these heavy issues for a boy is when he begins to enjoy masculinity among his fellows. There, in the later years of boyhood, before becoming a youth, masculinity has its greatest freedom. Some of it remains as a residue throughout a man's life. It may well be why this time in a boy's life has always caught the romantic imagination of writers, and, paradoxically, it is the period that analysts have written the least about.

While the conflicts of identification with the mother may have played out on the surface by early adulthood, there can be an enduring resonance of them in maturity, as the following example illustrates.

A late-middle-aged man, McKay, had made such a notable success of a business through his own efforts and inventions that he finally acquired complete ownership. After a number of years, in which he enjoyed his winnings, a large conglomerate enterprise made him a generous offer for its purchase. The proposal from the outset was tempting. It offered him undreamed-of financial rewards. The prospect of leisure time, which he had scarcely ever had and now could easily fill, was also appealing. Moreover, he was to remain with the company to continue to give it his direction. This was to be a real and not merely, as often happens, a titular position. To him, the only difference was that his company would become part of an aggregate. It was expected by the officers of the company and by the buyers that the sale would be consummated, but, to the astonishment of all, McKay refused to sell when they were on the brink of celebrating the occasion.

McKay was relieved by his decision, but he was left with doubts as to its wisdom. For nearly a year thereafter, the matter remained closed to discussion, although his doubts about what he had done remained. At times, he confided some of them to his associates. As the business continued to prosper, he drew on that for comfort, but his doubts were not dispelled as wisdom and riches became fused into further elevated success.

The matter was reopened by the reappearance of the buyers. They came this time with still better offers. McKay revealed to them his fears of relinquishing control of the company he had given so many years' work to acquire. With their reassurances that he would not have to give up the direction of his company, and although he was still somewhat fearful and uncertain about his anxiety when all the material aspects would be fully satisfied, he agreed and sold.

With the acquisition completed, McKay's apprehensions left him, and he became elated. His doubts were gone. He was wealthier than he had ever anticipated. He became an officer in the parent company, the director of his own company, and he saw at first hand that the new owners were pleased with him as their new possession.

Only he knew that the real basis for his reluctance to change was his private need, which was to have the company be solely his. He could not tolerate having anyone over him in authority. This was hardly a conscious idea, but more a vague and fleeting fear that was dispelled by the pleasure he had in the feeling of walking about the plant premises and sitting in his office when he knew he had no "boss" over him. Until he was himself the head of the company he had always worked well and compatibly with other men. Much of his reputation had been built on the cultivated good quality of his relationships with them. They were like "buddies" engaged in a mutual enterprise. As he rose to higher positions of authority, he was aware that the power he was acquiring made him less anxious and directly most amenable to those who worked under him. His associates were not rivals over whom he triumphed; they were a band who looked to him for his abilities and his leadership. He willingly and generously shared his rewards but not the command. Now, however, with the new state of affairs, his fears about a change in command were realized. He now had someone "over" him, even though this was only in the nature of the large corporate structure in which there were officers who ranked above him, but who were hardly aware of the nature of his work and gave him no direction to follow. He was responsible for his company, now a division of the conglomerate. Nevertheless, he had the fear that he was "under" someone; he became depressed; and he reluctantly came for help.

His first remarks were, "I have to adjust my level of vanity to the level of my reality. I can't seem to do it. I get ideas from it that I want to drop dead, get run over, be killed. I even feel like doing it myself. I thought I was strong enough to face anything. And I have faced a lot. But what will I do? Just sit by the fire like an old woman? Wait for the days to go by?

After some exploration into his feelings of a lack of strength and disillusionment with himself, he went on to explain that he was most depressed at work. Admittedly, there was no change made at the plant. "Where before I would decide how aggressive I was going to be, now I feel *I'm* being pushed. This kind of masculinity seems colder, crueler, more ruthless. People expect security from me. I like to give it. Now, it's not just up to me. I'd rather be dead. I have to make up for losing an image of myself. I fear some downtrend even when there is none. I'm watching, monitoring, observing myself; I always have. I enjoy it as keeping me alive. But, now, an image of myself with a big vanity seems gone. I'd rather drop dead with present achievements than just go on with the rewards of what I did. Will what I did in the last twenty-five years happen in the next twenty, or will I have to rest on what I got or did? My self-esteem depends on it. There are so many things I won't try now, because they may not be good enough or special enough. I have to be sure what I do is special. Before, at work, I was pretty sure it was, but not now.

"It must go back to my mother, who always treated me as special over my sisters, maybe it was that I was the only boy. But even more than my father, she filled me not only with what I was but what she expected of me. Not for her sake, but for mine. She was sure she could see how I was going to turn out. I filled her dream for me. If she could have lived to see me.

"I'm reminded that I always measure my competence; even in my wife's pleasure. I can't help doing it. I'm only comfortable when I know I have satisfied her sexually, even when it does not matter that much to her. Otherwise, I don't feel very masculine. I know I shouldn't mind this. She doesn't; I do. My image of masculinity is to possess a woman and not be concerned with her. In a way, that's what happens, but I have to be sure I'm wanted. I have to measure her reactions. I do the same at work. Can you imagine at my age thinking this way, questioning my masculinity? I insist on sex at times to have my way. Don Juan wanted to perform all over the place and all the time. I don't want to show I have that in mind. I don't want to act as if I have masculinity only on my mind. I don't. But, in a way, I guess I do.

"When I get depressed, I have to give up all these ideas about the success I had and that I could have. Some of the reason for not selling was selling out my success. That was what the sale of the business really had behind it. At the time, I was not so conscious of it as now. I had a lot of success or they wouldn't have been after me. I had to shrink from all that. It makes me look modest. I don't do that on purpose, but I can only stand success for a few days and then get moody. I have to escape from success is what it sounds like. I plot doing great things. Then I get scared I can't pull them off. When I do, which happens enough, I'm delighted. But then I think this is what I sold, I think I sold the machinery in me. My masculinity got sold.

"It's like a guy bought me. I have to be the big man. I enjoy being the boss. I've never admitted it. I'm even good at it. Even with more money than I'll ever need, it's not the same thing as before. I don't have the power. I feel less a man. It's like I made a marriage and have a man over me. It feels like slavery, womanly. And I weakened myself."

His capitulation and feelings of loss were contradicted by the actuality of what had occurred. They sharpened the fact that all his real gains, advantages, and freedom were not a cause of, but effected, deeper conflicts. Those lay in the allusions he made to losing masculinity, being feminine, weakened, and anxious. On the one hand, he was now more powerful and rich than before, and it gave him a freedom to exercise his ability and his strength that he previously had to curb while he was solely responsible in his own company. Now he could do as he wished, which was what he always wanted, but he feared that he had a "someone" over him who could do that with him, and who might wish to act as he so often wanted to in relation to others. This supported his notion of being masculine. He recalled how he hated authority when he was a boy and that he could hardly wait to get it for himself. "To give it up, even if only some of it, I guess, is what depresses me." Any yielding of it is not authority in a personal sense, but is masculinity. He felt he could ill afford to yield any. Forcing himself to submit, as he saw the transaction, was a cause for alarm. "To submit is a fright, a terror of somebody on top. This goes all the way back to being a boy."

After his recovery was well under way, he brought out his feeling that "all men want to get ahead, be on top and no underdog position." After going on in this vein, he said, "It's a scene from two dogs screwing. It's appalling. The other dog, when I'm on top, can't like it. I'm amazed I have this fear. It never happened. I guess I put myself in that place. To hand over the company for a takeover has nothing to do with the profits. It's lying down for those guys. My masculinity needs me on top or I won't survive. It's not the competition so much as the achievement that puts me where I have to be. So long as I can perform, my masculinity survives. I play a game with myself, privately. I can't remember when I started it. It was proving myself, pulling off something big. I was like this as a kid, maybe eight or nine. I felt I was watched by my mother and sisters, not so much my father, as to how I performed. I wanted to keep up the idea of being special. That's not so different from what I said about my work. It's ridiculous to enjoy prestige so much. It's not the hard work I mind as it is the burden of having to be great, having distinction. If I can't be terrific, I don't want to do anything.

"I knew all along what it meant privately to make that kind of bargain in the business. You sell yourself a deal. Then I can be told what to do. I feel like I'm on my knees in front of some guy. It's frightening to submit to that. I feel a disaster will occur. I have it in mind wherever I am. It crops up."

McKay's explorations of some of his oldest conflicts involved the demonstration of prowess, the development of mastery, and the rewards of achievement. To him, all were expressions of masculine development and some of its vicissitudes. It began, he tells it, with being watched by his mother and sisters in their attentiveness and pride in his prowess. This is more likely his fantasy in that period of his development, when he was absorbed in watching his own prowess. While the others may indeed have been as observant as he thought they were, he was also projecting on to them what he had early learned about himself and his unique differences from them, which he had certainly noted. He suggested that his father was little concerned with his performances or his prowess, and while this may have been the case, the fact that the women were intent on him had its particular importance. His impression, which he carried into manhood, was that, emotionally, they were invested in his achievements, much as, later, his wife was. He was very reluctant to admit that what he achieved gave him a "top-dog" position in relation to his admirers in the family.

After he disclosed his guilty pleasures, his impulses to be a "tough" dog to deal with, he feared that he would indulge them in his new job, which, in many respects, relieved him of direct responsibilities and somewhat loosened his employment of his talents. He was anxious about the removal of the restraints that had been on him when he was solely in charge of his company. He felt that his impulse was too masculine and that he had to retreat a bit from it. McKay's well-being depended, in large measure, unconsciously in the security that his masculinity was not weakened by all that he associated with femininity in himself through his identification with his mother and sisters, his wife, and even his men associates at work over whom he was "boss." Of course, his father was the "top-dog" ideal whom he longed to emulate as he was earning the admiration of the women in the family. We get his impression that his father was not very impressed with McKay, but the women were envious and proud of him. He performed for them.

The broad assumption that analysts have made is that a boy's identification with his mother, and his sisters, as is the case with McKay, menaces his masculinity. The further notion is that he has no alternative but to embrace the feminine identification. The reaction to that is overlooked. Most boys are goaded into a high masculine ideal to which self-esteem is nailed. McKay illustrates what we have observed in earlier periods of the masculine experience. It is that the identification with femininity is narrowly tolerated. It thus remains a menace to the masculine ego or self-esteem. He shows its vulnerability when circumstances take on a particular significance, i.e., when they impinge on conflicts of masculinity even when the conflicts have their setting in the marketplace rather than in the marital bed. McKay's masculine qualities needed to be reaffirmed not in relation to his wife and family so much as in relation to other men.

McKay's case is not unique. A completely different sort of family produced many similar problems in a man we shall call Phillips. A senior partner in a large business, he was inventive, clever, and had the productive capacity for long hours of fatiguing work that won his partners' envy. He was financially secure, which came in large part from his earnings, together with some small independent income of his wife. Phillips was nearly fifty years old. He was in very good condition and prided himself on his fitness. In short, he was a healthy, active, and vigorous man in early middle age.

He came to see me because he was having unaccountable periods of impotence and equally unpredictable outbursts of temper. At home, occasionally while driving his car, in raging at his wife, with whom he had a very good, devoted relationship, and at their three children, his impulsive anger burst out of bounds. He did not become violent but was reckless. Both the impotence and the rages pained him. He was left for days after with remorse. Although the impotence was not a common occurrence and aroused no complaint from his wife, who was on other occasions of their intercourse sufficiently satisfied, it was chiefly this that caused him to get help with his temper.

Unlike McKay, who never had more than modest means until he made his own success, Phillips came from a large, affluent, aggressive family in which, as far as he could recall, he was his father's favorite. The father, a model of aggressive success, was eager that his son continue in his place. His father had died years before, and Phillips, although favored, had earned his place.

One element in his aggression came early out of unconscious assocations. "I have a tendency to look for people like my father. I go out of my way to do it. I am not neutral. And look to see if someone is taking advantage of me. I'm on the lookout for aggressions against me and I'll feel like getting violent. Then I can't give vent to it." He realized his father was a model of aggression, but he was far less aware of being identified with him through aggression than of its being connected with his fears of being victimized. Phillips did not fear women; it was men he kept vigilant about.

On one occasion, he spoke of his father as "shitting on me to get me to do what he had in mind or what he wanted. He'd call me helpless for the slightest show of not doing best. I felt like nothing. I could murder him. As I think of him even now, I could do it. It didn't matter to me what good things my sisters and mother thought of me. Instead, I'd be thinking how to settle my score with him. I'd have in mind getting my independence. He'd hate that. I'll not have my freedom just handed to me. It's no good that way. I want it by force.

"I'd think of others being aggressive. I want to be the one to enforce the law. I've had those ideas since I can remember. But I'd have notions of being the victim, resisting and having to get tortured, or acting in self-defense. As a victim, I could do anything to justify my violence. I can picture myself now pretty violent. With that sort of excuse, I'd let myself loose. I can't stand being a victim.

245

"I have a contradiction in me. I can put myself in the place of the victim and feel what it's like. My wife's willingness gets me mad. In her place, I have to get revenge. As a victim, on the other hand, I feel like a little girl, submissive. Do I stand up to my father? He won't take it. Do I lie down for him? For my self-respect as a man, I don't take it. I think it means being buggered. My masculinity is at stake.

"I am not loved for what I am. Only for what I do. It's the same at work or in bed with my wife. I watch for it. How's the performance going to be judged? Could I be loved without a test or not for merit? The answer is the same: No! I get furious for being limited or having limits put on me.

"A limitation is in my mind a fault, and a fault is a flaw in masculinity; and I have a fault in me. I know this is an absurd notion to carry around. It depresses me. Even in intercourse, either I give myself medals or demerits.

"I imagine being with a woman to whom I have no commitment. I could be sexual without performance on my mind. It 'feminizes' me not to be tested for my prowess. I'd like to be free of that. With a strange woman, like a whore, I'd not be committed and be free, without limits. That's real manhood: to be without limits."

Retaining his boyhood image of his father, he said, "A guy who dominates men is a real man, more one than if he just dominates women. We used to play this as kids for hours and hours. What's the use of being king just to get a queen? It's to beat the other guys, too, that counts more. God willfully made man with limitations. No wonder Superman is a hero; he has no anxieties, no failures, no fears. Being a man is perilous and competitive. I'm that. It's important to self-esteem. I always wanted to be Superman as a kid. When I first read him, I thought, what will I do? How will I perform? I want to defy, defame, and feel like a demon when that part of me threatens to get out. Not to let it is masculinity in chains."

My comments to him were directed to his own experience living with a "superman," his father, as he saw him and as he

246

wanted to be so identified. His father had promoted it in his own son. It is from his father that, as a boy, Phillips conceived the idea that women, and men as well, are to be subordinated. Even as a small boy he abhorred these qualities in his father. Yet he now in part supported them in himself. Either he must feel he is a "superman" or else he must be subordinate. He was enmeshed in conflict either way. Recognizing this dilemma, he responded, "I guess Superman is still my ideal of a man. But I'm forced to accept less. My distance from Superman shows my failing. I'm no different from a woman. I have to grudgingly accept less. It's ridiculous to find I'm tied to a comic book myth. It debases all that I have, all that I do. I think it's a malignant myth of masculinity to be tied to that. Is being less being like Dr. Richards? [Phillips was referring to the transsexual, the man who had his genitals surgically removed, having complained that he was a woman in a man's body as in the case of James Morris.] He just carried it out to an extreme to make himself a woman, a penisless creature. Sometimes, I don't want to get too close to that repulsive wound. When I think that, then only a scrubbed whore, I imagine, or what I see in a porno magazine can get me excited.

"Do I want that a woman should not be limited? I know how much I hate it. I know how they must feel. And can they get by it by way of a man? They want what I have. It's not natural to be without a penis. I don't blame them for what they want. When I think of it, it makes intercourse with my wife a problem. This is when my whole sexual impulse disappears. After that, total impotence. The whole subject gets blocked. And good riddance. It's not just my wife. I want sex with no one. It's like the real thing is dangerous. Now I know what turns me off! It's liberating to hold a mirror up to myself but I don't like it. I'm living like a lot of men. This is no pipe dream, myth, or comic book type to feel if my masculinity goes, I have nothing, no incentive to work and forever cut out of any grand self. That's where relations with a woman are performance. It's a conceit, a judgment. I was brought up in it not to be content with less, the ordinary, that goes for the feminine. Can I stand that fate? Not to be straining to be Superman? I'll have to."

Phillips showed, only in sharper relief than we would find in less neurotic men, that a constant unconscious threat posed to masculinity is in the ineradicable identification with a woman. It is all the more plain inasmuch as he was groomed, exhorted, and rewarded for his identification with his seemingly "superman" father. Any faltering short of that ideal created the risk of being less a man, which meant being more a woman. As we see, the natural identification with her is not one simply confined to boyhood and then extended merely to periods of development. The unconscious conflicts in masculinity resist a lasting resolution. A man's femininity does not get expunged. Rather than compromising it, to spare himself fears, a man has to accept this quality of his masculinity.

Phillips's privately held, universal boyhood repugnance of the female genital continued to hold some of its original horror. Under duress from his discomfort over notions of the woman's genital, it remained a "cave." However, Phillips found that he could venture into it and find pleasure where previously he had only fleetingly enjoyed it. Although he could not altogether escape his unconscious childhood aversion, nevertheless he was able to become more loving and intimate with his wife than before seemed possible.

* * *

In our culture, divorce after decades of marriage is becoming increasingly common and is in fact the result of a particular problem of masculinity that develops in a man's middle years. The emotional importance of his work or pursuits divide his libido. It has always been the case. But in many instances, his work may absorb an increasing share. It is not necessarily the demands of the work itself, which has often been a man's rationalization for his condition, into which he has, as a rule, little insight. Rather, it is the increasing demands from his own masculine narcissism that drive him to wrest it from his occupation. His wife, however willing, cannot fulfill them. His immediate sexual activity or needs become less pressing than they were in decades past. The sexual focus in the earlier years of adult life is now shared to a greater degree with work. Masculine narcissism, however, does not diminish with this dispersion. Paradoxically, as the self-demand for performance and achievement, rather than sexual prowess, become pressed into satsifying the continuing demands of a man's narcissism, his increased coercion is reflected in the further gratification work must furnish.

Naturally, the realities of aging are resisted. However, the scope by which these realities may be held off is widened rather than narrowed. Work, a needed source of narcissistic gratification, makes it a broadened, valued source of such diverted satisfaction. Work that fails to furnish the deeper needs of compensation heightens masculine narcissism. In this case, it results in men who are often sad, feel aimless, are prone to periods of depression that may become clinically significant if unrelieved. The need turns to rest more heavily on social approbation to be found in the company of men rather than from women or from one's wife. The impaired self-esteem such men often suffer creates an underlying resentment that they project upon their wives as being inattentive or otherwise slighting them for pursuing their own interests. Of course, such attitudes are not strictly confined to their nearest relationships.

The waning sexual interest that men may feel in the second and third decades of marriage, which strains the relationship with a woman, is often variously attributed to being solely a natural function of the passage of time and emotional and physiological changes. The altered significance of work at this period of life, that has its profound effect on the man's ego, tends to receive the least notice as an increasingly important factor to satisfy masculinity.

A woman is as well but differently affected by her own fading self-image. She, too, has an increase in narcissistic demands for self-verification. However, as neither prowess nor achievement mean to her what they do to a man, she must turn to him for an endorsement of herself, even if she has a career equal to his. In short, while she depends on the man for her narcissistic affirmation, he depends less directly on sexuality for affirmation of his masculinity. That is, less on it as a demonstration of prowess, which he seeks from his work. This does not necessarily lead to diminished performance. His relation in work to other men represents an extended field for his achievement, where an added endorsement of his masculinity is gained. His wife's needs for him increase, but he turns more to work and its rewards for his masculine, narcissistic satisfaction. A woman's lament naturally often begins here.

We need to recall that, earlier in masculine development, the passage from being a small boy to boyhood showed a parallel dynamic. The small boy's need for a mother's endorsement of masculinity was associated with unconscious, grandiose expectations and extravagantly expressed, conscious wishes of exploits, prowess, achievement, and so forth. They all came to no fruition. This highly erotic, fanciful period ends in a colossal disappointment that falls on the little boy's narcissism. The intensity of this phase gives way to a recovery of narcissism and a start on its restitution through an impetus to activity. It is in the almost exclusively masculine company that this takes place.

The two phases are not identical. This later one is not a regression to the earlier one, although there is the temptation to regard some of the similarities as constituting a basis for that assumption. However, the dissolution of a marriage comes at a time when the man's narcissism is still tyrannically governed by performance, but it is one that depends less on his relation to his wife than on his performance at work or wherever else he may enjoy the esteem of other men or another woman related to his work as a colleague.

Few women perceive this shift in a man's narcissistic needs and tend to regard it as meaning an injury to their own worth or self-esteem, some failure on their part, or, if they are inclined to be less masochistic, they turn their hostility to feeling neglected and attribute their grievance to the man's apparent increased egocentric interests. The women are correct in their observations, but they cannot see what is around the corner, which is the narcissistic alteration in the man's ego that has taken place. The change is attacked as if it were a conscious choice the man has made. Both the man and his wife are aware of the change but ignorant of the motive.

*　　*　　*

We know little about the emotional conflicts of masculinity in aging. But there are sufficient consistent elements present in the conflicts throughout the development and maturity of masculinity that are carried into advanced years. The need for reaffirmed proof of prowess, performance, and achievement are, as we have seen, thoroughly present in a man's everyday psychology. We should not expect that they would be abandoned even though aging may impair their demonstration. A man's ruling emotional imperative remains his unique narcissism. As he finds those powers that he is accustomed to employ in its service dwindling, his narcissism increases. Where narcissism is concerned, aging is as insubordinate to time as it is to circumstance. In earlier years, the substitute for losses or the restitution that is found for them appeases one, but when restoration or reparations for resources depleted is no longer possible, narcissism is not placated, it is intensified.[12]

Aging assaults our narcissism. In his early years, a boy clearly perceives the precariousness of his self-esteem. Its friability is plain to the aging man and his narcissism has as significant a role as it had in the years before. However, as the substitute for losses is exhausted, narcissism is not appeased. With its increase, self-concern rises. Despite the burgeoning of both popular literature and scientific theories on the psychology of aging, i.e., the problems of the ego in aging, they have not illuminated or plumbed the depths and nature of the conflicts of a man's ego as he ages.

As much as aging is restive to circumstance, it nevertheless yields to it in one predominant way. Whereas in previous decades, the ego, the self, one's narcissism found expression to a significant degree in its investment in others, aging calls on reducing it in them. (This is not to suggest that dependence is diminished. We know it is not, but the dependence of this period represents an increase in self-interest that takes this form.) It corresponds unwittingly to being compelled to increase it in oneself. A man's narcissism is vulnerable to this course, and it has a particular propensity to take it. The point being made here is best illustrated in an essay of Freud's, "On Narcissism." He wrote that one's ego-interest and the libidinous may become indistinguishable from each other. He showed the familiar egoism of the sick person cover them both. One's interest then is devoted virtually wholly to oneself. "We find it so natural because we are certain that in the same situation we should behave in just the same way."[13]

A remarkable parallel takes place in aging. If we substitute the word "old" for the word "sick," Freud's statement exactly applies. The aging man, who yields unknowingly his previous critical judgment of himself, will in turn tend to overestimate in himself what he would have previously given less consideration, or he will dwell less preciously on his past achievements or prowess. He artlessly avoids what he fears might reduce his importance in his own eyes. It would weaken his self-esteem to do otherwise. Under these auspices, he refurbishes his past to be better than it was and retouches his body image so that it is not so vulnerable to the verdict his mirror reflects. To some extent, he thus becomes his own ideal, elevating himself and appeasing the demands his narcissism makes. It is a relentless need that presses a man for satisfaction he must search for and find in himself.[14]

A sixty-three-year-old, vigorous man, whom we will call Blaine, had a few extramarital affairs that he began during his forties. Married for nearly twenty years before he began them, he thought of them as hardly more than exercises in pornography. Recently, however, he had begun his first serious affair. He delighted in its accompanying grandiose fantasies. They were that he would leave his wife and at last enjoy a freedom he felt she had long stifled. He was bound to these fantasies without restraint, but for one obstacle: the burden of guilt. His wife had none of her usual suspicions of him, which paradoxically made him feel more guilty. It was at this point of depression that he came for treatment. He had become impotent.. It was this, as much if not more than his other depressive symptoms, that brought him to get help.

Blaine's previous illicit affairs had carried some important, unconscious, exciting meaning. The readiness with which women he pursued joined him and the private satisfaction he took in arousing their sexual appetites brought out a fascination with himself denied him by his wife's frigidity. It, moreover, aroused his disdain; he believed women were enslaved by their desires. (However, he did not apply the same measure to himself.) It was associated with the retained youthful fantasy that sex with women was for him an exercise in power. The deeper awareness of his fixation on sexuality as a cruel act a man enjoyed eluded him. He further rationalized his conduct with the notion that a woman takes abuse or may even solicit it. From other sources, I knew this was not the nature of his marriage, but I knew his wife was a neurotically fearful woman, timid, shy, and long-suffering with her children and her husband.

From the time that they had their children, Blaine felt that he had lost her deepest affections to them. His egotism was hurt by her choice. He was an indulgent father, but not intimate with his children. Throughout their years of marriage, he felt that his wife viewed their sexual relations with neither much enthusiasm nor any initiative. For a time, he blamed himself for it as a poor sexual performer, at fault because his wife made few or rare expressions of her sexual wishes. However, in time, he came to realize that she was a warm, but inhibited, anxious, and fearful woman. She was girlish in her close interests and shared most of them with a few women friends. He was excluded. He recalled that when he was a boy, his own mother was most engaged with her household and a brood of children, among whom he was not the favorite. Neither was he his father's favorite. The historical accuracy here is not so important as that Blaine carried the conviction that women, modeled on his mother, had little enthusiasm for sexual experience and more for children. His wife seemed to confirm his conviction. He was unaware, until he explored these reminiscences, how much his wife had the characteristics of his mother.

Blaine said of his relations with women other than his wife, "When a woman turns passionate, I am tempted not to give her anything, she wants a big man, craves it." The fantasy of being the master who tantalizes a slave was as irresistible to him in his advancing years as it had been in his earlier ones. His affairs had been brief. He would abruptly terminate them. There had been a few encounters with prostitutes when he was working away from home, but he was nearly always impotent. There were humiliating experiences: "The women were too professional."

During their entire married life, he said, he never escaped his wife's suspicions, although she had never discovered any actual evidence of his infidelity. However, his sexual adventures usually turned out to be hardly worthwhile because after them he would be guilty, contrite, and left with discontent compounded by his wife's suspicions.

Blaine and his wife became grandparents. His wife's attentions were increasingly engrossed with the arrival of each grandchild. The emotional distance between this aging couple widened. His wife's solution to their situation was to urge Blaine to retire from his work, which would permit them to spend more time with their grandchildren, who lived some distance away.

During his wife's excursions to visit their grandchildren, Blaine was angered that she was absorbed in her rejuvenated motherhood. She appeared to him to be more carefree in it than when she was herself a mother. It confirmed for him that she would rather be a mother than a wife, and, most of all, she wanted to be a grandmother.

As she insisted he work less and become more of a grandfather, he was angered. She was "forcing his age." He felt vigorous, enjoyed his very successful business with its variety of social obligations that his wife shunned. She continued to argue and finally prevailed on him to take extended vacations from work. After a few weeks of this regimen, during two winters, he found it unbearable. He said, "What could I do after a few games of cards, a couple of rounds of golf, and a few hours of sailing? Just sit around and call that a day with some old guys? No!" Each time, he returned to the city without his wife. Alarmed at the prospect of withdrawing into idleness rather than leisure, he emphasized to his wife that he was not prepared to "give up living," and that he felt that retirement was retiring from life.

The deeper emotional conflicts that these words concealed were that he felt his wife was encouraging him to deny himself the vigor he enjoyed and to accept passivity. It was to identify himself with her pursuits and aims. His rage increased. He believed she was fostering his giving up his activities to being "more a pussycat than a tom." It held one important meaning: to yield self-esteem and with it his masculinity. As he took an inventory of what he had long depended on in himself — that he showed few signs of his age and that his business was thriving — he had further proof that his wife's wishes were abhorrent proposals. He became less and less in a mood to relinquish what he had and what she would have him give up.

He kept himself physically trim with activities that had become part of his daily life. He took pride in his appearance. He was a bit of a dandy. He wore sports clothes somewhat more appropriate to a younger man. This was not a conspicuous display, but it was evidence of a resistance to his aging.

On the last occasion that he had left his wife behind on their "vacation," he began to have his first serious affair with a young middle-aged widow. In contrast to his wife's disinterest in sexual relations, this woman abandoned herself sexually. He felt with her as he had never before with a woman. His self-esteem soared. From having been far diminished by the threat of retirement and age that his wife had held up to him, he was relieved by his new feelings. His new experience was like a rejuvenation and the verification that his masculinity had not come to an end. He was in no mood to fall again into what he had so long resisted.

The woman did not press to marry Blaine, as he had proposed. She preferred the freedom outside marriage. I suspect that she had reason to suppose her relationship with Blaine would not be lasting. Not having to commit himself to her proved no relief to Blaine, as he had at first thought it might. Instead, the wish to be relieved of his wife, the fantasies that she might die, thinly veiled his wishes for license to pursue a new life. It also brought an increase of his depression.

Blaine had unwittingly made a Faustian bargain. For an escape from the limitations of age, he made his own private pact with this younger woman. In it, his self-esteem that depended on masculine prowess would be restored. But he would have to forfeit his married life and confirm all his wife's previously held suspicions. Unlike his earlier, transient peccadilloes when he was younger, as expressions of masculine narcissism, now his waning masculinity and diminished self-esteem made him more dependent on proving himself with a woman who would endorse it.

To satisfy his heightened narcissism required that he repudiate his wife and even be abandoned by his family for it. Its cost was in guilt, with the added anxiety of impotence. The consequence of his intentions was depression. From long experience, we know that depression has its roots in hostility toward one with whom we have an affectionate, close, or loving bond and with whom we are thus identified. The dictates of self-reproach turned the hostility away from his wife and away from the woman with whom he became impotent and toward himself as depression. Burdened by guilt, Blaine could not give up his wife, nor could he give up his newfound relationship at the expense of his masculinity.

His treatment uncovered that his renewed self-esteem was but barely reclaimed. It depended, he felt, on performance and prowess. Neither could be relied upon. His narcissism had not allowed him to live within his natural limitations. It made him reach for more than he could grasp. With his excessive narcissistic demands of himself exposed, they diminished. He quit the pact. It was a bargain he could not keep. His expectations that he would suddenly be burdened and aged magically did not occur, although he had feared this was part of the price he would have to pay for his delinquency. Somewhat wiser and not so much sadder, he returned to his work with renewed vigor, but he did not relish the role of grandfather. Its reality was beyond being altered.

Chapter 10

MANLY DESIRES

THE MIDDLE YEARS of masculine development are years of compensation. When a man enters middle age, he appears to yield the vigor of his earlier years for adopted substitutes: he places considerations of risk over reckless action, loss over attempts for nobler gain; and accepts submission to restraints. However, as Montaigne would say, the greedy appetite thus opposed turns loving eyes to Heaven for more. This cycle of loss and restitution, which begins early and continues without end, tends to be too narrowly conceived. Despite the appearance of complacency in a man of middle age, this period of masculine development initiates deep conflicts.[1]

Here we are concerned with the emotional conflicts that men of middle age begin to experience. After the restless exertions of the decades before, middle age begins with enclosures. What is the impact of these constraints on a man's commitment to prowess, performance, and the pursuit of achievement exhibited in every previous period? What substitutes, alternatives, exchanges, and new dimensions will be assigned to masculinity in a man's middle years?

In middle age, a man retains his critically important interest in a woman, but his interest does change more than is generally supposed. The results of my study show little doubt that, as the man's narcissism increases, his interest in women becomes narrower and more shallow in certain respects and thus strains his relations with them. The failure of a marriage of long duration is rarely because of great and open faults that have suddenly appeared or because of new, unsatisfied sexual struggles. Rather, it is the man's unique conflicts arising from petty, repeated annoyances to his ego, added to the increased demands of narcissism, that make the breach so severe.

When a man's narcissistic needs shift and find a gain elsewhere than with his wife, the effects of his marital loss are somewhat mitigated. This is not to suggest that the man cynically calculates the dissolution of his marriage or that he is not hurt by it. He is, but, as it is his narcissism that he unconsciously needs to restore, he is, as a rule, none the wiser for his experience. The sensitivity to an injured narcissism is heightened with middle age, and the case for compensation becomes more demanding. Men whose narcissism is most vulnerable, those in whom it is excessive, rarely develop insight when their attention is to their self-esteem and the need of its restoration that middle age usually requires.

As a rule, if the marriage is terminated, these men do not remarry, but they do not altogether forgo their erotic relations with women. Whether they marry, any commitment to a new partner is tenuous when the considerations of masculine narcissism are least compromising. Usually, the new woman is much younger than either the man or his former wife; often she is the age of his eldest daughter. (The occasional, fleeting awareness that the alliance with a young woman of his daughter's age has some incestuous significance seems not to be a source of significant emotional conflict. Despite the universality of this sexual taboo, it is the most frequently and widely violated.)

For the young woman, the sexual relationship with a man the age of her father is unconsciously contained within her own incestuous wishes. They are not sufficiently censored by her to forgo them, and, as we have seen in an earlier chapter, it is doubtful that they are ever altogether abandoned. But there is more to her relationship than the unconscious engagement of her incestuous desires. She knows, in general, what the older man needs. She awards him the compensation. As a participant in his restoration, she is closely identified with the masculine aims that are, as we have previously observed, also a fulfillment for herself. For such a young woman, this intimate connection with masculinity is more crucial than sensuousness, although she enjoys both aspects of the relationship.

For the man, the relationship in these circumstances tends to be strictly defined: it is sexual and is given little social importance. This is not to suggest that the relationship is without importance, but, once again, phallic prowess and performance are sought for their narcissistic gratification. Thus, the relationship must needs be shallow. The young woman seems ideally suited for the role such a man assigns to her. She may carry on her unresolved, incestuous, unconscious wishes and act them out, while her partner, the man who may be old enough to be her father or a surrogate, wants a lustful experience. He wants it manifestly free of incestuous significance, and, more important, the identification with her as a sexual partner. Unlike his wife or a woman his own age, the girl affords him a particular sort of erotic experience. He wants a sexual encounter without responsibility, with no real emotional engagement — one that he hopes will shore up his narcissism that strains against limitations. In short, it is to be a boy once again. Perhaps he wants to regain youth; possibly he wishes to rejuvenate an early promising manhood; but, above all, he wants escape from the flaws the middle years reveal.

There is, however, an eagerness to retain the relationship with his children, ostensibly to be a good father, as distinguished from a good husband. However, here, too, there is often a deeper, unconscious conflict, which is to compete with the mother. He wants to be a better mother than she. This stems from an unawareness of the identification with a woman as a mother. This is not then the sexualized identification with femininity, which when not normally anxiety provoking tends to cause a desired effeminacy in a man. Rather, it is identification with a mother as she is remembered from the man's boyhood period. This is the time when the mother is desexualized and when she acquires her sanctification and glorification. The nostalgia about her is woven from the threads of cherished memories and shreds of fantasies associated with this period that then unconsciously are stretched to blanket the earlier and the later conflicts about her.

It is rare in modern literature that we are given a deep insight into these conflicts in men. One notable exception is found in some of the novels by Saul Bellow. For example, beginning with his novel *The Victim,* and more fully developed later in *Herzog,* Bellow is at his best when he develops his character, Herzog, the victim of his middle years. Emotionally deep in his character is a worm eroding his self-esteem.

Bellow writes, "What sort of character? Well in modern vocabulary it was narcissistic; it was masochistic, it was anachronistic."[2] He goes on to show that Herzog's self-esteem is precarious. He is vain and is its victim, deploring his graying hair, his wrinkles, the dissolution of himself without maturation. He fears his narcissistic debt to his wife who would limit him and thus ridicules himself on reflection as a mere sexual drone to a queen. Lapsed into self-pity, Herzog in defense finds or tries to get solace from other men. As an added defense, he demeans women with whom he has had the shallowest relations and abysmal failures. By contrast, he is preeminently successful professionally. There are recollections at the same time of being cared for and indulged by his mother. He cannot resist wishing his wife or mistress had similarly nursed him. It evokes the fear, however, that their indulgence would identify him with them. "It would give the victory to the other side to let himself grow fat, jowly, sullen, with broad hips and a belly, and breathing hard."[3] His fear is that this would cost him his masculinity; loathing the gratitude of weakness, of the sufferer, he is furious underneath.

It becomes a female pursuit to look for fulfillment in another, thinks Herzog. "The occupation of a man is in duty, in use, in civility, in politics in the Aristotelian sense."[4] In the middle years, Bellow writes, a man risks the desire for love. "And the man who shops from woman to woman, though his heart aches with idealism, with the desire for pure love, has entered the female realm."[5]

There is, however, an identification with a woman that Herzog seeks to act out. She is an idealized mother: self-sacrificing, selfless, giving without restraint and dedicated only to gratifying her son's wishes. She is what Herzog wants to be as he is irresistibly compelled to visit his daughter. He thinks of his former wife as a whorish witch in whose custody the child is held. He is obsessed with saving his daughter and is mothering in the moments he is allowed to be with her. Given to self-reflection, Herzog, during his misadventures, thinks how "personal life is a humiliation."[6] By contrast, in public, he is rich, successful, and honored.

An example of this type of man we shall call Cooper. He had been divorced for years from a beautiful woman in whom he had lost interest soon after marrying her, although their marriage lasted nearly fifteen years. She quickly remarried, and their children were comfortably shared in regular visits and holidays. The property and children, like chattel, had been amicably parceled between them.

Cooper had persistent insomnia, as well as occasional nightmares that disturbed his sleep. As he was getting older, he seemed eager to get help for these symptoms. He was in an important, highly placed position, earning large sums because of his specialized technical gifts. His private agonies, except for the fatigue that had become more of a problem to him, seemed not to impair his work.

An attractive single man, he was sought after socially. Except for some social obligations that related to his work, he skillfully avoided social occasions as well as emotional commitment. He was soon aware that, although his anxiety focused on his problems at work, he could not verify his fears on them. He came to the undeniable and increasingly uncomfortable conclusion that they were unfounded in reality, but this did not illuminate their nature. His best periods, when he was free of his symptoms, were when he was alone with his children. He was happiest during their visits, taking care of them, cooking for them, planning their days, driving them about, and occasionally actively playing their games with their friends.

Cooper was very like his father, a reserved, distinguished man. The father said he had all he could have wished for in his son. As the old man aged and depended more on him, his pleasure increased. Their intimacy grew. He thrived on his conscious identification with his father whom he conspicuously resembled. His relations with his mother became antagonistic. After his divorce, he seemed to extend some of the decree in the divorce from his wife to her. The previously close relationship between mother and son became distant and, at times, openly hostile. Cooper expressed it only by his silence around her. To the extent he could, he isolated himself from her. Their previous, intimate relationship was reduced manifestly to a perfunctory one.

The respite from the conflicts of married, domestic life left him with a measure of freedom he welcomed. He found the company of young women "who are foreign-looking, with big breasts and big mouths . . . the sort you see in porno movies and magazines of high fashion. They all have their mouths wide open. All they need is a big penis shoved into them. Women are creatures after the most powerful. They like to get overpowered; even to get hurt. They sort of need pain, and sort of enjoy it.

"At home, as a kid, I used to tease our animals. I must admit I liked to inflict pain. I really don't actually want to hurt people, but I have to admit I like to see somebody humiliated. No one knows the pleasure it gives me. It's true at work when I find

263

someone doing wrong, I don't mind delivering the guy to the hangman. It goes with sex as sort of only one-night stands. I don't want to see the woman again. Because when I do, and if the girl begins to like me, I get as uncomfortable as when I get praise. I can take it at work because it has little to do with people. I don't want the commitment that being good or liked brings. And when it comes to women who want to get attached, I'd rather masturbate.

"I know no one would like that. I torture myself when I hate others and always feel guilty. That's why a short experience with a girl gets me into no big guiilt. What scares me is the importance a woman can come to have. She could say no to me. Am I willing to place my security in her hands? Can I let her shoot me down? With her refusal? I fight that. I can't let myself be in a woman's charge. My mother was the most indulgent woman you could ever imagine, and I was so dependent on her that I can't believe it. I felt I'd drown. It was the helpless feeling she gave me, doing everything for me, protecting me. It made me stand close to my father. I do the same thing with men I have worked for. I had to walk away from my mother. I had to be mean to her, even if it was painful to do it. To stay with her, she would feel seductive. It was like I was in a sexual arena. I had to get out of it.

"Getting married, I imagined, might be easier. It was not, even if my wife was nothing like my mother. She turned out to be like her in many ways — too many ways. The sexual arena was there again. The children are the best part of marriage. With them, I don't have any fears; with my wife, I feel like a victim with her, and weak.

"Some of this happens with men. I have some good friends among them, but when I am playing tennis, I can't bring myself to beat them. I know I can. I can get way ahead and have no relish to win. It's not that I don't want to win. It's somehow wrong. I remember my parents telling me that I was a smart kid and could have whatever I set my mind to get. This is still a scary idea. What if I want what I'm not supposed to get? Fortunately, at work, the sort of thing I do is so specialized, it's no problem. I always managed to avoid it by just being very good at what I was doing. There was no competition to beat, and, with luck, it worked."

The relations with young women to whom he had no obligation gave him the feeling of serving only himself. This admission and self-confrontation brought out the feeling that "people will hate that in me, if they knew it. They'd want to leave me. I would do that. I can't be trusted in feelings. The only security was my mother's dedication to me and that gave me plenty of grief. What a crazy ambition it gives a child. His father is powerful and to want to be in his place, put on his father's shoes, and be *the* father. That's the last thing I want from my mother. It's a dangerous relationship. I won't admit I need anyone. The divorce came as a relief." It took Cooper a long time to be aware of his inner contradictions.

In the course of treatment that had relieved his acute anxieties and insomnia, he met a woman ten years younger than himself, divorced and with three children. She seemed to want little more than a companion. Cooper must have appeared ideal. She was sexually undemanding. For Cooper, this was an irresistible situation. They began to live together. He enjoyed her children almost as though they were his own. She suited his neurosis so well he terminated his treatment.

Before he left for this new relationship, I learned that Cooper was a father lacking a family, a husband without marital obligation, and the motherlike figure with whom he was living was identified as feminine yet not sexual. He was without conflict over it. He was himself the idealized, indulgent mother to the children unconsciously denied him by his gender. It afforded him enormous gratification. Cooper illustrated that a man's identification with femininity need not represent a compelling conflict when it is without commitment and is expressed in a social context that wins approbation. Above all else, he was identified with an idealized mother, one whose sexuality is like the Madonna's, unearthly.

There are exceedingly rare references to this phenomenon of a man's identification with an idealized woman, a mother. I know of no authoritative reference of his finding it a source of gratification free of conflict. However, Helene Deutsch wrote of it as part of the psychology of a woman. She wrote that when a mother idealizes her son so that the ego-ideal is in harmony with other parts of the personality, it represents a specific relationship of a mother to her son. Deutsch does not take up the masculine aspect of this idealization as it is beyond the scope of her work, but it is appropriate here in consideration of masculinity. Deutsch had known well

Catholic families in which such a religious *folie à deux* was successfully acted out throughout life. The boy had been since his birth destined to become a saint via his profession as a priest. The expiation and idealization of the mother who gave him life, supposedly in an immaculate way, and his own professional chastity were the guiding spirits of his destiny. The gross reality of the mother, who may have borne many children were conceived not by lust by "pro maiorem dei gloriam." . . . [This is found in] the religious atmosphere of simple-minded, uncritical believers of Catholic dogma, where the Holy Virgin and the Christ-child play an immense role. The son as the future bearer of religious perfection and saintliness — will fulfil the mother's own fantasy of the immaculate conception and sanctify her to holy virginity.[7]

The form that the idealization takes will be from the particular culture that gives its coloring to the experience. A mother's idealization of a son may occur in any culture, much as he in turn may idealize her and identify himself through it with her. This was so in the case of Cooper, who illustrated in part what the process entails. Helene Deutsch mentions that she has noted, as we all have, that in "biographies of famous men, one very often finds such an idealistic union between mother and son. Here the ideals of cultural and aesthetic nature are the binding power."[8]

I have no personal instance to cite that shows this idealized union as part of masculine psychology to parallel what Deutsch described, but one outstanding example comes to mind to illustrate it. While we may all be aware of Monica's devotion to Augustine, it was his finally accepting her ideals that turned him to the destiny he was to find. I would suppose his is an experience in idealizing his mother, identifying himself with that aspect of her that brought him with his genius to Christianity where he was given sainthood. I know of no better account of it than the one Rebecca West gave us in 1933 in which she wrote: "For him there was then and thereafter to be nothing in the universe save his mother and her son."[9]

In the examples we have just cited, a remarkably fresh fidelity to the feminine identification is revealed to be contained in masculinity. The boyhood conflicts over it remain. The efforts to resolve them persist in assertions that would deny value to women. This is the typical, emerging, psychological reaction after having previously exalted a mother, as in Cooper's case, and it expresses the deep disappointment that the fruitless, passionate wishes bring on being thwarted. We see this, easily retrieved in men, as constituting a continuing conflict of those who are not homosexual (that is, who are not engaged in homosexuality as a perversion). As a conflict, the identification with a woman brings its derivative effects to men into a wide variety of influences on their everyday lives.

For instance, an unmarried experienced teacher was working to prepare new courses he was assigned to give. There was some pressure to complete his work for the curriculum. Despite his grasp of his subject and his natural diligence, he feared he could not finish the task. The added hours of work in libraries and his thorough familiarity with the subject seemed to bring him no relief. For every successful effort, he found fault with what he had done. Renewed efforts only repeated the frustration he already suffered. Dreading to overlook some seemingly essential detail, he became obsessed with doubts. They increased his industry, but did not diminish his anxiety.

In the past, there were always colleagues, often older ones, on whom he felt he would depend for guidance and support.

Actually, he needed the notion of their support more than the fact of it. He nevertheless had the inescapable feeling that he needed support in order to perform with excellence and to be valued. He felt a measure of comfort and ease and was able to form warm relationships with men who would sponsor him, support his efforts, guide him, and assure his interest in him. He was unconscious that this pleasurable, dependent, secure relationship was also the basis for his anxiety, as well as the relief of it. New directions in his work demanded more independence than he had previously experienced, and the limited piloting he could solicit left him anxious. As he had mastered the subject, he was all the more puzzled at his inability to go ahead with his project.

His major symptom was the fear of failing to make a tenured place for himself on the faculty. After some period of analysis, in which we reviewed the immediate circumstances of his plight, he revealed fears of long standing related to a private pursuit of his — testing himself. This was not confined to academic work, and he could not recall ever being without this process of reckoning and tallying criteria, which began consciously in his youth, chiefly in social experiences. Now he compulsively calibrated whatever engaged him with a yardstick that carried a critical measure, according to which he regularly fell short. He was well aware of monitoring himself, but he was not aware of the extent to which he was tyrannized by the compulsion to engage in it. His was a typical, obsessional, neurotic condition, but in this diagnosis, the masculine aspects are not revealed.

As we began to explore more deeply into his inner life, what was manifestly a compulsive testing of his mettle covered a vaulting ambition to have no peers. His work had to be the vehicle that would prove more than scholarship. Hence, it was neurotically obligatory to scrutinize it. It was to be of grand proportions. "I don't want to give that up. It's a powerful weapon that nothing could match. What a wonderful dominance I'd have. I think of it while riding the subways, in libraries, wherever I look at men. I think how I could make them jealous of my achievement. It's a triumph. I'd lose all fears. . . . I could do just what I want. I know it's very hostile, but it's worth it. I'd like to say I can do anything. I don't believe it, but I want to. I can't live with limits. Limits to capacities, not a genius, no raving talents or great intellect? I can't live with the limits of disappointment. They're intolerable."

Before the imperatives were so fixed on academic work, he had them about women. He had not modified them with respect to women any more than he had his work. He had many brief sexual affairs. "I want to be a real terror in bed, but, sometimes, I'd be impotent. That was a horror. Women expect commitments. I have them in work, not to women. Involvements are calculated to win gloriously. I'd prefer to be close with a man, share thought, feelings, wishes. Not the secrets — the sexual ones of impotence or homosexual wishes. I'm tempted, but I'd have to include ambitions of greatness and they go with hostility. Another man couldn't like that.

"I had one frightening homosexual experience: fellatio. It was to escape being more involved with a woman. I told her about it so she would expect less. I escape being a great fucker. Greatness is without a concern for others. Without greatness, I'd be ignored. It's a question of self-esteem, worthlessness that I can't stand. And homosexual is equated with it — a feminine man like a woman is degraded. You come from worthlessness to be great. No pride, no self-assurance, from all this comes great anxiety. It thrusts me to do things."

It is hardly necessary to explore for our purposes here what particulars of this man's early boyhood became established as a boy's conventional view of women. Studies of young children have made us familiar with it. What is important for us is that this man carried with him into adult life the derivatives of his early masculine conflicts. They are virtually intact. Like artifacts of some past era, they are buried in him, and, unearthed, they are seen to have been unaffected by the passage of time, as though impervious to the environment.

He was ridiculed by his own self-comparison with men, which he used to do as a small boy. The unconscious feminine identification was both reinforced and hated. Carried into adult life, the neurotic homosexual surrender, or at least the fantasies of it, served as a release from the exhortations of boyhood masculine demands. In the homosexual experience, he passively dreaded no less the similarly characterized demands of a rampant masculinity. These inhibiting conflicts vitiated his efforts.

The key to the underlying persistent problem was in the unconsciously held feminine identification that was incompatible with his masculine development. He had not been able sufficiently to relinquish it or find expression for it in a way that was relatively free of conflict. He illustrated that when masculinity remained exaggeratedly bound to its infantile aspirations for power, performance, and prowess, they become associated with the erotic aims of the same period. The moderating effect of intimacy is precluded by the ruling masculine narcissism. As a result, a fusion of infantile masculine and erotic aims occur. The feminine identification, normally a necessary, unconscious defense against extravagant boyhood masculine yearnings that are associated with brutal relations, remains ineffective. When he felt "feminine," he pictured himself a hapless victim. This was a small boy's fantasy of women in relation to men. As a man, he was bent on grandiose achievements. They happened to be academic ones since this was his occupational arena. Their emotional aim was to devastate his peers and argue into insensibility those who would oppose him or were over him.

As the evidence makes clear, a man's identification with a woman is not entirely relinquished. Beginning in boyhood, it is ordinarily held in abeyance, that is, repressed. While an active masculine development takes place, the unconscious or repressed feminine identification is retained. From its vestiges, a receptive medium is thus provided in which circumstances may effectively evoke men to open, rather than leave latent, their homosexual conflicts. An endless source of unconscious discord in masculinity is thus assured. It finds a wide variety of expression in hostility to women, to femininity, and to those signs of it suggested in the conduct of some men. The exception is in homosexual perversion, where femininity in a man is sought rather than shunned. Although the large subject of perversion is obviously related to some of the issues here, it is beyond the scope of this work.

* * *

We have become familiar with the resistance of boys and men to being identified with a woman. Whatever the source of the suggestion of identification, it is regarded as alien, repugnant, and it creates a xenophobic anxiety. There are, however, important exceptions to this reaction. In these cases, the masculine identification is well developed and actively retained while unconsciously a feminine version of the self is also sought. Although this phenomenon is wholly neglected in psychological studies of the dynamics of masculinity, it has a role in the everyday life of some middle-aged, married men. These are not instances of perversion of identification with a woman as in the case of James Morris and in certain types of homosexual men. Nor is it even the common neurotic attempt to gratify some remnant of femininity. These men experience an intensely intimate, passionate relationship very different from what they have experienced with their wives, and the identification with a young woman is an unconsciously imperative nexus.

The men I have seen who have exhibited this particular need for identification with a young woman were usually unexceptional in other ways. This type of man is gainfully and sometimes even lucratively employed in a variety of demanding occupations. He has been married for two or three decades and has children. He is a devoted husband without a specific, manifest incompatibility with his wife. While his wife has no direct role in his work, he does not wish or need such involvement from her. He is conventionally minded and in no way either socially exceptional or clinically remarkable but for one fact: he has become seriously, emotionally involved with a younger woman.

The leading complaints that brought these men for treatment were anxiety states and mild, recurrent periods of depression. They focused discomfort on a wide variety of somatic disorders and attributed them to early signs of age, whether cardiac disease, vague joint pains, or inordinate fatigue and other less well defined physical complaints. Thorough study showed the absence of organic pathology, and, in fact, the men were in excellent physical health, which they neither felt nor wholly believed. They were referred to me in states of moderate, but not disabling, clinical depression. In some instances, the man confessed an extramarital affair; many times this came out as part of a deeper, puzzling problem and was not a reluctantly acknowledged admission of marital infidelity. However, the relationship with the young woman was more readily recognized as a compelling one that incomprehensibly could not be terminated and was a disturbing dilemma.

While some of these men were mildly addicted to drugs previously prescribed to allay anxiety, and a few others found some relief from a mild dependence on alcohol, when the use of drugs and alcohol was terminated during treatment, most remained free of intensive feelings of deprivation or temptation to resort to them again, and, in fact, they became more easily accessible emotionally than they otherwise would have been. In those instances in which the dependence was not easily given up, there was still no discernible impediment to work. Often as a reaction to feeling impaired, they were driven to more zeal in their work.

The relationship to the younger woman was of such importance that serious thought had been given to abandoning or divorcing the wife. Some of the men needed to tell their wives frankly of their involvement, but gave assurances that the affair was or soon would be ended. In no instance did their extramarital relations actually lead to a dissolution of the marriage, although the young women often insisted they would not continue the relationship without the prospect of marriage. With interruptions, some of the affairs lasted nearly two years and others, a year or so longer.

The clinical problems these various men suffered — that is, their symptoms, whether anxiety, depression, and the often associated admixture of moderate alcohol and drug use — were in no way unique. In the throes of their guilt over their adulterous relations, their conventional rationalizations of discontent in a marriage were thin and gave them little more than brief periods of complete freedom. However, such times were deeply felt and the importance of the experience with the younger woman added to the conflict over giving her up. It was in the nature of the unconscious relationship to these women that the men revealed a problem of masculinity. It was outside the experience with their wives.

On the basis of a companionability experienced as previously utterly absent from his marriage, the man is led to the passionate conviction he is embarked on a new life. In certain respects, he is correct. However, he is remarkably unaware of its deeper, unconscious aspects. The woman, characteristically, is vigorous and physically attractive to him, although not necessarily more so than his wife, except that she is younger. She has more than these qualities that make her irresistible to the older man: he sees in her qualities like his own. When he sees her interest in him as compatible with his own egocentric interests, her eagerness to share them and her commitment to their mutual interests (that is, his interests), he is holding up through her a mirror to himself. Its narcissistic effect is inevitable.

The first hint of the powerful attraction she holds is that she has a career or potentially has one that she would bring and share with his own. Thus, it would expand or enlarge or further develop his aspirations. She is eager to participate in his expanded expectations of himself. They consciously engage in mutually developing their new joint existence. Hours of conscious fantasy about it gives them ecstatic pleasure that is then often carried over to their physical experiences, in which the man's sense of himself is unbounded, lost in the new dimensions that come with their sexual union. He wants her as a partner and as an associate in his occupation. He has ideas and takes great pleasure sharing them with her as mutual working ambitions. He is unaware of the depths of the partnership he wants. With her, he feels larger than life, as they construct his vaulting ambitions. She is set apart from his wife, with whom he never had more than fragments of such notions nor such exhilarating experiences. For both, it is a narcissistic ecstasy.

The wife's role as the mother of their children, associated with family or domestic life, even though she may have a new profession or work that is independent of the home, appears not to make her eligible for the partnership the man is enthralled in. Moreover, the actual moral betrayal of the wife, guilt producing as it is, gets overshadowed and has a remarkably small, if not absent, part in this drama.

In this type of man, the identification with the younger woman plays the most critical part in his pursuit of her. She is idealized in that she puts aside all consideration other than elevating him. She expressly forsakes her own prospects solely to promote his. It is not that she is selfless. They each believe his role with her exceeds the sum of their parts. Contrary to all that we have learned that an identification with a woman is hazardous and typically produces anxiety, the opposite is the case here. This is not to minimize the large consideration given by each of the partners to the importance of the sexual pleasure and freedom with one another.

Studying the women, I have learned that they enjoy the inflated pride of performance they can excite in the older man. Such a woman does not fully understand how central she is to the man's masculine narcissism that middle age promises to limit. However fully realized his ambitions may have been in reality, they are not felt so fully reached and even with greater possibilities until this experience develops. For the woman, it is an experience of her powers that with a young man she would be more obliged to share or divide rather than exercise. Her role creates the illusion that he will be transformed by her commitment. She is enchanted by the fantasy; it appeals to her own narcissism that she would have such powers. Nor is she insensitive to the heady effect on her own egoism their relationship provides. In the course of the man's deepest experience comes the expression of a profound sense that he is, as never before, and incomprehensibly to himself, at long last "complete." He is deeply moved by it. But he is far from understanding its psychological significance.

He is unaware what dynamic forces affect him as he undergoes in this relationship an inarticulated, unconscious sense of self-fulfillment. What previously eluded him left him with a lingering, egoistic discontent brought to light by middle age. As a younger man, he narcissistically entertained the possibility of this discontent's being dispelled. Even the most joyous moments before were sufficiently overcast with privately held thoughts that such exhilarating experiences could only be transient. It was the feeling of transience that germinated the seeds of discontent. He wanted more. Now at last the flush and exulting moments seem caught in this relationship. It is an elated feeling of being "complete," like "joined to a wonderful twin," as one man said. The tie that binds him to the younger woman bewilders him.

It is, to him, inexplicable in its intensity, alarming in its passion, and sobering in its seriousness. To maintain it, the man considers sacrificing his marital life. The possible price adds to the conviction of the importance that the woman holds. No insight comes to him from staring into his obsessive ruminations, reviewing and commandeering rational resolutions to abandon his compelling fervor. He is desperate to hold it. Theseus could not have been in a more torturous maze, nor hung more tightly to Ariadne's string to thread his way out. The woman has become part of him. Can a man seek the very identification that all his life he has shunned?

The clue to this paradox lies in when the woman is, in the mind's eye, like the mother that nostalgia contrives. She is the one who, in his fantasy, through dedicating herself to his achieving his ambitions, his wishes, and prospects, thus makes secure his masculine narcissism that all men from boyhood know is precariously balanced. Far from forgoing her own needs, the younger woman lives them out through the middle-aged man's reaching. Moreover, as one young and vigorous, she shares his ambitions as an ally through the promise to help him and engage with him in his quest. She is more than a Sancho to his Quixote. For each partner, the other fulfills a counterpart; each completes the other. Their compatibility is jointly experienced. Their vanity is mutually shared. Neither one is an individual in his or her own right. They are joined in an enterprise where she is for the man an idealized woman whose chief object is to help him to transcend himself, to become the hero in whose shadow stands the woman with whom he made the Faustian pact. She is a part of what he gains. His masculine narcissism soon becomes reluctant to share and the unconscious demands resist the obligations the relationship implicitly incurred. So, like Faust, he cannot get the self-satisfaction he seeks and the compact finally comes to nothing. He emerges unrepentant. The therapy lays no moral burden but aims at bringing him to desist from the proposal that he might have more than "earthly meat and drink." (How different he is from the middle-aged man who wants to defy his limitations and vainly to rejuvenate himself by way of using a young woman as a vehicle and once again to be a boy.)

The younger woman who plays a lead here illustrates a variation on what we have learned in the earlier chapters. She enjoys the fantasy and translating it to the real role of participating in a masculine enterprise. And perhaps even more in the rehabilitation of one who seems failing. We found that universally a woman wants to enjoy masculinity. She may do so on a narrow and shallow basis merely sexually as an intimate partner, or, being capable, have a more profound role, as we have just recounted. A woman may enjoy her husband's as well as her father's masculinity and it need not be simply incestuous. Rather, it is an extension of femininity expanded to embrace the qualities of masculinity without herself becoming mannish. In some instances, when she is not too envious or conflicted, her pleasure in masculinity may extend to being identified with her brothers. There are, of course, exceptions. We are only concerned here with the rule. It would dwell too much on the psychology of women, inappropriate here, to do more than call attention to it. However, it is well known that some women marry, yet do not enjoy their husbands. I cited examples here in the early chapters, in particular one of a woman who enjoyed her son's masculinity but not his father's. We know women who enjoy neither their husband's nor their son's masculinity. We are also familiar with the mothers who are deeply attached to their sons, each becoming tightly bound to the other.

What of the women to whom masculinity in their husbands is no pleasure, but rather a source of criticism and grievance? Does it tend to make their husband hostile to women? Logically, this may be reasoned to be the case. We have seen such intimate relationships between a mother and son especially in homosexuals. There is a large literature that verifies that such a condition of intimacy bears a heavy influence on the development of homosexuality. Some of it I have cited here, but what appears not to have been considered is the effect on a son whose mother was hostile to the father and was as critical of her son for his masculinity. If she has more than one son, she may exonerate one while retaining her hatred of men in the other. Such a woman feels herself hurt, demeaned, and as if made to feel or believe herself worthless. The son for whom she spares her criticism, especially when he is a young boy, tends to identify himself with her and her plight closely. They develop a mutual likeness of hurt, self-hate, criticism, and burdensomeness. With this legacy, which is little influenced by the father inasmuch as the boy is closely attached to his mother and the father is alienated by her, he, too, develops a demeaned self that is not conscious and is expressed in a hostile defensiveness and, like his mother, is anxious that the world is hostile. Also like his mother, he is unaware of how much he projects his fury on those whom he fears harbor hostile intentions. These are not clinically paranoid states, but the condition is one of a distant caution toward others, distrusting of them, and allowing no genuine intimacy.

Hence, as such a boy leaves home for relationships outside the immediate family, they are not close or intimate. The experience at home extends into the new relationships that are soon to carry similar qualities to the previous, familiar ones. I have known men with such histories who marry and have stable marriages to women from whom they expect no attack and with whom they are relieved to have escaped the hostile encounters their masculinity has suffered. Their wives tend to be bland, long-suffering, and masochistic.

As these men become middle-aged and successful in work or a profession, the relationship with their wives leaves them with no shared experiences in regard to their work. Thus, they are left with feeling episodes of success but no definite sense of achievement that is shared. Although the facts would often contradict, and there are substantial accomplishments, the sense of it is absent. It is a solitary feat. The unconscious struggle against identification with the woman who demeaned one's efforts continues. He is no heroic son, but one to satisfy his mother even if he met his father's expectations in some measure, although he is not without doubts about that, too. The relation to the real or material acheivement seems not to modify discontent. He adds the concern of his middle years to the struggle to escape the lack of satisfaction his masculinity furnishes.

The relationship to his wife and family suggests that little has changed. His wife may be a devoted, dependent woman who grows more so with the decades of marriage. He is prone still to long unconsciously for relief from the self-denigration he continues, unaffected by outward success and the satisfaction of friends. It is as if he had a tapeworm in him. No matter how much he is nourished, he is left starved. In this condition, circumstances in the form of a much younger woman offer a tantalizing promise of a longed-for respite.

The younger woman who finds such a man attractive is one who is eager, vigorous, and ambitious. She is herself an active woman in the sense that she strongly identifies herself with a man, his goals, and his aspirations. They inspire her. She wants a share in them and is ardent to contribute to their jointly realizing his wishes, which become her own.

The man has the fantasy that she has no weakness, does not demean herself, and is not masochistic or desirous of being dependent. The differences from his mother, the self she cultivated, which his wife was ignorant to dispel, seems swept away by the young woman who idealizes him. The effect is profound; he is transformed by her ambition. It enhances and fires his own aspirations to a point where he is at a loss to know where his begin, and hers leave off. It brings a passion he seems never to have experienced.

The woman's commitment to advancing his masculine narcissism promises him more than an expanded prowess and achievement. She is dedicated to it. She actively shares in his performance sexually and each emotionally and eagerly loses the self-boundaries. They become fused with one another — as a subjective experience. None of the man's old fears of identification with femininity discredited unconsciously arouse his repugnance. He feels they both are dedicated to his notions of an enlarged career. His ideas are not merely conjectures. The young woman makes it evident that she is deeply engrossed, invested, and aims to profit from their joint venture. His narcissism is heightened. He feels a freedom and exhilaration he never experienced before. The young woman and he enter into a pact; its unconscious clauses are that they share in his masculinity, i.e., its narcissism. He feels heroic and often with that vision accomplishes more than he otherwise had. She

279

enjoys his activities vicariously by way of her own unconscious masculine wishes that are thus fulfilled. It becomes a heady experience for her. She becomes more demanding, expressing in it an increasing dependence on him for her fulfillment, much as he previously felt and came to realize he needed her. It is their mutual but not similar, dependence that raises new conflicts and strains the relationship. They begin to consume it. The narcissism that was shared does no longer inherently lend itself to being merged. Grief and discontent follow.

From the example of a middle-aged man whom we shall call Dorsey, it will become evident that his relationship with such a woman brought his masculine narcissism to a level of excitement in a way that his wife had unknowingly failed to do. In fact, she had inadvertently diminished it. Dorsey came for treatment because of persistent hypochondriacal symptoms that had become acutely painful and emotional problems resulting from fears that he was facing an uncertain future as a result of them. Any underlying cause for his fears, uncertainties, and gloom was not readily disclosed. Dorsey had been in very good health, and, until a recent bout of illness, he had been in unusually good condition for the past few years.

Dorsey came from a conventional middle-class family in which no member achieved more than a moderate, respectable success. Dorsey's accomplishments resulted from the most prosaic qualities. Following college, he was inducted into the army at the end of World War II. After being demobilized, he found work in a large company. He worked hard and earned his deserved recognition. In the meantime, he married a girl of a similar background and education. It was not a passionate affair but a steady one of growing affection and shared social interests that led to their marriage. In his work, as in his marriage, Dorsey's main ambition was to be secure, to feel there was certainty. From it, he drew comfort that dispelled doubts he was otherwise prone to suffer. Contentedly, he advanced in his work and, together with his conventional aims, beliefs, and his tightly knit family and a small circle of friends,

280

he enjoyed a degree of satisfaction he liked. Where he may have lacked spirit, he applied zeal.

His wife evidently enjoyed her domestic life. They soon had a number of children and lived a rather uneventful suburban existence. Their sexual life, while satisfying to them as far as Dorsey knew, had little that was more than occasionally passionate, but neither he nor his wife seemed to demand much more of each other than they were giving. What discontent he entertained about his wife he tended to keep to himself. He was inclined to feel that such notions were too petty to express, and, with such denials, their life was fairly tranquil.

Dorsey was neither so shy nor so even-tempered as he made an effort to appear to be. It was not that he was dissembling; he was fearful of his temper. On those occasions when he came home from work in a rage, his wife tried to pacify him, and, usually in a short time, she succeeded. Dorsey could not bring himself to confront his subordinates when they often failed to carry out his orders. He feared his own fury, feared losing control and humiliating himself. It was the humiliation he really feared.

Among his oldest fears, from when he was a boy, was that he would prove himself wanting, inadequate to his expectations of himself. It made him cautious in what he ventured. Keeping close to convention seemed to give him some assurance among these fears. The dread of humiliation he still felt caused him anxiety, which was limited to short attacks of apprehension that he related to immediate problems at work rather than to his fears. There were longer periods of being morose after which he was not frankly depressed.

After a period of exploring his present complaints, Dorsey explained that at work one day, he had become intent on a recently employed young woman, who was in a minor executive position in another department. What had struck him was that she was very attractive, but, more than that, she was so regarded by others. He became conscious that this was especially important to him. He soon began to develop a fantasy

281

about her. It intruded into his consciousness with repeated frequency at various, odd hours of the day. This fantasy was that she chose him for her favors over the others. He said, "I know this is absurd, but I endow her with superhuman qualities. Her choice of me would endow me, too. . . . I'd feel no faults. It's preposterous the feeling of a kind of assurance it gives me. I don't have many demands and they are modest, my needs don't seem excessive and I am content with what I have without extravagance. So why do I need to be above all this? The only relief that comes from feeling limited is in thinking of winning this girl's approval. With that, she would endorse me. She has the power over my self-esteem that I can't control. When she chooses me, I am changed."

With these compelling fantasies, Dorsey cautiously proceeded to begin an affair with her. She was about fifteen years younger than he, and he referred to her as a girl and thought of her more in those terms. They began to see each other regularly. Dorsey found ways to arrange his time clandestinely away from home evidently without arousing his wife's suspicions; at least she accepted his explanations of his absences without much question. He came back from these excursions in an excitement he found difficult to mask in view of his accustomed, rather bland and unobtrusive conduct. Although he did not know that there were in fact any rivals for her attention, he was certain that he had been chosen over them. "I embrace her and feel myself better. I feel I am liked by her as a great person, and I feel I am great! My voice sounds different to me. Physically, I feel vigorous.

"It seems grotesque. She gives me a new importance. She completes me. I can't give her enough to express my gratitude for this. I feel she rescues me. I'd feel with her I had no limits, be what I wanted. What matters most in this is performing — I don't mean just sexually — I feel I have to put out a performance. What I've done already or will do with her is part of me, this girl completes. Somehow she completes me. She has to have a record of achievement. None of the women in my family have it. All that I demand of myself, that I lack somehow, I look for and find in her. She turns them on in me.

"She is not like a wife. I want her as a resemblance of an expectation. She has exaggerated notions, qualities that transform me. With her, all that goes on in family life, daily life, and material things all drop away. I'm excited by her, I want to put it into myself, have her freedom, be her. I love it!

"I admit I get furious when I know by myself I am not enough. She holds a part I need. When I can take on what she feels, the high esteem she has for herself, I acquire it as part of myself.

"It's not the same with my wife, who respects and admires me no less, but she is dependent on my performance and not a part of it. My self-esteem depends on being responded to and not just depended on. I can't stand that quality which does not demand the performance. I need to go about with a mirror that reflects performance. It tells me whether my masculinity is deprived or nourished. I want to fuse with this girl. I'll feel more complete to fuse with her. It is an extension of myself so that I would not know where she left off and I begin. I lose myself, that's true. I'm loving myself extending myself into her. She was the half I was looking for in myself. It completes me — makes me warm, affectionate, like I have not been, and was deprived without it. I live through her. As I fuse with her, I'm part of her. It's a partnership. I admit I don't bring to her what she gives me. She *completes* me.

"I feel no guilt, no shame — I feel warmer toward my wife and children and at work, but it will all terminate. It won't last. What will happen is I'll have a terrible loss. The liberation, the getting away from the limits would be all gone. It's a threat to myself to lose all this. Look how much I have gained."

The relationship was not sustained. The young woman became demanding. She wanted Dorsey for herself, free of his wife. Her own ambition began to invade his. From here, she wanted a more durable relationship. It was irresistible to share vanity. As a vehicle, she seemed to transport him to a fantasied destiny, a charmed life, a vigorous self-fulfillment, a narcissistic experience he had not before realized. The only disquiet he had was a sense of a shift in the balance of the relationship.

A sudden, crushing blow struck Dorsey. From it, his anxiety came in a rush that made him feel he was dragged near the edge of panic. The "girl," the partner, the one who "completed" him, who had turned him from a toad to a title, began to plead that she needed him. The "partnership" shattered. She was now no ally, no amalgam; the fusion was split. Thus transformed, she was alien, no longer as if a part of himself. She declared she needed him and wanted to be dependent for her own sake. So long as the desire, the need, and the impetus was his, he was in a headlong, mindless rush to join her to complete himself. But at the confrontation with her own need and desire, his was quenched. So long as the need was his, he was unfettered to find a partner, whom he unconsciously needed to be a young woman who would complete him. So well had he succeeded in satisfying her that he aroused her own, intense, narcissistic need. His was extinguished. The unconscious covenant was broken. The promise of an exhilarating fulfillment exploded. Puzzled as to how so real and important an experience could so quickly vanish, Dorsey was left no wiser. With only the wispiest of romantic recollections reflecting about himself as having a brief encounter that he had to abandon, the "affair" ended.

Who "needed" Dorsey, lost him. Whether it was his wife or his "partner," he accepted with resignation and without pleasure that a woman's need of him depleted him. He showed that the emotional significance to a man of being needed by a woman represented a complex requirement. It brought out that a woman's dependence on him, on the one hand, supported his masculine narcissism. On the other, however, when it meant that he was to share it, his oldest fears were aroused: that he must compromise some of his masculine attributes with a woman who enjoys them and wants them or at least an active share in them. His "partner" needed to gain for herself a participation in Dorsey's masculinity. Their joint participation became an enterprise in which it was his masculinity that was apportioned. Dorsey's wife was content to be dependent on it. Dorsey, however, had entered unwittingly into a pact with a woman who, through him, would further the masculinity she sought for herself, and he would "complete" himself with a masculine, striving woman. She, however, was bent on a parallel course to complete herself with what she lacked and what Dorsey would share. When he finally realized her need was for his masculine role in which she had to have a part that became a dependence on him for it, the alliance broke. It apparently ended without rancor. Dorsey felt the loss as a severe one, and it was at this time that his hypochondriacal symptoms became sufficiently severe and his depression superficially associated with them brought him to treatment.

While Dorsey may indeed be an exception in certain respects, he proved the rule that for a man a woman's dependence has its particular importance in masculinity, and that, for some men, a relationship with a woman who is unconsciously seeking a share of his "masculinity," who may manifestly be very feminine, brings identification with her to an irresistible attraction. However, when she no longer shares in it so much as she wants to be dependent for her own narcissistic needs, she loses what drew Dorsey to her. The illusion burst. The relationship ended. The rationalization used to explain its termination cannot reach into the deeper motives that gave the experience its ecstatic moments. What was a union for each in identification with one another became a brief, exquisite, intense love affair that had to be abandoned.

Ordinarily a man's narcissism thrives on his being needed by a woman. He loves her for the particular value she places on him. But, when his self-esteem depends upon its endorsement from a woman whose own need is then heard as a demand to relinquish his own aims in favor of hers, or what she may require for her own narcissistic needs, their conflict is reduced to a contest of narcissistic goals. It entails, under such conditions, a sacrifice of some of the self, the ego, and narcissism is threatened. The self-defenses go up and the relationship is in jeopardy.

Dorsey's deep relationship to the young woman appeared to be a love affair, if we confine ourselves to observing their conduct, but our further scrutiny shows it to be a powerfully motivated, mutually narcissistic one. We cannot know to what degree this was the case in the psychology of the young woman. For Dorsey, however, once we learned her role was to "complete" him, be like a "twin" to him and as an extension of himself that makes her a part of him, we find this is no union of a man and woman mutually committed to each other. The enormous value he placed on her was sincerely meant, but it was for him, as its unconscious intention in this type of identification showed us, that he was "elevated" in prowess, power, and achievement. That is, his self-esteem was advanced by it. When this is unsettled, the linchpin of the relationship gets pulled, and the vehicle falls apart.

When the woman made a claim for herself, Dorsey found he could not honor it. He resisted it. He felt it compromised him. Instead of feeling the new "wholeness," he felt limited, reduced, "trapped" by her. He was unaware that it was his deep commitment to himself that trapped him. He spoke of it as not enhancing his ego. Should he honor such a claim, his manhood would be impoverished. He fully understood the woman had every reason to expect that he would honor her demand and that she had a right to make it, but it felt menacing. He could not do it. Dorsey's identification with a woman was in this respect one that he first acquired as a small boy, which was repressed but never quit. When he was put to the test, the relationship was broken.

It is generally assumed in psychoanalytic theory that the revival of the Oedipus complex, in the course of a man's development, somehow gets reworked to at long last give him the gratification that as a boy he had to forgo. He consciously experienced it as a repugnant intimacy he escaped. In maturity, he expects that in his choice of a woman for himself, she will be unassociated with those unconscious conflicts from which he took flight into boyhood and that he will be launched into an intimate, loving, sexual freedom. The course of psychological events or wishes follow no such ordered sequence. We have seen that in each early phase of masculine development, and even in maturity, its oldest conflicts may be readily reactivated, retrieved from repression, and thawed out to produce conflicts with the freshness as before the repression took place. They may again and again be removed from awareness — repressed — only to return, given the proper provocation.

Some men who enjoy extramarital affairs draw on them as an aspect of their masculinity from which their wives are excluded. Dorsey demonstrated this phenomenon. There are others, unlike him, who could not tolerate the identification he developed with a woman. The masculinity of many men thrives on the pleasure certain women enjoy on being dependent on them. That women find it a compatible condition is often thought to be a basis of comparison with those passive, dependent men who wish to submit to women. It is mistakenly conceived merely as a simple reversal of roles. There is also a tendency that accompanies this reasoning to drop into the fallacy that conduct may be taken as an indication of an actual role change. A man's role reversed, considered on a deeper level than simply his conduct, suggests problems of his masculinity are the governing influences, rather than a mere choice, of behavior.

*　　*　　*

With the onset of middle age, new real enclosures naturally begin to take place. With them, as harbingers of a waning masculinity, narcissism heightens, bent on buttressing itself with more dedication to performance, mastery, and achievement. While the result may be often rewarding, nonetheless the conflict is joined. However acutely self-perceived, the dilemma seeks to escape full disclosure. Throughout a man's existence, we have observed his unique sensitivity to restrictions of performance that impose limits on mastery and achievement that would compromise the contemplation of masculinity unbounded. Resistant reactions appear, demanding and receiving expression.

The universal need, born of the human wish to transcend one's limits, is never more insistent than when the psychology of loss is evoked. Losses test our measure of the self, of achievement, and of mastery. Our entire history shows there can be no contentment with our limits. And a restless exertion for liberation, from whatever we feel circumscribes us, compels our efforts. We learned some of its implications during early boyhood. With the passage of time, later in life, its significance is even further intensified. Moreover, it is the human condition to accept neither loss nor deprivation without searching and requiring restitution.

The common incidence of despair, anxiety, and periods of clinical depression at this time of a man's life are notorious. Commonly, they are termed, in the present vernacular, "mid-life crises." The strain a man puts toward exceeding his limits makes him more than ever a hostage of his own narcissism. This is the nexus with so-called crisis.

How ordinarily a woman may find a way to elude her own limitations through a husband's or a son's masculinity is familiar to us. But the opposite is not the rule for a man. Much as he vicariously may enjoy a son's prowess and achievements, his unconscious immodest need for them himself is not relieved. It is not from envy, as may be popularly or theoretically supposed, so much as from the masculine tenacious narcissism that tyrannizes, especially when circumscribed, that fails to be sublimated in another's accomplishment. Thus he rarely finds gratification for his own narcissism in a woman's achievement unless, as we have seen, she is joined to promote his. A woman finds it a source of pleasure; a man's narcissism blocks it.

In the course of his extensive psychoanalytic explorations,

Freud posed a vexing question that he discovered no answer to fit. "What does a woman want?" The same inquiry was not framed for a man. Should we put it to him, his reply is predictable. *Evermore!*

NOTES

Chapter 1

1. George Foot Moore, *Judaism in the First Centuries of the Christian Era* (Cambridge: Harvard University Press, 1970), vol. 1, p. 484.

2. P. Faergeman, "Fantasies of Menstruation in Men," *Psychoanal. Quart.* 24 (1955): 1–19; F. Boehm, Femininity Complex in Men," *Int. J. Psychoanal.* 11 (1930): 444–469.

3. J. Lampl de Groot, "The Preoedipal Phase in the Development of the Male Child," *Psychoanal. Study Child.* 2 (1948): 75–83; E. Jacobson, "The Development of the Wish for a Child in Boys," *Psychoanal. Study Child.* 5 (1950): 139–152; J. Kestenberg, "On the Development of Maternal Feelings in Early Childhood," *Psychoanal. Study Child.* 11 (1956): 257–291; M. Sperling, "Analysis of a Boy with Transvestite Tendencies," *Psychoanal. Study Child.* 19 (1964): 470–493; R. J. Stoller, "The Mother's Contribution to the Infantile Transvestite Behavior," *Int. J. Psychoanal.* 47 (1966): 384–395; C. A. Socarides, "A Provisional Theory of Aetiology in Male Homosexuality," *Int. J. Psychoanal.* 49 (1963): 27–37; Panel (1970), "The Development of the Child's Sense of Identity," V. L. Clower, reporter, *J. Am. Psychoanal.* 18 (1970): 165–176; M. S. Mahler, F. Pine, and L. Bergman, *The Psychological Birth of the Human Infant* (New York: Basic Books, 1975).

4. Gregory Rochlin, *Man's Aggression* (Boston: Gambit, 1973; New York: Dell, 1974), pp. 173–174; "Child Analysis Number," *Psychoanal. Quart.* (1935); T. Benedek, "Parenthood as a Developmental Phase," *J.*

Am. Psychoanal. Assoc. 7 (1959): 389–417; P. Greenacre, "Considerations Regarding Parent-Infant Relationship," *Int. J. Psychoanal.* 41 (1960): 571–584; D. W. Winnicott, "The Theory of the Parent-Infant Relationship," *Int. J. Psychoanal.* 41 (1960): 585–595; J. Bowlby, "The Nature of a Child's Tie to His Mother," *Int. J. Psychoanal.* 39 (1958): 350–373; J. D. Lichtenberg, "The Development of the Sense of the Self," *J. Am. Psychoanal. Assoc.* 23 (1975): 453–484.

5. T. Berry Brazelton, *Infants and Mothers* (New York: Delacorte, 1969).

6. Erik H. Erikson, *Identity, Youth and Crisis* (New York: Norton, 1968), p. 82; M. S. Mahler, "Thoughts About Development and Individuation," *Psychoanal. Study Child.* 18 (1963): 308–310; B. D. Lewin, *The Psychoanalysis of Elation* (New York: Norton, 1950).

7. Sigmund Freud, *Standard Edition Complete Psychological Works*, vol. 1, pp. 222–227.

8. Ibid., vol. 10, pp. 5–147.

9. Gregory Rochlin, *Griefs and Discontents* (Boston: Little, Brown, 1965), pp. 336–337.

10. Freud, "The Ego and the Id," *Works*, vol. 19, p. 27.

11. Jean Piaget, *The Child's Conception of Physical Causality* (London: Kegan Paul, 1930), p. 272.

12. Ibid., p. 272.

Chapter 2

1. Sigmund Freud, *Works*, vol. 15, p. 206.

2. Ibid., vol. 22, p. 133.

3. Ibid., vol. 14, "Narcissism: An Introduction" (1914), p. 91.

4. E. R. Geleerd, "A Clinical Contribution to the Problem of the Early Mother-Child Relationship," *Psychoanal. Study Child* 11 (1956): 336–351; Sylvia Brody, *Patterns of Mothering* (New York: International Universities Press, 1956); T. Benedek, "Parenthood as a Developmental Phase," *J. Am. Psychoanal. Assoc.* 7 (1959): 389–417; I. C. Kaufman and L. A. Rosenblum, "The Reaction to Separation in Infant Monkeys," *Psychosom. Med.* 29 (1967): 648–675; M. S. Mahler, "A Study of Separation-Individuation Process," *Psychoanal. Study Child* 26 (1971): 403–424.

5. Helene Deutsch, *Psychology of Women* (New York: Grune & Stratton, 1945), 2 vols.

6. Ibid, vol. 2, p. 297.

7. Ibid, p. 136.

8. George Eliot, *Daniel Deronda* (London: Penguin, 1974), p. 123.

Chapter 3

1. Rochlin, *Griefs and Discontents,* pp. 1–33.
2. Ibid., pp. 225–232.

Chapter 4

1. Freud, *Works,* vol. 10, p. 61909.
2. Rochlin, *Man's Aggression,* p. 24.
3. Freud, *Works,* p. 7.
4. Ibid., p. 9–10.
5. Ibid., p. 11.
6. Ibid., p. 24.
7. Ibid., pp. 24–25.
8. Ibid., p. 16.
9. Ibid., p. 39.
10. Ibid., pp. 39–49.
11. Ibid., pp. 86–87.
12. Ibid., p. 93n.
13. Ibid., p. 110.
14. Ibid., p. 5.
15. Ibid., pp. 6–7.
16. Ibid., p. 22.
17. Ibid., p. 146.
18. *The Plays of Nathan Field,* ed. William Perry (Austin: University of Texas Press, 1950), vol. 2, p. 197.
19. Daniel Schreber, *Memoirs of My Nervous Illness,* trans. Ida MacAlpine and Richard Hunter (London: Dawson, 1955).
20. Freud, "Psycho-analytic Notes on an Autobiographical Account of a Case of Paranoia (Dementia paranoides)," *Works,* vol. 12, ed. note (1958) and Introduction (1911).
21. Ibid., pp. 18–19.
22. Ibid., p. 21.
23. Ibid., p. 32.
24. Ibid., p. 73.
25. Ibid., vol. 17, p. 17.
26. Ibid., p. 15.
27. Ibid., pp. 15–16.
28. Ibid., p. 17.
29. Ibid., p. 46.

30. Ibid., p. 6.

31. Ibid., p. 64.

32. Ibid., p. 78.

33. Ibid., p. 78.

34. W. B. Yeats, "Crazy Jane Talks with the Bishop," in *The Collected Poems* (New York: Macmillan Co., 1970), p. 255.

35. Joseph C. Rheingold, *The Fear of Being a Woman* (New York: Grune and Stratton, 1964), p. 263.

36. Freud, *Works*, vol. 18, Group Psychology, VII, Identification, pp. 105–106.

37. M. S. Mahler, "On Human Symbiosis and the Vicissitudes of Individuation," *J. Am. Psychoanal. Assoc.* 15 (1967): 740–764; M. S. Mahler and B. J. Gosliner, "On Symbiotic Child Psychosis: Genetic, Dynamic and Restitutive Aspects," *Psychoanal. Study Child.* 10 (New York: International Universities Press, 1955); C. A. Socarides, "A Provisional Theory of Aetiology in Male Homosexuality: A Case of Pre-oedipal Origin," *Int. J. Psychoanal.* 49 (1968); Charles Socarides, "The Historical Development of Theoretical and Clinical Concepts of Overt Male Homosexuality" (Panel Report), *J. Am. Psychoanal. Assoc.* 8 (1960): 552–566; Charles Socarides, *American Handbook of Psychiatry*, 2nd ed. (New York: Basic Books, 1974), vol. 3, *Adult Clinical Psychiatry*, Ch. 14, pp. 295–296.

38. R. von Krafft-Ebing, *Psychopathia Sexualis* (New York: Physicians and Surgeons Book Co., 1922).

39. H. Barry, Jr., and H. Barry, III, "Homosexuality and Testosterone," *New Eng. J. Med.* 293 (1972), 38–81.

40. Jean Baker Miller, ed., *Psychoanalysis and Women* (Baltimore: Penguin, 1973); Juliet Mitchell, *Psychoanalysis and Feminism* (New York: Random House, 1974).

41. Freud, "From the History of an Infantile Neurosis" (1918) (1914), *Works*, vol. 17, pp. 105–106.

42. Rochlin, *Griefs and Discontents*, pp. 35–62.

43. Melanie Klein, *The Psychoanalysis of Children* (London: Hogarth, 1932).

44. R. J. Stoller, "The Mother's Contribution to the Infantile Transvestite Behavior," *Int. J. Psychoanal.* 47 (1966): 384–395.

45. Ibid., p. 394.

46. Freud, *Works*, vol. 11, Leonardo Da Vinci and a Memory of His Childhood, p. 100.

47. Ibid., p. 99fn.

48. R. J. Stoller, "Adult Transsexualism," *Int. J. Psychoanal.* 54 (1973), 215.

49. J. Money and A. A. Ehrhardt, *Man and Woman, Boy and Girl*

(Baltimore: Johns Hopkins Press, 1972); G. Weidman, "Homosexuality, A Survey," *J. Am. Psychoanal. Assoc.* 22 (1974): 651–696.

Chapter 5

1. Rochlin, *Griefs and Discontents,* pp. 1–164.
2. Anna Freud, *The Ego and the Mechanisms of Defense* (1948) (New York: International Universities Press, 1948), pp. 132–133.
3. Freud, *Works,* vol. 4, "Infantile Material as a Source of Dreams" (1900), pp. 191, 199; vol. 8, "Jokes, Dreams, and the Unconscious" (1905), p. 161; vol. 11, "Five Lectures on Psychoanalysis: Third Lecture" (1910 [1909]), p. 34.
4. Ibid, vol. 15, "Lecture VIII: Children's Dreams" (1916 [1915–1916]), p. 126.
5. Rochlin, *Man's Aggression,* pp. 176, 234, 236–242.
6. John E. Mack, *Nightmares and Human Conflict* (Boston: Little, Brown, 1970).
7. Ibid., p. 117.
8. Ibid., p. 119.
9. Ibid., p. 121.
10. Ibid., p. 127.
11. *The Confessions of St. Augustine,* trans. E. B. Pusey (London: Oxford University Press, 1853), pp. 4–5.
12. J. J. Rousseau, *On Education,* trans. Barbara Foxley (London: Dent, 1911), pp. 28–29, 70–74.
13. Freud, "Character and Anal Eroticism," *Works,* v.p. (1901), p. 169.
14. Mack, pp. 151–153.
15. Rochlin, *Man's Aggression,* p. 83.
16. Ibid., p. 184.
17. Freud, "Mourning and Melancholia" (1917 [1915]), *Works,* vol. 14, p. 252.
18. Rochlin, *Griefs and Discontents,* pp. 255–256, 283, 286.
19. Freud, "Analysis of a Phobia in a Five Year Old Boy" (1909), *Works,* vol. 10, pp. 5–149.
20. Jan Morris, *Conundrum* (New York: Harcourt Brace Jovanovich, 1974).
21. Rebecca West, *New York Times Book Review,* April 14, 1974.
22. Morris, p. 3.
23. Ibid, p. 4.
24. Ibid., pp. 7–8.
25. Ibid., p. 13.

26. Ibid., p. 20.

27. Ibid., pp. 23–24.

28. Ibid., p. 24.

29. Ibid., p. 31.

30. Ibid., p. 49.

31. Ibid., p. 93.

32. Ibid., p. 141.

33. (1913), vol. 13, pp. 1–161.

34. "The Sexual Theories of Children" (1908), *Works*, vol. 9, p. 207; "Leonardo Da Vinci and a Memory of His Childhood" (1910), *Works*, vol. 11, pp. 78–79; Rochlin, *Griefs and Discontents*, pp. 225–319.

Chapter 6

1. T. H. Gaster, *The Oldest Stories in the World* (Boston: Beacon, 1958), pp. 21–51.

2. Ibid., p. 27.

3. Robert Graves, *The Greek Myths* (Baltimore: Penguin Books, 1955), vol. 1, pp. 63–65.

4. R. B. Y. Scott, *The Anchor Bible: Proverbs, Ecclesiastes* (New York: Doubleday, 1965), p. xxiii.

5. Ibid., p. xlvii.

6. Ibid., pp. 41–42:ii. 1. 22.

7. Ibid., p. iii. 1–31.

8. Ibid., p. 57: vi. 16–19.

9. St. Augustine, *The Confessions,* trans. Rev. E. B. Pusey (Oxford, London: John Henry Parker, 1853).

10. Ibid., pp. 8–10.

11. Ibid., p. 17.

12. *Rebecca West: A Celebration* (New York: Viking Press, 1977), p. 172.

13. Ibid., p. 174.

14. Ibid., p. 174.

15. St. Augustine, *The Confessions,* p. 23.

16. Bernard De Voto, *Mark Twain at Work* (Cambridge: Harvard University Press, 1942), pp. 3–24.

17. Ibid., pp. 18–19.

18. *Neurosis and Character Types* (New York: International Universities Press, 1965), pp. 218–225.

19. *Don Quixote,* trans. J. M. Cohen (Baltimore: Penguin, 1972), p. 32.

20. Ibid., p. 34.

21. Deutsch, *Neurosis and Character Types,* p. 220.

22. Ibid., p. 220.

23. Ibid., p. 223.

24. Philippe Aries, *Centuries of Childhood* (New York: Knopf, 1962), pp. 34–51.

25. Robert Lee Wolff, "Children's Literature: The Victorian Age" (unpublished ms.), general introduction to vols. 4 and 5.

26. *Early Children's Books and Their Illustration* (Pierpont Morgan Library) (New York: Godine, 1975), p. 31.

27. (London: E. Newbery, 1781).

28. Peter Coveney, *The Image of Childhood* (Baltimore: Penguin, 1967), pp. 40–41.

29. Ibid., pp. 111–161.

30. Ibid., p. 91.

31. Ibid., p. 240.

32. *The Steranko History of Comics* (Reading, Pa.: Supergraphics, 1970), vol. 1, pp. 1–84.

33. Marvel Comics Group (April 1977).

34. Marvel Preview, no. 8 (Fall 1976).

35. Gaster, *The Oldest Stories in the World,* p. 69.

36. Ibid., p. 231.

37. (New York: Harcourt, Brace & World, 1951).

38. (New York: Bantam Books, 1968), pp. 226–227.

39. (New York: Bantam Books, 1972), pp. 88–98.

40. Ibid., p. 1.

Chapter 7

1. "An Outline of Psychoanalysis" (1949 [1938]), *Works,* vol. 23, p. 153.

2. "Character and Anal Eroticism" (1908), ibid., vol. 9, p. 171.

3. "A Short Account of Psychoanalysis" (1924 [1923]), ibid., vol. 19, p. 208.

4. "Inhibitions, Symptoms, and Anxiety" (1926), ibid., vol. 20, p. 116.

5. "Formulations on the Two Principles of Mental Functioning" (1911), ibid., vol. 12, p. 222.

6. Berta Bornstein, *Psychoanalytic Study of the Child* (New York: International Universities Press, 1949), vol. 3/4, pp. 181–226.

7. Charles Sarnoff, "Ego Structure in Latency," *Psychoanal. Quart.* 40 (1971): 387–414.

8. Bornstein, *Psychoanalytic Study of the Child,* vol. 6 (1951), pp. 181–226.

9. Peter Blos, *On Adolescence* (New York: Free Press, 1962), pp. 54–55.

10. Freud, "Beyond the Pleasure Principle" (1920), *Works,* vol. 18, pp. 3–123.

11. Anna Freud, *The Ego and the Mechanisms of Defense* (New York: International Universities Press, 1948), p. 121.

12. Rochlin, *Man's Aggression,* pp. 213–214.

13. I. Handelman, "The Effects of Early Object Relationships on Sexual Development: Autistic and Symbiotic Modes of Adaptation," *Psychoanal. Study Child.* 20 (1965): 376–383; H. W. Loewald, "Psychoanalytic Theory and the Psychoanalytic Process," *Psychoanal. Study Child.* 25 (1970): 54–68; Ted E. Becker, "On Latency," *Psychoanal. Study Child.* 29 (1974): 3–11; Elizabeth Bremner Kaplan, "Manifestations of Aggression in Latency and Preadolescent Girls," *Psychoanal. Study Child.* 31 (1976): 63–78; Theodore Shapiro and Richard Perry, "Latency Revisited: The Age 7 Plus or Minus 1," *Psychoanal. Study Child.* 31 (1976): 79–105; Fredrick L. Meisel, "The Myth of Peter Pan," *Psychoanal. Study Child.* 32 (1977): 545–563.

14. Jean Piaget, *The Language and Thought of the Child,* preface by Professor E. Claparede (London: Routledge & Kegan Paul, 1926), p. xv; *The Child's Conception of Physical Causality* (London: Routledge & Kegan Paul, 1930).

15. Freud, "On the Sexual Theories of Children" (1908), *Works,* vol. 9, p. 216.

16. Ibid.

Chapter 8

1. Thomas Hughes, *Tom Brown's School Days,* Ed. Kaye Webb, (New York: Macmillan, 1856; New York: Puffin Books, 1971), p. 240.

2. Joseph Conrad, *Great Short Works* (New York: Harper & Row, 1976), p. 185.

3. Erik H. Erikson, *Identity, Youth and Crisis* (New York: Norton, 1968); "Youth: Change and Challenge," *Daedalus* 91 (Winter 1962); "Twelve to Sixteen: Early Adolescence," *Daedalus* 100 (Fall 1971).

4. J. M. Tanner, "Sequence, Tempo, and Individual Variation in the Growth and Development of Boys and Girls Aged Twelve to Sixteen," *Daedalus* 100 (Fall 1971), no. 4, p. 925.

5. P. Blos, "The Initial Stage of Male Adolescence," *Psychoanal. Study Child.* 20 (1965): 146.

6. Rochlin, *Griefs and Discontents,* p. 318.

7. Anna Freud, "Adolescence," *Psychoanal. Study Child.* 13 (1958): 255–278.

8. Ibid., p. 263.

9. Ibid., p. 267.

10. C. W. Socarides, "Theoretical and Clinical Aspects of Overt Male Homosexuality," *J. Am. Psychoanal. Assoc.,* vol. 8 (1960), Scientific Proceedings, pp. 552–566.

11. P. Blos, pp. 145–164.

12. Ibid., p. 151.

13. Franz Kafka, *The Complete Stories* (New York: Schocken Books, 1972).

14. Ibid., p. 95.

15. Ibid., p. 122.

16. P. Blos, p. 161.

17. Sigmund Freud, *Works,* vol. 7 (1905), pp. 125–243, 1963.

18. G. H. Wiedman, "Homosexuality: A Survey," *J. Am. Psychoanal. Assoc.* 22 (1974): pp. 651–695.

19. C. W. Socarides, "Transsexualism and Psychosis," *Int. J. Psychoanal. Psychotherapy* 7 (1978–79): 372–383; H. Greilsheimer and J. E. Groves, "Male Genital Self-Mutilation," *Arch. Gen. Psychiatry* 36 (April 1979): pp. 441–446.

20. Erikson, *Identity, Youth and Crisis* (New York: Norton, 1968).

Chapter 9

1. "Neuroses and Character Types," *Clinical Psychoanalytic Studies* (New York: International Universities Press, 1965), 353–357.

2. Joseph Conrad, *Lord Jim* (Baltimore: Penguin, 1974), p. 9.

3. Ibid., p. 11.

4. Ibid., pp. 21–22.

5. Ibid., p. 25.

6. Ibid., pp. 65–117.

7. Ibid., pp. 229–230.

8. Ibid., p. 134.

9. Ibid., p. 150.

10. Ed. Bernard De Voto (New York: Harper & Row, 1962), p. 40.

11. C. W. Socarides, *American Handbook of Psychiatry: Adult Clinical Psychiatry* (New York: Basic Books, 1974) p. 297; P. Blos, *On Adolescence* (New York: Free Press, 1962), pp. 21, 105, 109, 185.

12. Rochlin, *Griefs and Discontents,* "The Loss of Function," pp. 321–361.

13. Freud, "On Narcissism" (1914), *Works,* vol. 14, p. 82.
14. Rochlin, pp. 378–379.

Chapter 10

1. Rochlin, *Griefs and Discontents*, pp. 121–164.
2. *Herzog* (New York: Vanguard, 1964), p. 10.
3. Ibid., p. 46.
4. Ibid., p. 119.
5. Ibid., p. 233.
6. Ibid., p. 323.
7. "Some Clinical Considerations of the Ego Ideal," *J. Am. Psychoanal. Assoc.* 12 (1964): 514.
8. Ibid., p. 515.
9. "St. Augustine" (1933), in *Rebecca West: A Celebration* (New York: Viking Press, 1977), p. 203.

INDEX